and Tourism

Dr Robert Prosser

Lecturer in Recreation and Tourism Studies
University of Birmingham

Collins Educational
An imprint of HarperCollinsPublishers

Collins Educational
77–85 Fulham Palace Road
London W6 8JB
An imprint of HarperCollins*Publishers*

First published 1994
Reprinted 1995, 1996, 1997
Second edition 2000

ISBN 0 00 326650 8

Edited by Ron Hawkins
Designed by Jacky Wedgwood
Design production by Adrienne Lee
Picture research by Caroline Thompson
Computer artwork by Jerry Fowler
Index by Judith Moore

Printed and bound by Printing Express, Hong Kong

References

Baud-Bovy, M and Lawson, F (1977), *Tourism and Recreational Development*, Butterworth Heinemann.
BBNPA (1995), *Structure Plan 1995*, Brecon Beacons National Park Authority.
BTA (1992), *Selling Britain to the World*, Annual Report 1991/92, British Tourist Authority.
BTA (1997), Annual Report 1996/97, British Tourist Authority.
Chapman, K (1979), *People, Pattern and Process*, Edward Arnold.
CIPFA (1999), *Annual Statistical Report, 1999*, CIO/HMSO.
Comedia (1991), *Out of Hours*, Comedia.
Cooper, C, Fletcher, J, Gilbert, D and Wantill, S (1993), *Tourism: Principles and Practice*, Pitman.
Countryside Commission (1992a), *Parish Paths Partnership: An Outline*, Countryside Commission.
Countryside Commission (1992b), *Pennine Way Survey 1990: Use and Economic Impact* (CCP361), Countryside Commission.
CPRE (1995), *Tranquil Areas Study*, Council for the Preservation of Rural England.
Dartmoor NPA (1991), *Structure Plan 1991*, Dartmoor National Park Authority.
Edwards, J (1992), *Fit For the Future*, Countryside Commission.
Open University/Countryside Commission (1985), *The Countryside Handbook*, Croom Helm.
Ryan, C (1991), *Recreational Tourism*, Routledge.
Shaw, G and Williams, A M (eds) (1997), *The Rise and Fall of British Coastal Resorts*, Cassell.
Shoard, M (1987), *This Land is Our Land*, Paladin.
Social Trends (1996, 1999), Central Statistical Office, HMSO.
Standeven, J (1991), 'Against the tide', *Leisure Management*, August.
TRRU (1987), *Outdoor Activities in Scotland: A Survey*, Tourism and Recreation Research Unit.
Tucker, D (1991), 'Themes and schemes', *Leisure Management*, February.
WTO (1997), *Yearbook of Tourism Statistics*, World Tourism Organisation.

Dedication

My thanks to Sue Truman, University of Birmingham, without whose organisational skills this book would have taken much longer to complete.

Acknowledgements

Every effort has been made to contact the holders of copyright material, but if any have been inadvertently overlooked, the publishers will be pleased to make the necessary arrangements at the first opportunity.

The publishers would like to thank the following for permission to reproduce photographs and publicity material (T = Top, B = Bottom, C = Centre, L = Left, R = Right):

Aerofilms Ltd, Fig. 2.46; Airtours, Fig. 6.22; Alton Towers, Fig. 5.31; Argyll, the Isles, Loch Lomond, Stirling & Trossachs Tourist Board, Figs 3.10, 3.11, 3.12; AP Photo/Anat Givon, Fig. 6.16; Barnaby's Picture Library, Figs 5.4, 5.9, 5.12; Beamish: The North of England Open Air Museum, Fig. 5.30; Photos from www.JohnBirdsall.co.uk, Figs 1.13, 2.3, 2.8, 2.10, 2.12, 2.21; Bournemouth News & Picture Service, Fig. 5.17; David Brinn/Brecon Beacons National Park, Figs 4.28, 4.33; The CBSO Society Ltd, Managers of the City of Birmingham Symphony Orchestra, Fig. 2.32; J Allan Cash Ltd, Fig. 7.8; Champneys, Fig. 2.4; Churchtown Outdoor Adventure Centre, Fig. 1.28; Coventry Racquet Centre, Fig. 2.9; Stuart Currie, Fig. 3.31; Prodeepta Das, Fig. 2.22; Dean Heritage Museum Trust, Fig. 5.26(R); Ted Ditchburn/*Daily Telegraph*, Fig. 5.2(T); Ecoscene/Andy Hibbert, Fig. 5.10; The English Riveria Tourist Board, Fig. 5.19; Environmental Images/Chris Westwood, Fig. 7.5; Jim Holmes, Fig. 7.37; Format Photographers/Roshini Kempadoo, Fig. 1.14; Carole Wright, Fig. 1.15; T Waltham/Geophotos, Fig. 4.10, 4.26; Stuart Gill, Fig. 5.21; *Guardian*/Don McPhee, Fig. 3.24, Liz McGregor, Fig. 7.29; Guzelian Photography/Steve Forrest, Fig. 3.13; John Harlow/*Daily Telegraph*, Fig. 5.2(B); David Hollis, Fig. 1.27; Inspirations Holidays, Fig. 7.7; Kuoni Travel, Fig. 7.9(R); Langdale Leisure Ltd, Fig. 4.13; James McEvoy, Fig. 5.27; Mansfield District Council, Figs 2.11, 2.13; John Mills Photography, Fig. 2.28; NHPA/ANT, Fig. 7.46; Noble Caledonia Ltd, Fig. 6.31; Northern Ireland Tourist Board, Figs 2.1, 5.28; Oasis Forest Holiday Village, Figs 5.22, 5.23; Oxford Scientific Films Ltd/R Price/Survival Anglia, Fig. 7.38; Robert Prosser, Figs 1.2, 1.3, 1.4, 1.7, 1.8, 1.11, 1.16, 1.20, 2.15, 2.17, 2.19, 2.24, 2.25, 2.26, 2.30, 2.35, 2.38, 2.39, 2.43, 3.3, 3.4, 3.16, 3.32, 4.2, 4.3, 4.4, 4.5, 4.7, 4.19, 4.20, 4.21, 4.25, 4.30, 4.31, 4.34, 4.35, 4.38, 5.16, 6.2, 6.3, 6.7, 6.10, 6.14, 6.15, 6.33, 6.28, 7.17, 7.18, 7.25, 7.26, 7.34, 7.35, 7.47; Ramblers' Association, Fig. 3.27; Riveria Centre, Torquay, Fig. 5.20; Royal Caribbean International, Fig. 6.26; Carl Royle, Fig. 3.28; South Tyneside District Council, Fig. 5.26(L); Tomorrow's Leisure plc, Figs 2.27, 2.29; Tony Stone Images, Figs 1.17, 1.30, 6.36; Stewart Thompson, Fig. 1.26; The Walt Disney Company, Fig. 5.32; Watermeadows Swimming & Fitness Centre, Fig. 2.6; Jacky Wedgwood, Fig. 2.34; West Air Photography, Fig. 5.6; Mike Williams, Figs 3.18, 4.15; World Expeditions, Fig 7.9(L).

Cover photograph: Jumbo jet landing at St Martin, Leeward Islands (Camera Press)

Maps:
Birmingham City Council, Fig 2.30 (T); Butterworth-Heinemann, Oxford, UK, Fig. 7.12 (from an article first published in *Tourism Management*, Vol. 14, No. 4); Denali National Park, Fig. 7.19; Kingsbury Water Park, Fig. 4.5; Ordnance Survey, Fig. 2.30(B) reproduced from the 1974 Ordnance Survey 1:1250 Plan SPO686 NW map with the permission of the Controller of Her Majesty's Stationery Office; Ordnance Survey, Fig. 4.29, reproduced from OLM No 12 © Copyright with the permission of the Controller of Her Majesty's Stationery Office; Saltwells Nature Reserve, Fig. 2.43; South East London Green Chain Working Party, Fig. 2.45.

Contents

1 Leisure demand and supply

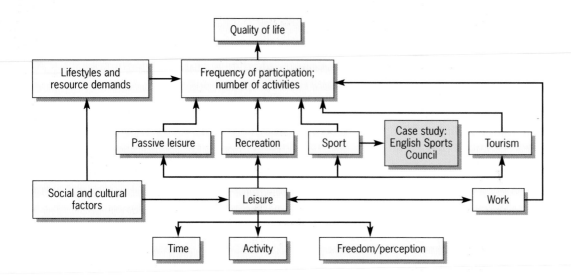

1.1 What do we mean by 'leisure'?

Leisure is one of those words we all use, think we know its meaning, but find it difficult to define. It is used in this book as the general term which encompasses passive leisure, **recreation**, sport and **tourism** (Fig. 1.1). Passive leisure may be simply sitting around, relaxing. Recreation includes some form of activity. Sport involves activity within a formal set of rules etc. Tourism involves travel away from the home environment. However, as the Venn diagram in Figure 1.1 suggests, the distinctions are not clear-cut. For instance, your recreation may include watching a sporting event such as an athletics meeting, but if you watch it at home on television, it could be defined as 'passive leisure'; if you play pitch-and-putt golf while on holiday, then your activity can be seen as both tourism and recreation (Fig. 1.2). Equally, the same activity can be sport or recreation: competition swimming is a sport, while casual swimming in a leisure pool is a recreational activity.

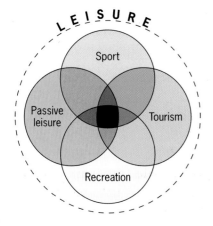

Figure 1.1 The leisure domain

Figure 1.2 When recreation and tourism mix: playing mini-golf while on holiday at the seaside

Figure 1.3 'Sun-sea-sand seekers' on Miami Beach, Florida

Figure 1.4 'Wilderness' seekers on a canoe trek in the Everglades National Park, Florida

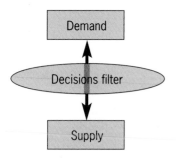

Figure 1.5 The leisure system

1 Under the headings of each of the four components of leisure shown in Figure 1.1, list two things you have enjoyed doing during the past year.

2 Use the photographs in Figures 1.2–1.4 to illustrate the definitions of leisure given in Section 1.1 to support this statement: 'People engage in a wide range of leisure activities for a wide variety of reasons.'

3 Here is a list of reasons or motives for taking part in a leisure activity: relaxation; getting fit; socialising and making friends; looking good; challenge; excitement; getting away from it all; improving skills; adventure.
a For the people in Figures 1.2–1.4, suggest two motives.
b Suggest two additional possible motives for engaging in a leisure activity.

Key themes
This book focuses upon recreation and tourism, and explores three main themes:

1 The resource demands and environmental impacts resulting from the leisure 'explosion' (Figs 1.3, 1.4).

2 The decision-making processes involved in the **demand** for (who does what, where, when, with whom and why) and the **supply** of (who provides what, where, how, for whom and why) of leisure opportunities and experiences (Fig. 1.5).

3 The relationships between the 'Four Ps' of leisure: policy; planning; provision; participation.

Leisure: A simple definition
Here are four apparently quite different definitions of leisure:

As time: time free from work and other obligations.

As activity: things you choose to do in your spare time.

As freedom: the relatively freely chosen non-work area of life.

As perception: relatively self-determined experiences that occur in those parts of your life when you are free from 'work', that you see as 'leisure', and you enjoy across a wide range of intensity and commitment.

From these various elements, we can suggest a single, straightforward definition of leisure: *action relatively freely chosen within time and space.*

1.2 Leisure–work relationships

Definitions make it clear that it is difficult to think about leisure without considering the idea of 'work'. In traditional societies, 'work' means the direct production of the necessities of life – food, clothing and shelter. Today, when we use the word 'work' we most commonly mean 'earning a living' or 'employment'. But this narrow definition ignores the vast range of unpaid work, such as running a home and family. Thus, a more useful definition of work is: *productive activities, paid or unpaid, which are expected to be completed, and to which there is some contract or obligation.*

Figure 1.6 Japan's new leisure world (*Source: Time* magazine, 5 July 1993)

?

4 We can think of our lives in terms of leisure–work relationships: things we are paid to do (job); things we need to do (obligations, chores, duties); things we like to do (leisure).
a Give an example of each of these that you have experienced during the past week.
b Suggest how the balance between these elements may change as you move through the stages of your life (think of the lives of your parents and grandparents, for example).

Work, therefore, seems to involve limited choice or freedom and, for many people, limited pleasure or satisfaction – think of the 'jobs' you have to do at home, or your Saturday job! Yet western societies give high status to this idea of work, based on Victorian Christian and moral **values**: work is 'good' and leisure is a 'reward' only to be enjoyed when you have earned it, e.g. 'You can go out to play when you have finished your homework.' This so-called 'Victorian work ethic' is found, too, in other religions and cultures, such as the well-known Japanese 'work ethic'. From this viewpoint we gain self-respect and status through work, while loss of work brings a sense of failure and loss of status – this was the theme of the film *The Full Monty*.

Yet **attitudes** are changing: those who enjoy high-status lifestyles now give comparable importance to both work *and* leisure. Across the world, people are beginning to adopt this leisure ethic (Fig. 1.6). Prestige homes are built around marinas and golf courses (Fig. 1.7). As a quick scan of the shelves in newsagents and bookshops reveals, being healthy and taking part in leisure activities is becoming fashionable across all age groups – from kids on roller-blades to retired people travelling the world.

Figure 1.7 The leisure lifestyle: houses built around a golf course, Phoenix, Arizona

1.3 The leisure industry

The economic potential of this emerging leisure ethic is enormous: today we spend approximately 18 per cent of our total expenditure on leisure. The leisure industry – including tourism – is the world's largest industrial sector, generating over 10 per cent of global GNP. During the 1990s the growth rates averaged 6 per cent per year. The industry contains both secondary and tertiary components (Fig. 1.8) and covers an immense range of products and services (Fig. 1.9).

Lifestyles and resource demands

Leisure is more than simply 'things I do in my spare time'. It is about experiences: *choice, fun, freedom, doing my thing, getting away from it all, personal challenge, feeling good,* and so on. For increasing numbers of people in many countries, leisure has become an important element in *lifestyle* and so a crucial factor influencing **quality of life** (Fig. 1.10).

Figure 1.8 The provision of this private-sector swimming pool involves both the service (tertiary) and manufacturing (secondary) dimensions of the leisure industry

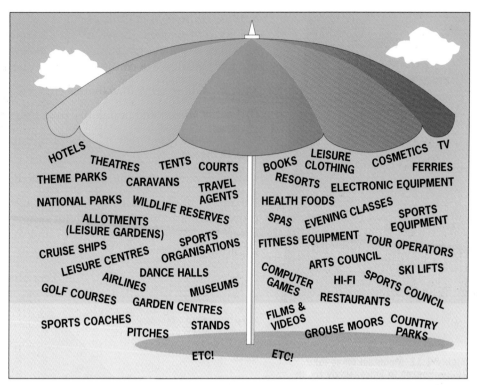

Figure 1.9 The leisure industry (above right)

HOTELS THEATRES TENTS COURTS BOOKS LEISURE CLOTHING COSMETICS TV
THEME PARKS CARAVANS TRAVEL AGENTS RESORTS ELECTRONIC EQUIPMENT FERRIES
NATIONAL PARKS WILDLIFE RESERVES HEALTH FOODS
ALLOTMENTS (LEISURE GARDENS) SPAS EVENING CLASSES SPORTS EQUIPMENT
CRUISE SHIPS SPORTS ORGANISATIONS FITNESS EQUIPMENT TOUR OPERATORS
LEISURE CENTRES DANCE HALLS ARTS COUNCIL SKI LIFTS
AIRLINES MUSEUMS COMPUTER GAMES HI-FI SPORTS COUNCIL
GOLF COURSES GARDEN CENTRES RESTAURANTS
SPORTS COACHES STANDS FILMS & VIDEOS COUNTRY PARKS
PITCHES GROUSE MOORS
ETC! ETC!

Figure 1.10 Chinese families enjoying a display in the Cultural Villages theme park, Shenzhen, China

Social and cultural factors

When we study how people enjoy their leisure, two key understandings quickly appear: first, leisure behaviour is socially and culturally moulded; second, it is strongly influenced by fashion. For instance, in 1985 mountain bikes were a rarity; by 1990 they were seen as 'crucial' urban transport; by 1995, mountain biking was becoming a very popular form of outdoor recreation (Fig. 1.11). In response, **Country Park** and Forestry Commission managers have waymarked special bike trails and routes in order to control erosion and reduce tensions with other recreationists. But by 2005, will the trails be unused and will the bikes be car-boot sales offerings?

Figure 1.11 Mountain bikes take recreationists to increasingly rough and remote places. This photograph was taken in the Chugach National Forest, Alaska

?

5 For a Friday evening to a Sunday evening, keep a diary of your out-of-home leisure activities, i.e. behaviour and experiences that you think of as leisure. For each episode, record:

a The activity or activities engaged in.

b Where you were and the **facilities** and resources you used, both your own (hockey stick; snooker cue) and those provided for you.

c Who provided the resources or facilities.

d If it was free (in which case, who funds it?) or if there was a charge.

e How far you travelled to take part.

f The transport you used – who provided it, and paid for it.

g Who you were with.

h Why you did it, e.g. relaxation, fitness, meeting people, etc.

Figure 1.12 Leisure lifestyles and resource demands

Resources and opportunities

For decision-makers, therefore, the fundamental issues are that of *allocating* resources – money, space, materials, people – and *managing* leisure provision and participation are complex processes because of:

• the incredible *range* of activities enjoyed by *increasing* numbers of people;

• *swings of fashion* and popularity over time;

• the *inequalities in society* which result in unequal opportunities for leisure participation;

• *economic* and *demographic conditions* which change over time.

The model in Figure 1.12 uses two variables – the *frequency* of participation (how often) and *numbers* of activities (how many) to illustrate the diversity of leisure participation (consumption) and some of the implications for policy, planning and provision.

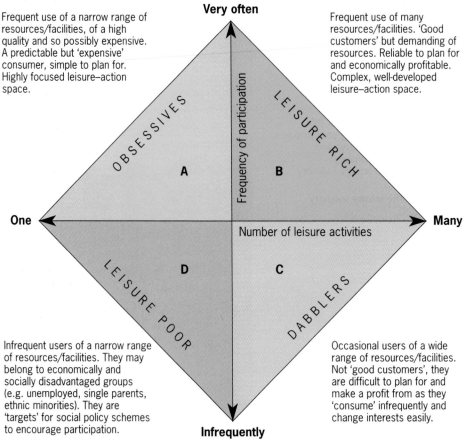

Frequent use of a narrow range of resources/facilities, of a high quality and so possibly expensive. A predictable but 'expensive' consumer, simple to plan for. Highly focused leisure–action space.

Frequent use of many resources/facilities. 'Good customers' but demanding of resources. Reliable to plan for and economically profitable. Complex, well-developed leisure–action space.

Infrequent users of a narrow range of resources/facilities. They may belong to economically and socially disadvantaged groups (e.g. unemployed, single parents, ethnic minorities). They are 'targets' for social policy schemes to encourage participation.

Occasional users of a wide range of resources/facilities. Not 'good customers', they are difficult to plan for and make a profit from as they 'consume' infrequently and change interests easily.

EXAMPLES

A Competition swimmer who requires the use of a competition-style pool for several hours a day, with few other people present. Therefore is an 'expensive' customer for these specialised facilities. Holidays usually associated with competitions.

B Professional couple who belong to several clubs and societies. They are 'joiners': out regularly in a theatre group; play squash and tennis each week at a health club; jog most days; attend weekly music concerts. Two holidays a year – skiing and sailing.

D Single parent with young child, no car and a part-time job. Has severe constraints on time, money and mobility, so although lives in a large city, makes little use of leisure resources/facilities. Few opportunities for holidays.

C Family who 'do something together' each weekend – sometimes a country picnic or walk; sometimes shopping; sometimes tennis or pitch-and-putt; sometimes cinema; sometimes eating out. Holidays vary from camping to coach tours.

?

6 Analyse this brief spell in your leisure life in terms of the model in Figure 1.12. If this weekend is not typical, then place yourself within the model and suggest reasons for your placement.

7 Compare your leisure lifestyle with others in your group and place them on the model. Do your placements correspond to where other group members placed themselves on the model, and if not, why not?

8 The model suggests that the more leisure activities you take part in, the better your quality of life. What are the values and attitudes behind this suggestion? (Refer to leisure–work relationships on p.5.)

9 Essay: All definitions of 'leisure' include concepts of 'freedom' and 'choice'. Outline the main factors that influence the degree of freedom and choice you have in your leisure life.

10 From Table 1.1,
a Describe briefly the patterns of time availability shown.
b Does the data support the claim that women are 'disadvantaged' in terms of their leisure opportunities?
c What are the main implications of the patterns shown for the providers of leisure facilities?

11 Outline the distinctive needs of (a) active retired people and (b) shift workers, and assess the extent to which they may be described as 'advantaged' or 'disadvantaged' in terms of their leisure opportunities.

1.4 Leisure participation in the UK

The basic factor underlying our leisure behaviour is *time*. For instance, a common reason given for ceasing to use a leisure centre is, 'Oh, I don't have the time any more.' Such a person may have a more demanding job, has got married, has started a family, etc. Your age, gender, job status and stage in the life cycle are important factors influencing how much free time you have, when it occurs and in what time blocks (Table 1.1), and hence what activities you can take part in. For example, a round of golf may take three hours, plus travelling time. For many people, such a time block is available only at weekends. As a result, many facilities show heavily peaked patterns of use – overcrowded at weekends, underused on weekdays. These patterns of time availability and use affect policies adopted by owners and managers of leisure facilities (see the case study, Coventry Centre, Chapter 2, pp.24–25). Groups such as the active retired are thus advantaged: they can enjoy less crowded and often cheaper activities at off-peak times (Fig. 1.13). In contrast, some groups, such as nurses, security guards, police, factory and hotel workers, have jobs which may distort leisure opportunities (Fig. 1.14).

The activity requiring the longest time block is, of course, going away on holiday, and one factor influencing the growth of tourism has been the increase in the length of paid holiday leave. In 1975, 75 per cent of full-time employees in the UK were entitled to three weeks' paid holiday or more; by 1995, over 90 per cent had at least four weeks – significantly more, for example, than is common in the USA. Although four in every ten people in the UK do not go away on holiday in a given year, more people are taking at least two holidays and are increasingly likely to go abroad (see Chapter 5).

Table 1.1 Free time by age, gender and job status (hours per day)
(*Source: Social Trends*, 29, 1999)

	Males		Females	
Age	16–44	45+	16–44	45+
Weekday	4.44	6.07	4.28	6.11
Weekend day	7.32	8.56	6.02	6.42

	In full-time employment		In part-time employment	Non-working homemakers
	M	F	F	M/F
Weekday	4.5	3.1	4.5	7.0
Weekend day	10.4	8.5	8.0	8.7

Note: Categories chosen according to available data

Figure 1.13 Retired people can enjoy leisure facilities at off-peak times

Figure 1.14 When do shift workers have time for leisure?

Table 1.2 Participation* in leisure activities away from home in the UK: the top ten, 1998 (%) (*Source: Social Trends*, 29,1999)

Activity	Age group					
	16–24	25–34	35–44	45–59	60+	All adults
Visit a public house	82	85	81	74	55	74
Meal in a restaurant	63	69	65	75	70	69
Library	41	38	43	37	43	40
Cinema	65	51	31	23	11	34
Visit a historic building	24	30	35	39	30	32
Disco or night club	68	47	20	9	3	27
Spectator at sports event	31	34	36	22	11	26
Visit a museum/art gallery	21	18	27	26	19	22
Funfair	27	29	23	16	6	19
Theatre	14	18	15	18	17	17

*In the three months before the survey

Table 1.3 Participation* in sports and physical activities in the UK, by age and gender: the top five, 1998 (%) (*Source: Social Trends*, 29,1999)

Activity	Age group						
Males	16–24	25–34	35–44	45–54	55–64	65+	All adults
Walking	57	50	53	51	50	37	49
Snooker/pool/billiards	50	29	19	13	9	5	19
Cycling	30	19	18	12	8	5	15
Swimming	18	17	20	10	7	5	13
Soccer	47	28	17	10	2	1	10
Females							
Walking	44	44	45	49	43	25	41
Keep fit/yoga	29	24	20	14	12	6	17
Swimming	22	26	22	14	12	5	16
Cycling	12	10	12	7	4	2	8
Snooker/pool/billiards	21	6	3	1	—	—	4

*In the four weeks before the survey

Patterns of participation

Tables 1.2 and 1.3 set out our most popular leisure activities. At first glance they seem a mass of figures. But even such relatively brief tables are a valuable database, and we can extract useful information by asking specific questions, such as: What effect does your age have upon your leisure activities? Is age more important than gender in influencing leisure behaviour? However, official statistics often have frustrating limitations. For instance, Table 1.3 allows us to distinguish leisure behaviour by gender and age, but the data in Table 1.2 is broken down by age only. Furthermore, the age groupings in the two tables are not identical – yet they are from the same publication! Notice, too, that the timescale of participation is different for the two tables. None the less, we can extract several important understandings:

• People lead very different leisure lives, shown by the generally low participation levels for individual activities.
• Men and women enjoy quite distinct leisure lives, with women tending to have a narrower range and lower levels of participation.
• Informal, social activities dominate.
• Participation levels in sport and physical activities are generally low.

These findings lead us to further questions, such as: What resources and facilities are needed and who does and should provide them? Does the finding that there is a demand for a wide range of activities by relatively small numbers of people create problems for planners and providers? What are the environmental demands and impacts of various activities? What variables not included in the data might influence whether someone can take part in a

12 From Tables 1.2 and 1.3,
a Illustrate the four understandings about leisure participation patterns extracted opposite.
b What evidence is there in the data to support the assertions that (1), participation levels fall off with age? (2), some leisure activities are more age-specific than others?
c Suggest three factors which influence the participation patterns, and give examples of their possible effects.

Figure 1.15 Social and cultural backgrounds sometimes play little part when young people go clubbing

particular activity, e.g. social and cultural factors? (Fig. 1.15). How can participation levels of particular groups and for individual activities be improved?

1.5 The supply of leisure opportunities and facilities

All forms of leisure make some demands on resources, from your tiny 'personal space' on a beach to high-tech arenas. In turn, leisure must compete for these resources with other potential uses and users: houses, factories, roads, farms, wildlife, etc. (Fig. 1.17). Issues arising from this competition provide one of the central strands running through this book. A second strand is the concept of **access**: what it is; who controls it and provides it, and on what terms. Whether you want to walk the dog, practise windsurfing, lie on a beach, or go 'clubbing', you require access to natural or human-made resources and facilities.

Resource supply and management

When demands are made on resources, those who own and/or control them will respond. They either deny access ('Keep out – private property'; 'Trespassers will be prosecuted') or adopt policies which make the resources available on certain terms ('Members only'; 'Entry £5'; 'Open Monday to Friday only') (Fig. 1.16). We can think of this process of *supply* to meet *demand* while protecting ownership rights as a sequence or 'cascade' of concepts, with one idea spilling into the next, as in Figure 1.19. You may find this cascade useful as a framework for your examination of the issues and case studies throughout this book.

Demand–supply relationships are dynamic – they are constantly shifting. The four graphs of Figure 1.18 summarise basic relationships. In response to increases in demand, suppliers create additional capacity. They also have to react to decreases in demand. We must remember, too, that the providers also make efforts to promote and increase demand, e.g. marketing campaigns to increase the numbers who participate.

Figure 1.16 Access control, Mt Rainier National Park, USA. A firm but light-hearted way of saying 'Keep off the grass'. The sign is protecting fragile mountain meadows

Figure 1.17 Recreation must compete for resources and space: Central Park, New York

Figure 1.18a,b Demand–supply relationships

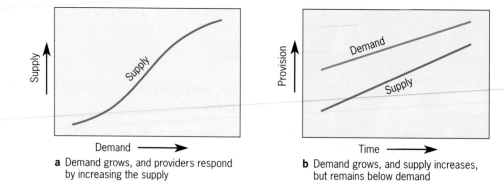

a Demand grows, and providers respond by increasing the supply

b Demand grows, and supply increases, but remains below demand

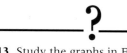

13 Study the graphs in Figure 1.18. For each of the graphs in turn, describe in not more than two sentences the trends and demand–supply relationships shown.

14 To which of the graphs does the following statement apply? 'In 1990 there were 974 golf courses in England, and 195 of them had been built since 1970. There are over a million golfers in the country, half of whom do not belong to a club, and have little hope of joining one. An average waiting list of between five and ten years is not unusual. In some clubs there is a 25-year queue.'

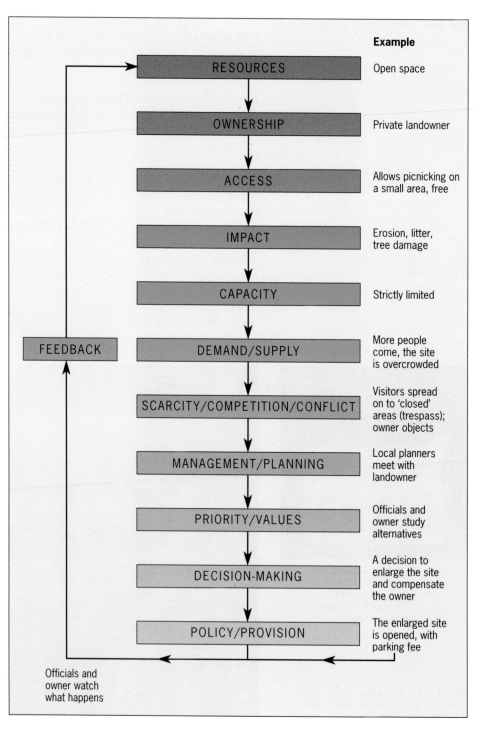

Figure 1.19 A concepts cascade for resource management

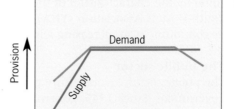

Figure 1.18c,d

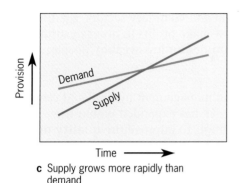

c Supply grows more rapidly than demand

d Demand grows, and supply increases to meet demand, but then demand decreases, while supply remains static

1.6 Providers of leisure resources and facilities

The providers of leisure opportunities fall into two major categories: the **private sector** and the **public sector**. The private sector then divides into two sub-types, according to their purpose and motivations – the **commercial sector**, whose primary concern is making a profit (from a farmer who charges rent for caravans and tents, to major holiday companies such as Thomas Cook plc), and the **voluntary sector**, made up of groups who organise themselves to provide specific forms of leisure activity, where social benefit outweighs profit margins. This voluntary sector contains a vast assemblage of clubs and societies, from suburban tennis clubs and choirs to national bodies such as the Caravan Club or National Trust. In Birmingham alone, a city of approximately 1 million people, it has been estimated that there are at least 3000 voluntary clubs and societies. This mixture of private and public sectors can be found in most countries of the world (Fig. 1.20).

Figure 1.20 Private enterprises advertising leisure opportunities on Hinchinbrook Island, a National Park in Queensland, Australia

Table 1.4 UK membership of major voluntary environmental organisations, 1995 (*Source: Social Trends*, 1996)

Organisation	Membership (thousands)
Civic Trust	280
CPRE (Council for the Preservation of Rural England)	50
Friends of the Earth	130
National Trust	2000
National Trust for Scotland	220
Ramblers' Association	100
RSNC (Royal Society for Nature Conservation)	200
RSPB (Royal Society for the Protection of Birds)	800
Woodland Trust	70

?

15 Draw a simple tree diagram to represent leisure providers. Make your diagram large enough to add notes as you study the rest of the chapter.

Not all voluntary organisations provide leisure opportunities directly; many act primarily as political lobbies, communications networks, controlling bodies, etc., e.g. Ramblers' Association, Royal Yachting Association, Football Association. The size of their membership is a significant factor in their ability to exert influence upon resource owners, politicians and planners (Table 1.4). For instance, the Ramblers' Association has been a powerful lobby group for increased countryside access (See Chapter 3, p.54). Some organisations

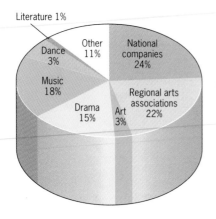

Total expenditure £180 million

Note: 'National companies' includes the English National Opera, National Theatre, Royal Opera, Royal Ballet, Royal Shakespeare Company

'Other' includes local arts centres and community projects

Figure 1.21 Arts Council support in the UK, 1996, percentage of total expenditure (*Source: Social Trends*, 1997)

?

16 Look at Figure 1.21.
a Make a list of possible reasons why some forms of activity receive more support from the Arts Council than others.
b The Arts Council has been accused of 'élitism' in its funding policy. What is there in the data to support this claim?

combine the characteristics of the commercial and voluntary sectors, e.g. the Youth Hostels Association (YHA), which must make profits in order to sustain its commitment to increasing leisure opportunities for less-wealthy people.

The public sector

The public sector covers leisure provision and management by local and central government. Since 1945, government influence has expanded within the sphere of Welfare State policies, with its attempts to improve the **quality of life** for all sections of society. Social fairness, and not financial profit, has been the primary intention.

This philosophy dominated until the late 1980s, since when the financial rules and levels of government funding have been increasingly tightened (see Chapter 2). None the less, when you use the local park or youth club, borrow a book from a library, go for a swim, picnic in a Country Park, take pottery classes or practise guitar in a local arts centre, or pedal your mountain bike across the hills of a National Park, your enjoyment will owe much to both the local authorities and central government.

Much government input is indirect, through separate bodies such as *quangos* (quasi-autonomous non-governmental organisations). Government supplies money and guidelines, and the semi-independent quangos distribute the money and implement the policies. In the world of leisure, two principal quangos are the Arts Council (Fig. 1.21) and the Sports Council (see case study, opposite). Since 1995, an increasingly important influence has been the National Lottery, with grants to a broad range of cultural, recreational and sports projects. Countryside policy and funding is channelled through the Countryside Agency (until 1999, the Countryside Commission).

Other government money is allocated to local authorities, which then add funds from local taxes (Council Tax) to provide and support facilities such as parks, libraries, pools, leisure centres, picnic sites, footpaths, etc. (Fig. 1.22).

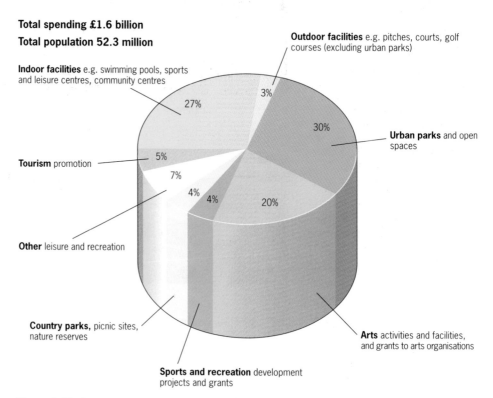

Total spending £1.6 billion
Total population 52.3 million

Indoor facilities e.g. swimming pools, sports and leisure centres, community centres — 27%

Outdoor facilities e.g. pitches, courts, golf courses (excluding urban parks) — 3%

Urban parks and open spaces — 30%

Tourism promotion — 5%

Other leisure and recreation — 7%

Country parks, picnic sites, nature reserves — 4%

Sports and recreation development projects and grants — 4%

Arts activities and facilities, and grants to arts organisations — 20%

Figure 1.22 Spending by local authorities in England and Wales on leisure, recreation and sport, 1998–9 (*Source:* CIPFA, 1999)

The English Sports Council (ESC) and the National Lottery, 1999

What the English Sports Council does

- **Young people** The ESC, in partnership with the Youth Sports Trust and others, targets resources through the National Junior Sport Programme to schemes which support youth sports in schools, partnerships, sports bodies and youth agencies.

- **Development of excellence** The ESC works to develop performance and excellence, through support to sports governing bodies, the six national Sports Centres and the proposed British Sports Academy.

- **National Lottery** The ESC distributes grants from the Lottery Sports Fund (LSF) and provides advice to LSF applicants on sports facility planning, design and management.

So – More people involved
More places to take part
More medals through high standards

Figure 1.24 Where the money comes from

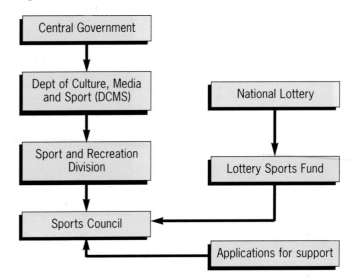

Sport Centre crisis: Lottery threatens to ask for cash back

LEOMINSTER'S flagship Bridge Street Sports Park has been threatened with closure little more than 18 months after its opening. And the director of the Lottery Sports Fund, which contributed almost £2m to the project, has intimated that an attempt may be made to force the troubled centre's trustees to repay the money invested by the LSF: 'The English Sports Council hereby gives notice of its intention to claw back the LSF award unless the trustees can satisfy the English Sports Council that the centre is financially and operationally viable.'

Herefordshire Council leader Terry James confirmed that the Council had been approached to get involved in rescuing the beleaguered centre but that they had been denied access to the books.

'It's very sad, as it is a magnificent facility, but it obviously needs dramatic changes in management,' said Councillor James. 'To be involved we would need the authority to change the management and also to have some sort of financial guarantee.'

Figure 1.23 Newspaper report on sport centre funding (*Source: Hereford Times, 25 March 1999*)

LSF awards, 1995–8 The top five winners

		(£m)
1	Association football	178
2	Swimming	175
3	Multi-sports	105
4	Cricket	54
5	Tennis	48

Figure 1.25 Where the money goes to

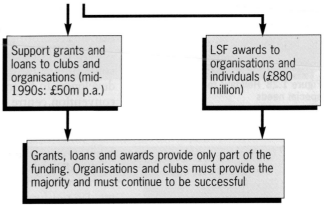

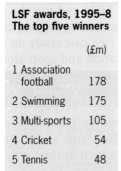

Figure 1.26 Leominster's Bridge Street Sports Park – can it be made successful enough to keep it open?

2 Leisure and the urban environment

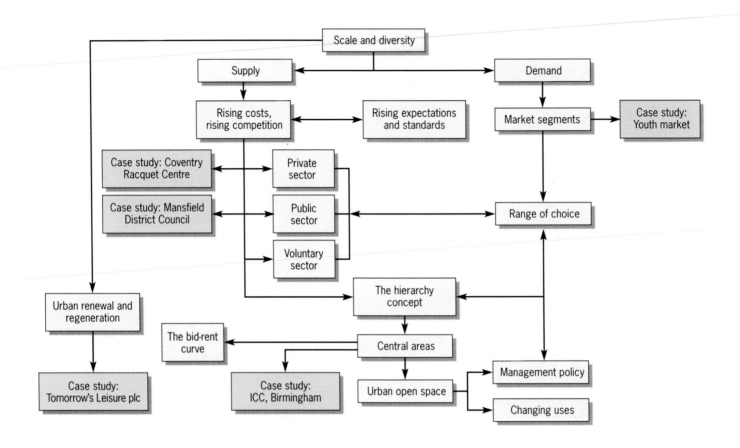

2.1 Scale and diversity

Approximately 80 per cent of the UK population lives in, or on the fringes of, urban areas. Thus, for most of us, towns and cities are both where we live and where we enjoy much of our leisure. This chapter will show that our demands for leisure and the provision of leisure opportunities are significant influences on urban land-use patterns, morphology (shape and form) and planning policy. For example:

• Where should major sports facilities such as athletics and football stadiums be located, and what impacts do they have on surrounding communities?
• What part can leisure developments play in urban regeneration programmes?
• As shopping emerges as an important leisure activity, how does this affect planning policy for the location and layout of retail centres?

Because cities concentrate people, they encourage the clustering of leisure facilities. Urban dwellers, therefore, should be 'advantaged' in terms of opportunities for leisure, especially in cities that attract large numbers of tourists. The case study of the leisure lives of two young people in Birmingham helps us to 'test' this hypothesis (pp. 20–21).

Market segments

The leisure industry (the suppliers) in both the public and private sectors understands that the use an individual makes of leisure facilities (the demand) depends upon a number of variables: age, gender, education, mobility, income,

Table 2.1 The most popular visitor attractions in the UK, 1997
(*Source: Social Trends*, **29, 1999**)

Attraction	Visitor (million)	Sector	Admission
Blackpool Pleasure Beach	7.8	Private	Free
British Museum, London	6.1	Public	Free
Strathclyde Country Park, Glasgow	5.6	Public	Free
National Gallery, London	4.8	Public	Free
Palace Pier, Brighton	4.3	Public	Free
Alton Towers	2.7	Private	Charge
Madame Tussaud's, London	2.7	Private	Charge
Westminster Abbey, London	2.5	Private	Free
Eastbourne Pier	2.2	Public	Free
York Minster	2.0	Private	Free
Pleasureland, Southport	2.0	Public	Free
Tate Gallery, London	1.9	Public	Free
Tower of London	1.8	Public	Charge
Chessington World of Adventures, London	1.8	Private	Charge
Natural History Museum, London	1.8	Public	Charge
Canterbury Cathedral	1.6	Private	Charge
Science Museum, London	1.5	Public	Charge
Legoland, Windsor	1.5	Private	Charge
Blackpool Tower	1.3	Partnership	Charge
Windsor Castle	1.1	Public	Charge

Note: These are specific facilities, not broad destinations such as resorts or National Parks

Figure 2.1 The 'Paradise Lost' nightclub, Belfast. A survey of young women regulars found that the main reasons they went there were to meet 'boys', the music, the opportunity to dance and be with friends in a relatively safe environment. Factors which influenced their attendance were money, social class, parental approval and the accessibility of the club

culture, stage and status in the family life cycle, personality, interests. The industry uses these variables to classify the population in terms of **market segments**. Each segment has a distinctive leisure lifestyle, e.g. 'Dinkies' ('Double-income-no-kids'), are seen as having considerable leisure consumption potential. Cities, with their large and diverse populations, contain a broad range of market segments of sufficient size to support a diversity of leisure facilities and attractions.

Perhaps the most high-profile segment is the 'youth market'. Young people, such as Mike and Siobhan in the case study (pp.20–21) are identified as having active leisure lifestyles, with ample time, motivation and spending power, e.g. the 'pubbing and clubbing' boom of the 1990s. It is to attract this market that major brewery companies have invested heavily in restyling pubs with music, 'pop' themes etc. Young women in particular have been targeted (Fig. 2.1).

1 From Table 2.1,
a How many of the top attractions are in cities?
b How many of the attractions are in London and SE England?
c Describe briefly the location and character of the attractions.
d Discuss the demand–supply relationships illustrated by the character and distribution of these attractions.

2 In 1988, entry to the Natural History and the Science Museums was free, and visitor numbers were 2.7 million and 2.4 million respectively. In 1989 the government adopted a 'user pays' policy and introduced entry charges. Make out the case *for* and *against* charging for entry to publicly owned leisure facilities.

3 For each of the following market segments, identify three leisure facilities whose primary target is (*a*) young people; (*b*) 'active retired'.

Birmingham: leisure diaries of two young people

The diary extracts in Figure 2.2 allow us to look more closely at the ways in which young people enjoy their leisure. Siobhan and Mike, two young adults who live in Birmingham (Fig. 2.3), have recorded their out-of-home leisure activities over a weekend. They have engaged in a range of activities in a range of settings with no round trips of more than 20km. Table 2.2 analyses their leisure experiences in terms of the demands made on resources and facilities, and their providers.

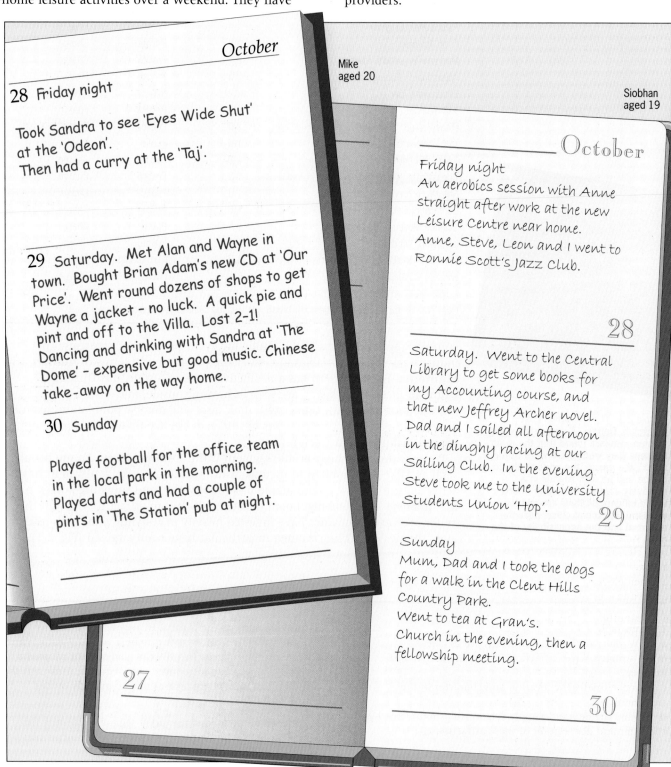

October

28 Friday night

Took Sandra to see 'Eyes Wide Shut' at the 'Odeon'.
Then had a curry at the 'Taj'.

29 Saturday. Met Alan and Wayne in town. Bought Brian Adam's new CD at 'Our Price'. Went round dozens of shops to get Wayne a jacket - no luck. A quick pie and pint and off to the Villa. Lost 2-1! Dancing and drinking with Sandra at 'The Dome' - expensive but good music. Chinese take-away on the way home.

30 Sunday

Played football for the office team in the local park in the morning. Played darts and had a couple of pints in 'The Station' pub at night.

_27_

Mike
aged 20

Siobhan
aged 19

October

Friday night
An aerobics session with Anne straight after work at the new Leisure Centre near home.
Anne, Steve, Leon and I went to Ronnie Scott's Jazz Club.

_28_

Saturday. Went to the Central Library to get some books for my Accounting course, and that new Jeffrey Archer novel. Dad and I sailed all afternoon in the dinghy racing at our Sailing Club. In the evening Steve took me to the University Students Union 'Hop'.

_29_

Sunday
Mum, Dad and I took the dogs for a walk in the Clent Hills Country Park.
Went to tea at Gran's.
Church in the evening, then a fellowship meeting.

_30_

Figure 2.2 The leisure diaries of two young people

Figure 2.3 Mike and Siobhan – two typical young leisure users?

4 Compare and contrast the leisure lives of Siobhan and Mike. Think carefully of the variables and factors you will use to make this assessment.

5 In what ways might their leisure lives change if they were:
a married
b unemployed
c lived in a rural area?

6 What other factors might influence how they spend their free time?

7 What 'messages' would the two diaries send you if you were:
a a leisure services officer in a local authority?
b a market researcher in a commercial leisure company?

Table 2.2 An analysis of leisure activities

A MIKE				
Activity	**Venue**	**Location**	**Provider/owner**	**Free/pay**
Watching film	Cinema	Major radial road	Private commercial company	Entrance charge
Eating out	Restaurant	Suburban High Street	Private enterprise	Pay for meals
Shopping	Various shops	City centre	Private commercial companies	Free entry
Eating out	Pub	Inner suburb	Private commercial company	Free entry; payment for consumption
Watching professional sport	Football stadium	Inner suburb	Private company	Entrance fee
Dancing, social entertainment	Nightclub	City centre	Private commercial company	Entrance fee
Eating out	Fast-food outlet	Major radial road	Private enterprise	Pay for meals
Playing sport – football	Public park pitch	Outer suburb	Local authority	Free to individual. Team rents pitch
Recreational game and social entertainment	Pub	Outer suburb	Private commercial company	Free entry

B SIOBHAN				
Activity	**Venue**	**Location**	**Provider/owner**	**Free/pay**
Physical exercise – aerobics	Leisure centre	Suburb	Local authority	Payment session
Listening to music and social entertainment	Club	City centre	Private enterprise	Entrance fee
Selecting reading material	Library	City centre	Local authority	Free
Outdoor activity – sailing	Reservoir	Urban fringe	Private club – voluntary sector; renting private water space	Free on day but annual subscription
Dancing and social entertainment	University club	Suburb	Private club with public funding	Entrance fee and guest fee. Annual subscription
Outdoor activity – walking	Country Park	Urban fringe	Local authority and National Trust (public and voluntary sectors)	Free
Visiting relatives	Family home	Inner suburb	Local authority (public sector)	Free
Religious service	Church	Outer suburb	Voluntary sector – Church institution	Free
Discussion	Church meeting room	Outer suburb		

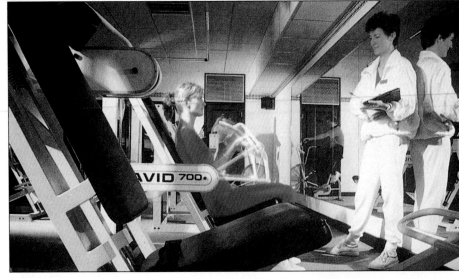

Figure 2.4 The health and fitness craze has led to the spread of private fitness centres and clubs. The quality expected and the expense of the facilities, the equipment and the staff constantly push up costs and prices. So, competition for trade becomes tougher

Rising expectations – rising costs – rising competition

Over the past 25 years the commercial leisure industry has changed in three significant ways: first, it has become dominated by a small number of large companies; second, it is offering an ever-wider range of leisure opportunities; and third, it is responding to customers' expectations of higher-quality facilities and equipment across all market segments (Fig. 2.4). Leisure provision has become increasingly capital intensive. This has raised a number of issues for providers in the private and public sectors (Fig. 2.5). Swimming is one of the most popular activities across a broad age range, and illustrates the issues and trends vividly (Figs 2.6, 2.7).

The commercial sector has been able to respond to this expanding and increasingly affluent market by continued investment (see the Indoor Centre in

What is our target market and how do we make a profit?

Director of a commercial company

How can we raise money to upgrade?

Committee member of a voluntary club

How can we afford to offer opportunities for all local people to enjoy our leisure facilities?

City councillor

Figure 2.5 Questions for the providers

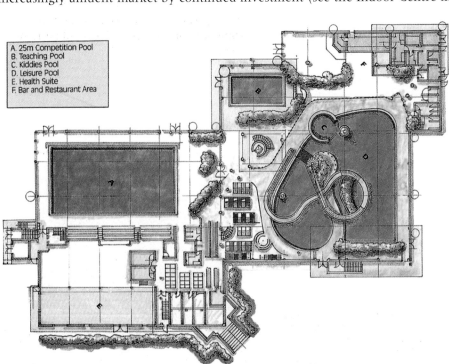

A. 25m Competition Pool
B. Teaching Pool
C. Kiddies Pool
D. Leisure Pool
E. Health Suite
F. Bar and Restaurant Area

Figure 2.6 Mansfield Water Meadows Leisure Pool complex

Figure 2.7 Changing trends in swimming pool provision (*Source:* Standeven, 1991)

Trends

For swimming, flexibility, fun and fitness characterise the spirit of the new decade. An increasing trend over the past few years has been to design pools for more flexible use. The Suncentre at Rhyl, which opened in 1980 with all pools dedicated to fun, summed up a decade of relatively affluent lifestyles. Leisure pools boomed in the 1980s, and have undoubtedly been partly responsible for the increase in swimming among women.

Changing provision is illustrated by the recently opened Ponds Forge complex in Sheffield. The three pools in this international facility – a diving pool, warm-up pool, and what is claimed to be the most versatile 50m pool in the world – allow maximum flexibility. Although the complex has been designed for world-class competition, the warm-up pool is located within a 650sq.m water area which has a wave machine, a river ride and twin 90m long flumes. The facility combines a high-level performance pool with fun-based leisure pools within the same complex.

Water play does not appeal to all, and providers have become increasingly aware of the need to provide separately for more 'athletic' swimming. Ponds Forge is one way to achieve this flexibility.... Flexibility can also be achieved by a mix of facilities within a district. 'Playing' in the water will maintain its appeal, but facilities that provide only for play may find it increasingly difficult to be cost-effective.

Social welfare objectives are high among councils' reasons for providing swimming facilities, but they are increasingly attempting to balance such objectives against the need to improve their income–expenditure balance.

Profitability seems to depend not so much on type of pool as on pricing structures and programming of sessions. The need to control costs, and the deterioration of ageing swimming pools, indicate that modernisation and refurbishment programmes will predominate over replacement in the next decade.

Coventry case study, pp. 24–25). Increased competition, with its emphasis on quality, is one reason why local authorities have been forced to raise the standards of their facilities, while attempting to achieve success for all groups in society (see Mansfield District Council case study, pp. 26–27, and Fig. 2.8).

Figure 2.8 Facilities are now required to provide ramp entrances as well as steps to allow accessibility for people with disabilities and encourage their participation in sport and leisure activities

An indoor centre in Coventry

The Coventry Racquet Centre is a high-quality indoor facility for racquet games and fitness activities. Figure 2.9 sets out extracts from their publicity material. It tells us a great deal about their marketing strategy, what opportunities they supply and for whom. The company's decision-making process will be guided by the fact that this is a private commercial enterprise which needs to make consistent profits. We can follow the company through six important elements of this process.

Location
The company seeks a *highly accessible location*. The maps in Figure 2.9 present the image of the centre at the heart of a road network, within a city of 250 000 people and a well-populated sub-regional **catchment area**.

Demand, supply and accessibility
The company selects *activities growing in popularity* – squash, badminton, keep-fit – plus a well-established activity, tennis, with a *shortage of indoor facilities*. Notice, too, that the participant profile (i.e. the types of people who take part) comprises mainly car owners with some money to spend. These activities, then, are accessible to them via their mobility and their ability/willingness to pay.

Capacity
From the publicity material in Figure 2.9 we can see clearly that the company wants all the facilities to be used fully. Courts and activity rooms have a **physical carrying capacity**, that is, they are designed to hold a certain maximum number of people at one time. This is their **at-one-time capacity** – two people on a squash court; four on a tennis or badminton court. The centre's managers, therefore, need to decide upon *(a)* the length of the booking period, and *(b)* how many hours per day and per week they will keep the facility open. Thus, if they keep a badminton court open for 10 hours a day, and it is used for doubles play continuously in a series of one-hour bookings, then 40 people will have used the court. This is its **throughput capacity**.

Pricing policy.
The next step in the decision-making process then becomes: 'How much shall we charge?' This decision is affected by *(a)* how much income the company needs to cover its invested capital, its running and maintenance costs, and to make a profit, and *(b)* how much people are willing to pay. This may be affected by the nature of the local competition. The company decides upon a *pricing policy* which takes into account

that some times are more popular than others, some activities are more popular than others, and some facilities cost more to build and run than others.

Target market
Now the company needs to decide upon the market segments it is aiming at – what demand it is hoping to satisfy, and how it can attract its targeted customers. Once it has selected the range of activities it will offer, the next step becomes the 'no membership; pay-as-you-play' decision. Thus, access to the centre is not restricted by membership but by ability and willingness to pay, or by qualification through a social programme (e.g. 'Access to Leisure' passes for the unemployed). It is important, too, to attract customers from as broad a market as possible in terms of age, gender and family status. Thus, the company may target certain groups and ease **accessibility** for them by pricing and timing of activities. To extend appeal still further, all skill and commitment levels are provided for. For example, the centre has received money from the Sports Council (a central government agency) to support a 'Badminton Development Programme' for young people.

Facilities
Finally, the company aims to provide a *high-quality environment*. So, the centre has saunas, sunbeds, excellent changing and shower facilities, bar and restaurant. In order to make best use of the expensive facilities and to increase profits, the company also provides rooms for conferences, business meetings and receptions.

8 Examine the publicity material in Figure 2.9 carefully, and give examples of how the company aims are being carried out, e.g.:
a How do the pricing and timing policies try to raise use levels towards capacity? Why do pricing levels vary?
b Make a list of customer types being targeted.
c Why are certain groups being targeted at certain times?
d In what ways do the maps suggest that the centre is not a local 'community' facility, but a facility which aims at a broader catchment area?

9 Essay: Assess the relative importance of the main factors that influence the location and the **management** policy of private leisure clubs such as the Coventry Racquet Centre. (Use the Coventry example and, if possible, an example from your local area to illustrate your general points.)

Figure 2.9 Examples of the Coventry Racquet Centre's publicity material

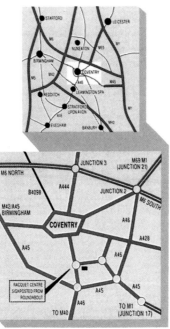

5 OUTDOOR TENNIS COURTS
7 INDOOR TENNIS COURTS
15 BADMINTON COURTS
8 SQUASH COURTS
RHYTHMIC GYM
STEP REEBOK
AEROBICS
SUNBEDS
SAUNA
STEAM
YOGA
KARATE
BUMBLE BEES
BAR & RESTAURANT
LOVETT SPORTS SHOP

NO MEMBERSHIP
PAY AS YOU PLAY

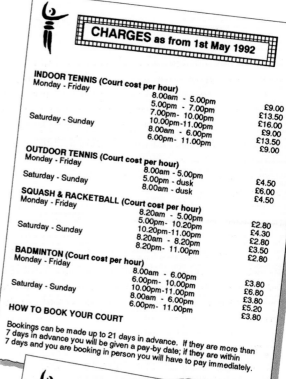

CHARGES as from 1st May 1992

INDOOR TENNIS (Court cost per hour)

Monday - Friday	8.00am - 5.00pm	
	5.00pm - 7.00pm	£9.00
	7.00pm - 10.00pm	£13.50
	10.00pm-11.00pm	£16.00
Saturday - Sunday	8.00am - 6.00pm	£9.00
	6.00pm- 11.00pm	£13.50

OUTDOOR TENNIS (Court cost per hour)

Monday - Friday	8.00am - 5.00pm	£9.00
	5.00pm - dusk	£4.50
Saturday - Sunday	8.00am - dusk	£6.00
		£4.50

SQUASH & RACKETBALL (Court cost per hour)

Monday - Friday	8.20am - 5.00pm	
	5.00pm- 10.20pm	£2.80
	10.20pm-11.00pm	£4.30
Saturday - Sunday	8.20am - 8.20pm	£2.80
	8.20pm- 11.00pm	£3.50
		£2.80

BADMINTON (Court cost per hour)

Monday - Friday	8.00am - 6.00pm	
	6.00pm- 10.00pm	£3.80
	10.00pm-11.00pm	£6.80
Saturday - Sunday	8.00am - 6.00pm	£3.80
	6.00pm- 11.00pm	£5.20
		£3.80

HOW TO BOOK YOUR COURT

Bookings can be made up to 21 days in advance. If they are more than 7 days in advance you will be given a pay-by date; if they are within 7 days and you are booking in person you will have to pay immediately.

coventry
racquet
centre

SPECIALS

BUMBLE BEES

Come and join our
Pre School Play Activity
climbing, balancing & co-ordination
forty five minutes of fun

9.30am only
10.30am & 2.00pm
11.30am & 3.00pm

1-2 years
2-3 years
3 years to school age

"FAMILY FIVER"

£2 adult £1 child
£5 per family
max. 2 adults
& 4 children

SATURDAY   6.00pm - 10.00pm
SUNDAY   2.00pm - 6.00pm

a variety of sports for all the family
Use any available courts
gym/sauna/steam

Family Fiver

KEEP FIT/AEROBICS

Day	Time	Instructor	Cost
Monday	1.30pm - 2.30pm	Ricky	£2.50
	6.00pm - 7.00pm	Ricky	£3.20
Tuesday	7.15pm - 8.15pm	Ricky	£3.20
Wednesday	7.00pm - 8.00pm	Julie	£3.20
Thursday	7.15pm - 8.15pm	Ricky	£3.20
	10.00am - 11.00am	Ricky	£3.20
	7.00pm - 11.00pm	Ricky	£2.50
Friday	8.00pm - 8.00pm	Julie	£3.20
	10.00am - 9.00pm	Ricky	£2.50
Saturday	6.00pm - 11.00am	Karen	£3.20
	11.00am - 12noon	Ricky	£2.50
		Ricky	£2.80

SPECIAL SESSIONS

Monday	CIRCUIT TRAINING 6.00pm - 7.00pm	£2.70
Monday	FEMALE FITNESS 7.30pm - 10.00pm ladies girls (12-18yrs)	£3.00 £1.50
Monday & Tuesday	'VETS' OVER 45's 2.00pm - 4.00pm	£2.20
Tuesday	ANTE & POST NATAL (ladies only) 10.00am - 11.00am	£3.00
Tuesday & Thursday	FEMALE FITNESS 10.00am - 12 noon ladies girls (12-18 yrs)	£3.00 £1.50
Tuesday & Thursday	'FIT FOR WORK' 7.00am - 9.00am	£3.00
Saturday	TEENAGE TRAINERS (12-18 yrs) 2.00pm - 8.00pm	£1.50

Mansfield District Council

Because people are no longer satisfied by a narrow range of activities, outdated buildings, and poor-quality courts and pitches, the costs of providing and running facilities are rising. Further, government policy and increasing competition from private leisure companies (see pp. 22–25) are forcing local authorities to make hard decisions. One council that is strongly committed to providing a wide range of high-quality leisure opportunities for all sections of its population is Mansfield.

Mansfield is a Nottinghamshire town with a population of approximately 104 000, at the centre of a County District on the Nottinghamshire coalfield (Fig. 2.11). Under the rule of compulsory competitive tendering (CCT), the Leisure Department put in a bid to its own District Council to run the town and district public-sector leisure services. It succeeded, and since January 1992 it has had the contract to manage all leisure facilities, including the parks, 16 community centres, a lottery, the Civic Theatre and Museum. The materials in Table 2.3 illustrate the range and quality of the opportunities for recreation. Notice, too, how expensive it is to provide the top-quality experiences necessary to attract people and compete with the private sector.

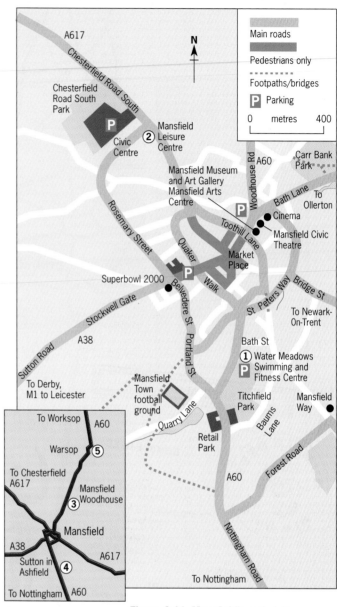

Figure 2.11 Mansfield's main leisure facilities

Figure 2.10 Meden Sports Centre

Table 2.3 Examples of leisure provision by Mansfield District Council

1 The Water Meadows at Titchfield Park: An investment of £6.5 million has produced a 500sq.m leisure pool with wave machine, water channel, weir and beach-effect area; a 6-lane competition pool with seating for 250 spectators; a 10m teaching pool; a health-fitness centre; a bar and restaurant overlooking the pool.

2 The Mansfield Leisure Centre: Facilities include a 9000sq.ft multi-purpose hall for sports, theatre and concerts, seating up to 1500 people (e.g. for plays, cabarets, fashion shows, volleyball and badminton tournaments); a social hall for table tennis, martial arts, yoga and keep-fit; solarium; squash courts.

3 Manor Park: The council has invested £3 million to turn a disused sewage works into a sports complex. Some of the money comes from the Sports Council and government 'derelict land support grants'. There is a new sports pavilion and tennis courts, cricket nets and an artificial playing surface with floodlights used for a wide range of competitive, recreational sports and coaching. There are also two outdoor bowling greens and ten grass pitches. The site has been landscaped and provides trails for walking and jogging, with car parking and facilities for the disabled.

4 Berry Hill Park: £9 million has been invested to build a pavilion and international-standard athletics track: a synthetic, all-weather surface with eight lanes and a ten-lane straight. The park is run as a Social Welfare Centre, managed by a joint committee involving a partnership between the coal companies, the Mining Union and Mansfield District Council.

5 Meden Sports Centre: A dual-use facility at Warsop Meden Comprehensive School, funded jointly by the District and County Councils to allow educational use during school hours and community use at other times. There is a 20m swimming pool; a 27m x 16m sports hall (badminton, football, basketball, volleyball, hockey, netball); a gym; squash courts; multi-purpose children's play room; tennis courts.

Figure 2.12 Water Meadows

WATER MEADOWS
Tel: 22507

Tuesday 8.00am-8.45am
Wednesday 12 noon-3.00pm
Thursday 8.00am-8.45am

SHERWOOD BATHS
Tel: 663082

Monday and Friday
8.00am-8.45am – 12 noon-1.15pm
School Holidays 8.00am-3.00pm
Wednesday 12 noon-1.15pm

Summer Holidays only
Tuesdays and Thursdays
8.00am-3.00pm
Wednesdays 8.00am-12 noon

MEDEN SPORTS CENTRE
Tel: 842865

Monday and Friday
12.30pm-3.00pm
Squash and Weight Training
Swimming *(School Holidays only)*

OAK TREE LANE CENTRE
Tel: 23926

Monday and Friday
9.00am-3.00pm
Badminton, Table Tennis
Weight Training only

CONDITIONS OF SCHEME

1. All facilities SUBJECT TO AVAILABILITY
2. Concessions only available at the stated facilities and at the stated times
3. These concessions are only open to the following people:

*UNEMPLOYED AND ACCOMPANYING CHILDREN
(to include those engaged on EMPLOYMENT TRAINING SCHEMES – on production of Form B83)

*SENIOR CITIZENS
Aged 60 and over

*REGISTERED DISABLED PERSONS
(on production of a Green Card)

*EARLY RETIRED/JOB RELEASE
(on production of an Income Support Order Book or a Family Credit Order Book)

*SINGLE PARENTS AND ACCOMPANYING CHILDREN
(on production of an Income Support Order Book or a Family Credit Order Book)*

Please Note:
- Concessions only available to recipients of Family Credit or Income Support.
- Applies only to residents living within the boundaries of Mansfield District Council.
- Please ring and confirm your attendance.
- Please contact facility before intended use.

Figure 2.13 The Mansfield district – leisure provision

WILLIAM KAYE HALL COMMUNITY CENTRE

MONDAY	Bingo	7.15pm-8.45pm
TUESDAY	Wine Making (every 3rd Tuesday)	7.00pm-10.00pm
	Dance School	5.00pm-10.00pm
THURSDAY	Fellowship Group	1.30pm-4.00pm
	RSPB (Juniors)	6.00pm-7.00pm
	RSPB (Seniors) (every 1st Thursday)	7.30pm-9.30pm
	Aerobics/Step Aerobics	6.00pm-9.00pm
FRIDAY	Bingo	7.15pm-8.45pm

One of the largest Community Centres in Mansfield, the William Kaye Hall has a main hall which seats 200 and staging suitable for concerts and shows.

The smaller room is ideal for children's parties, family get-togethers, meetings or classes.

Close to the Town Centre, the building is easily reached on foot or by bus and there is ample parking space to the rear of the building.

For further information/bookings contact Mr P Norman on 658471

As of April 1992

MANSFIELD LEISURE SERVICES

?

Use the materials in Figures 2.11 and 2.13 and Table 2.3 to answer the following questions:

10 List the range of activities provided.

11 Why do you think that many of the facilities are located some distance from the town centre?

12 In what ways do the examples given illustrate the increasing emphasis upon high quality and standards of opportunities?

13 What evidence is there of policies to attract from all sections of the community, especially those who might be described as 'disadvantaged'?

14 Which of the council facilities involve partnerships with or are supported by other organisations? Suggest reasons for these partnerships.

15 Which types of leisure activities appear *not* to be provided by the District Council? Can you suggest reasons why this might be so?

Examples

1 A local authority leisure centre may have some of the services run by a commercial company, while a number of voluntary clubs may rent the facilities as their base.

2 A voluntary club may receive a grant from central government or local authority.

3 Pitches in a public park may be rented by commercial firms and voluntary clubs for sports league matches.

Figure 2.14 Interrelationships of the providers

We must remember that, although the public sector invests massively in leisure (see Fig. 1.22), local authorities vary widely in their spending (Table 2.4). In turn, these trends put pressure on voluntary clubs and societies – after all, who wants to play badminton in a church hall, with no showers, when the local public or private leisure centre offers high-quality courts, changing rooms and social facilities? One increasingly common response to the competitive and financial pressures has been closer interrelationships between the sectors.

Table 2.4 What London local authorities spent on leisure, recreation and sport in 1998–9 (*Source*: CIPFA, *Leisure and Recreation Statistics 1998–9 Estimates*)

Expenditure (£/head of population)						
Authority	**Population ('000)**	**Indoor sport and rec.**	**Outdoor sport and rec.**	**Other rec. and leisure**	**Arts**	**Total**
Camden	187	6.3	10.0	1.6	5.4	23.3
Greenwich	212	23.3	22.7	10.0	4.8	60.8
All Inner London boroughs	2230	10.7	18.1	4.9	5.0	38.7

2.2 Leisure facilities and the hierarchy concept

Two important ideas put forward by urban geographers are:

1 The larger the city, the greater the number, variety and quality of services available.

2 Within a city there will be a number of service centres offering a different number, range and quality of services.

Following from these ideas, urban settlements and service centres have been grouped into a set of levels called a *hierarchy*. Centres of the highest level offer the full range of goods and services including the highest quality and most specialised, known as 'high-order' goods and services. Medium-sized centres offer only up to 'middle-order' level, while small centres contain only 'low-order' goods and services. Equally important, high-order goods and services are few and far between and attract custom from long distances, while at the other extreme, low-order facilities occur frequently and attract only local custom.

This general hierarchy model has been used most commonly to study retail and professional services, but it can also be applied to leisure. For example, we

Figure 2.15 All over the world, major cities are the location of high-order leisure facilities. The famous Opera House occupies a spectacular site in the centre of Sydney, Australia

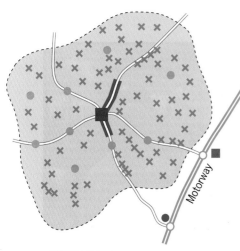

■ City centre, high-order facilities

● Suburban, middle-order facilities

✕ Neighbourhood low-order facilities

▧ High-order peripheral facilities

● Middle-order peripheral facilities

▬ Middle-order facilities along radial road

Figure 2.16 The urban leisure hierarchy: a model

16 To test the usefulness of the leisure model (Fig. 2.16), apply it to a town or city with which you are familiar by studying the distribution of dance and disco clubs. (For a large city you may be able to examine one sector or transect, extending outwards from the CBD, and use one residential neighbourhood.)
a Plot the venues (Yellow Pages or advertisements in the local newspaper can be useful) on a base map and decide whether they are 'high-', 'middle-' or 'low-order' facilities.
b Describe the resulting pattern. Say whether it has a spatial and hierarchical structure similar to that suggested by the model in Figure 2.16.

17 Does the model work for other leisure activities – e.g. swimming pools, libraries, leisure centres, parks? (Check this by using Yellow Pages.) If not, can you suggest reasons why the model works for some activities and not for others?

can use this starting hypothesis: *high-order facilities are few in number, large in size and widely spaced, with large threshold populations and extensive catchment areas.* So, Table 2.1 shows the broad scatter of the top attractions, but with the dominance of London. Think, too, of the location of the highest-order sports facilities: London has Wembley for football, Twickenham for rugby union, Wimbledon for tennis, and Edinburgh, Cardiff, Belfast and Dublin are all bases for high-order facilities and events (Fig. 2.15).

Do not forget, however, that one element of UK government regional development policies for many years has been to give grant-aid support to help disperse major facilities (e.g. Sheffield athletics stadium; the aid that was promised to Manchester in their unsuccessful bid for the Olympic Games in 2000).

Figure 2.16 suggests an urban model based on our starting hypothesis. The **Central Business District (CBD)** contains a cluster of high-order facilities whose sphere of influence is city-wide, and indeed may extend to the surrounding region. Major suburban centres contain middle-order facilities with a district catchment area, while residential neighbourhoods are dotted with low-order 'local' facilities.

The model diagram shows two significant modifications to this simple pattern: first, there are linear strips of middle-order facilities along main roads (e.g. hotels, clubs), and second, there are high-grade facilities in peripheral locations – near bypasses or motorway junctions – to take advantage of land availablility and accessibility.

We can take dance and disco clubs as an example of how this model works. The city centre has large, high-quality, expensive nightclubs, with perhaps one or two located along a radial road or accessible fringe site (Fig. 2.17). In suburban centres, moderately priced and equipped venues are found, often attached to larger pubs. In residential districts, local pubs may have disco or 'live music' nights, or a community centre or youth club might have 'disco nights'.

The key understanding is that the location and distribution of leisure facilities are not haphazard – there is a pattern. This pattern depends upon a number of factors: history of the area; land values; government policy; local planning policy; transport networks; population distribution; commercial company decisions; fashion, etc. The materials in Section 2.4 (pp. 34–38) explain these issues.

Figure 2.17 The 'Dome' nightclub, Birmingham: a high-order facility in an accessible location on a radial road at the edge of the CBD, which can be seen in the background

2.3 Leisure as a competitor for space in the city

Factors that influence the location of leisure facilities in urban areas are: land values, the availability of suitable sites and the planning policies of local authorities. These factors interact and we can see the results of this interaction in any town or city in the UK.

Land values and the bid-rent curve

One explanation for the hierarchy model of Figure 2.16 is given by economic geographers through the bid-rent curve (Fig. 2.23). This states that land values, as measured by the rent that can be obtained for a site, fall as distance from a central point (the PLVI = peak land value intersection) increases. This simple curve is modified by subsidiary peaks along radial roads and at suburban centres. This idea is based upon accessibility: the more people that have ready access to a site, the more valuable that site is for businesses that rely on customers coming to them. So, leisure facilities that need or wish to attract people either have to compete for the most accessible sites (e.g. high-grade nightclubs) or have been placed there by historical events (e.g. civic concert halls built in the nineteenth century; older professional football grounds).

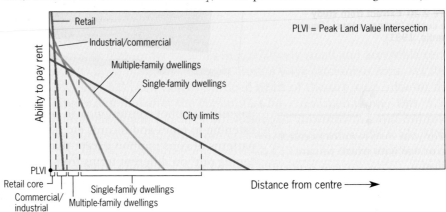

Figure 2.23 The bid-rent curve and land-use patterns (*Source:* Chapman, 1979)

Availability of land and buildings; planning policy

Other factors which influence location are the availability of land – clearly related to who owns it – and of suitable existing buildings (e.g. cinemas converted into bingo halls) and above all, planning policy. City development and structure plans are based on **zoning** principles: the city is subdivided into areas according to preferred land uses. Any landowner or developer wishing to bring a 'non-conforming' land use into an area faces the difficult task of justifying their proposal before gaining planning permission. In this way, planning policy has a significant influence upon the distribution of leisure facilities, e.g. semi-continuous strips of pubs, restaurants, clubs and hotels along some radial roads leading to a city centre, which are zoned for commercial use (Fig. 2.24).

Leisure in the suburban High Street

The outcome of the interaction between planning policy and competition for space and place (i.e. location) is easily visible in the typical suburban High Street, where lines of commercial, professional and personal service businesses include a range of leisure-based enterprises. Figure 2.25 illustrates a number of the key features to look out for in such a High Street: (*a*) the *range* and *level* of leisure facilities and services; (*b*) the relatively small site size and hence restriction upon provision; (*c*) accessibility problems caused by traffic congestion and lack of parking space; (*d*) the interspersion of leisure-based facilities among buildings with other uses; (*e*) the predominance of the commercial sector in this relatively high-rental location.

Figure 2.24 Hagley Road, Birmingham. A major radial road to the city centre, originally lined by elegant nineteenth-century houses. Planning policy has zoned this strip for commercial use. Thus today there is a linear development of hotels, wine bars, pubs, restaurants, clubs etc.

21 Essay: To what extent can the leisure facilities hierarchy shown in Figure 2.16 be explained in terms of the bid-rent curve? You will find it useful to look again at your results from question 4.

22 Look at Figure 2.25 carefully.
a Divide the leisure-related facilities into not more than four categories and place each facility into one of your categories.
b Describe the pattern of leisure provision in Harborne High Street. Compare this with a suburban High Street with which you are familiar and suggest what range and character of leisure provision appears to be typical of such High Streets.

23 For a suburban High Street with which you are familiar, carry out a leisure land-use survey, and build up a set of field notes based upon the features identified for Harborne High Street (Fig. 2.25). (If you wish to make this the basis of an assessment project, then you will find it useful to contact the district planning officers about the local plan.)

Figure 2.25 Harborne High Street, Birmingham. A large suburban High Street along a radial road from the city centre. Originally it was a residential street – the buildings have been modified or replaced. Sites are small and parking is limited. The leisure-related facilities are scattered along the frontage, and shown on the map

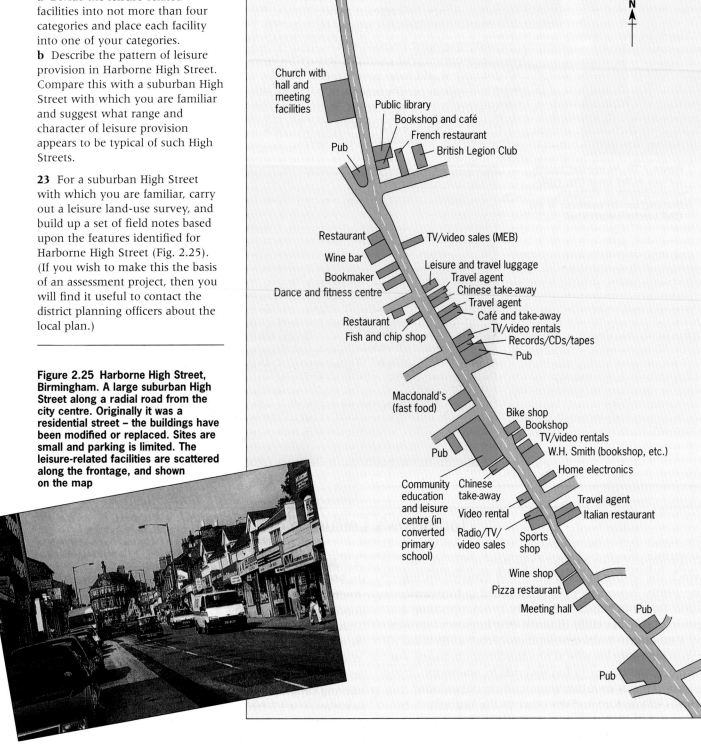

The International Convention Centre (ICC), Birmingham

The 'conference trade' combines both business and leisure and has been growing rapidly worldwide in recent years. It brings in large sums of money, creates jobs, raises a city's 'image'. It is not surprising that many cities – from **resorts** such as Brighton to industrial cities like Birmingham – have entered this competitive market by encouraging the development of conference centres.

In 1991 the ICC opened in central Birmingham. As Figure 2.30 shows, it is a massive, multi-facility complex of the highest quality, approached through an outdoor piazza (Convention Place). The complex stands on the edge of the CBD and astride a major road lined with pubs, restaurants and clubs. The ICC combines leisure (e.g. concerts, sporting events, eating out) with business (e.g. conferences, exhibitions), and so increases the usage and hence the economic benefits.

In the field of leisure, the high-order facilities of the ICC attract top-quality performers and events (e.g. the Indoor Arena hosts international sports meetings, and the concert hall is one of the finest in Europe, using high technology to produce excellent acoustics). Thus, local people as well as the regional population and international visitors enjoy improved opportunities for leisure.

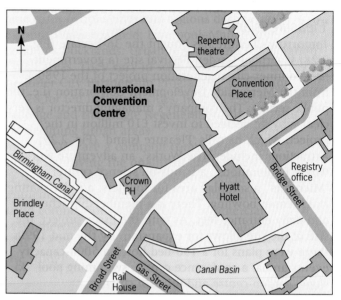

Figure 2.30 The International Convention Centre site in Birmingham, before (below) and after (above) redevelopment. The photo shows a view from the CBD. The new buildings of the complex can be seen in the middle ground, beyond the car park. On the left is the shining tower of the Hyatt Hotel, linked to the main ICC buildings by a bridge over a main road. On the right is the darker bulk of the National Indoor Arena

?

26 Give brief descriptions of the ICC site before and after the redevelopment. Pay particular attention to the size and shape of individual sites.

27 There have been criticisms that the improvements in the road and parking infrastructure in the ICC project are not good enough. Suggest reasons for this under-provision. (Think of space requirements, costs, what makes the profits, who owns the land.)

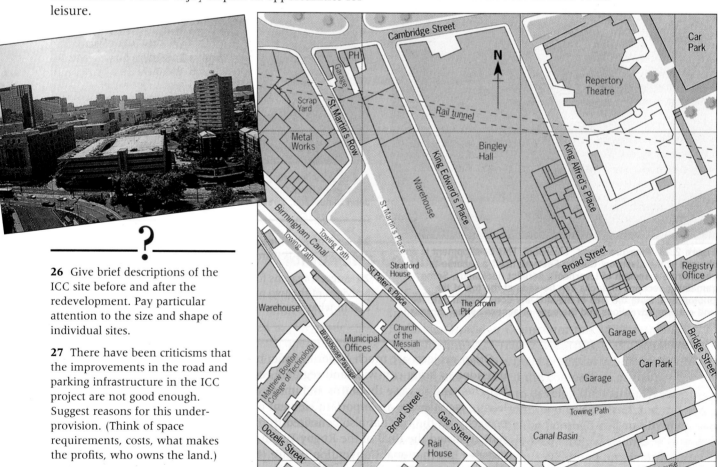

Figure 2.31 Newspaper report questioning the benefits of high-cost prestige projects (*Source: Express and Star*, 14 June 1993)

But is it worth it?

Loftman and Nevin's findings show those projects will never be profitable and will suck funds away from basic services for decades.

In Birmingham subsidies to the ICC and NIA came to nearly £46 for every adult in the city in 1992/3 – a total of £33.6 million. It has eaten up the £11.5 million profits from the NEC and left another £22.1 million to be paid by council tax payers.

Loftman and Nevin's aim was to find out whether projects like the ICC really do enrich local populations – who after all eventually have to pay the bills.

Patrick Loftman said: 'Prestige projects like the ICC are based on the theory of Trickle-down Economics.

'The idea is that if you invest in a high-profile scheme it will create jobs and attract investment.

'The benefits will eventually trickle down to all levels of society.'

This idea, imported from the USA, has been enthusiastically adopted by British local authorities.

'But,' says Mr Loftman, 'they have adopted it so keenly that it will cause massive over-capacity.'

Birmingham's NIA, for example, faces competition from the £100 million-plus worth of facilities built by Sheffield.

Soon it will face more problems, with Manchester planning a £30 million sports arena, a £9 million velodrome and other facilities for its Olympic bid.

All will be competing for the same limited number of national and international sports events.

The ICC – already the subject of huge subsidies – will from 1995 have to compete with a new facility in Edinburgh.

A similar project is proposed for Rainham Marshes. That would be ideally placed for Continental traffic via the Channel Tunnel and would surely attract business from both the NEC and ICC.

Birmingham's world-class Symphony Hall is already rivalled by another in Glasgow and a similar one planned for Manchester.

Despite these apparent benefits, there is growing concern over the wisdom of such high-profile, high-cost projects (ICC = £180 million, National Indoor Arena = £46 million). Figure 2.31 summarises key points from a 1993 study by two university lecturers, Patrick Loftman and Brendan Nevin.

CBSO

The issue of how to provide the opportunity to enjoy what is often called 'high-culture' experiences at reasonable (i.e. accessible) costs are illustrated by the example of the City of Birmingham Symphony Orchestra (CBSO). Its home base is the new concert hall in the ICC (before the ICC development it was the nineteenth-century Town Hall (Fig. 2.19) in the CBD).

A top-quality orchestra is very expensive, and if income comes solely from seat sales, then only wealthy people can afford them, and there may not be enough wealthy people around to support the orchestra (the concert hall seats 2200 people). Thus, the CBSO is supported partially by grants from the Arts Council (central government), the City Council (local government), and by sponsorship from commercial companies (Fig. 2.32).

As Figure 2.33 shows, the ICC has extended the CBD in a south-westerly direction, an example of the highly dynamic quality of a CBD. The complex has replaced a collection of out-of-date buildings, derelict sites (a previous, old exhibition hall had been destroyed by fire)

Figure 2.32 Private commercial support for the arts: sponsorship of the City of Birmingham Symphony Orchestra

?

28a Select three areas of urban open space you have visited within the past four weeks. For each, give brief descriptions of: (i) character, including approximate size; (ii) location in relation to your home; (iii) what you used the area for; (iv) ownership and management.

b If you have not used any such urban spaces, then give your reasons. If you have used such an open space, suggest what changes/additions need to be made. Who should and could provide these facilities?

29 From Figure 2.37,

a Suggest two factors which would help to explain the patterns shown on the maps.

b To what extent does the Leicester example support the assertion that inner-city communities are relatively disadvantaged in opportunities for outdoor recreation?

c For your own type of outdoor recreation interests, which part of Leicester would you prefer to live in? Why?

d What additional information would you require in order to answer this question: 'Does the pattern of outdoor recreation facilities provide effectively for the needs of the people of Leicester?'

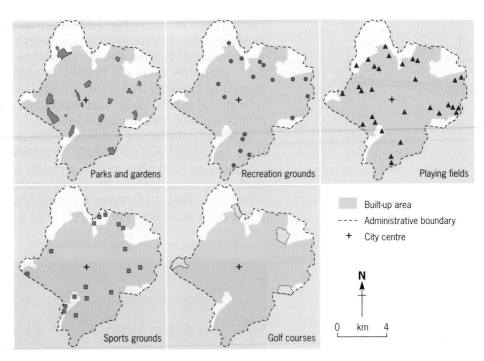

Mean distance (in km) from the city centre of different types of recreational space (Leicester)

Parks and gardens	Recreation grounds	Playing fields	Sports grounds	Golf courses
2.9	3.6	3.5	3.7	4.6

Figure 2.37 Spatial patterns of outdoor recreational facilities in Leicester

Figure 2.38 Birmingham City Football Club, St Andrews. The stadium lies within a kilometre of the CBD. Once at the heart of a densely populated district of nineteenth-century housing, it has become increasingly isolated by redevelopment schemes and outward movement of people. Despite extensive modernisation, the facilities and the access/parking infrastructure struggle to keep up with modern needs

Development pressures and land-use change

Councils, voluntary organisations and commercial businesses are aware of the value of their recreational and sports facility sites. Recreational spaces tend to be spacious, level, well drained, with a full infrastructure (road access, electricity, sewerage etc.) and in single ownership, making them relatively straightforward to develop. They are more attractive than derelict, awkwardly shaped inner-city 'brownfield' sites.

The temptation for a sports club, whether amateur or professional, to sell land can be strong, especially when it has occupied the site for a long time. Today the site may be poorly located for its customers, or inadequate in quality, scale and accessibility by modern standards and expectations, e.g. long-established professional football clubs (Fig. 2.38). Similar pressures and responses occur across a broad range of sports. In 1988, Hampshire County Cricket Club sold their Southampton ground and moved to a cheaper 25ha suburban site. In 1990, Hull Kingston Rovers Rugby League Club sold its traditional ground for £4 million and built a new stadium on the edge of the city. In some cases, where clubs have rented their grounds, owners have forced a move in order to sell off the land for more profitable uses (Fig. 2.39). Financial pressures caused by expanding professionalism also trigger sales and relocation, e.g. in 1997, Moseley Rugby Club was forced to sell its traditional ground in suburban Birmingham to a large housing development company.

This process affects inner-city and suburban districts particularly severely and reduces recreational space. However, where policy is strong enough, it is possible to reverse the loss of public recreational space. For instance, during the 1990s, Paris completed the Parc Citroën, on an old car factory site alongside the River Seine.

Figure 2.39 Stourbridge Rugby Football Club, West Midlands. The Club used to lease land inside the town from a church organisation. In the 1960s the owners bought out the lease and sold the ground at a high price for housing development. Fortunately, the Rugby Club received a sum large enough to be able to acquire land outside the town, but inside the West Midlands Green Belt. They gained planning permission for change of use from farming, and have been able to develop the present excellent facilities

Table 2.5 Hierarchical pattern of public open space (*Source:* London Planning Advisory Committee, 1988)

Type and main function	Approximate size and distance from home	Characteristics
Regional park Weekend and occasional visits by car or public transport	400 hectares; 3.2–8km	Large areas of natural heathland, common woodland and parkland. Primarily providing for informal recreation with some non-intensive active recreations. Car parking at strategic locations
Metropolitan park Weekend and occasional visits by car or public transport	60 hectares; 3.2km but more when park is larger than 60 hectares	Either natural heath, common, woods or formal parks providing for active and passive recreation. May contain playing fields, provided at least 40 hectares remain for other pursuits. Adequate car parking
District parks Weekend and occasional visits on foot, by cycle, car or short bus trip	20 hectares; 1.2km	Landscaped settings with a variety of natural features providing for a range of activities, including outdoor sports, children's play and informal pursuits. Some car parking
Local parks For pedestrian visitors	2 hectares; 0.4km	Providing for court games, children's play, sitting out etc. in a landscaped environment. Playing fields if the park is large enough
Small local parks Pedestrian visits especially by old people and children, particularly valuable in high-density areas	2 hectares; 0.4km	Gardens, sitting-out areas, children's playgrounds etc.
Linear open space Pedestrian visits	Variable; where feasible	Canal towpaths, footpaths, disused railway lines etc., providing opportunities for informal recreation

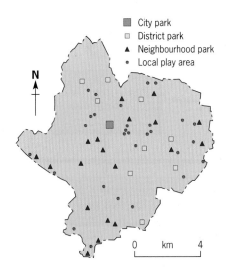

Figure 2.40 The hierarchy of public open spaces in Leicester (*Source:* Leicester City Council, 1991)

- ■ City park
- ☐ District park
- ▲ Neighbourhood park
- • Local play area

N

0   km   4

The use of urban parks

In many cities, a *hierarchical system* of parks can be identified, based upon size, location and character. Thus, a metropolis such as London supports a complex hierarchy (Table 2.5), while in medium-size cities such as Leicester there is a simpler structure (Fig. 2.40). District and local parks serve communities generally within a 2km radius: most users are regular visitors, walk to the park,

Figure 2.41 The use of a typical urban park for informal recreation during a summer week-day in fine weather

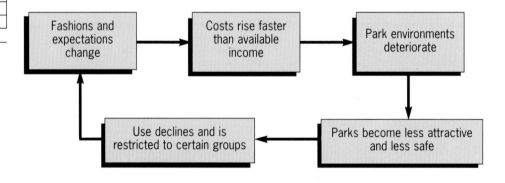

Note: This shows 'informal' use, and excludes bookings of tennis courts, bowls greens, 'pitch-and-putt' golf and all-weather playing surface.

30 Identify one example from your own or a nearby town/city where open space has been acquired for development. Describe the location, character, ownership change and the land use for which it was acquired.

31a Describe the pattern of use of an urban park shown in Figure 2.41, and detail the ways in which the various groups use the park.
b Which groups might come into conflict with each other over their use of the park? Draw and complete a compatibility matrix like the one below, using a cross to indicate where conflict might arise.

	Joggers	Dog walkers	Parents and babies	Retired people	Workers	Unemployed people	Teenagers	Cricketers
Joggers								
Dog walkers								
Parents and babies								
Retired people								
Workers								
Unemployed people								
Teenagers								
Cricketers								

engage in informal activities and stay for less than one hour, although usage patterns vary through the day (Fig. 2.41).

Demand is constantly shifting, causing recurring maintenance and improvement costs. For instance, children's paddling pools, which were once common, are rare today (health and safety regulations) and have been replaced by equipped play areas. Fashions such as BMX bikes and skateboards have been accommodated; the health trend is reflected in the appearance of jogging tracks and 'trim trails'. Grass playing surfaces are being replaced by all-weather pitches and courts, which are more expensive to install but cheaper to maintain and raise more money because of their high **carrying capacity**. None the less, in recent years, parks in many cities have deteriorated and have become perceived as less attractive, unsafe and 'threatening' environments (Fig. 2.42). In order to reverse this decline, in 1998 the government launched an initiative and support funding to revitalise urban parks, with the focus on four main themes:

- Extending the appeal of parks, e.g. provision of better toilets, refreshments, information; new facilities such as fitness trails, bike tracks; events and entertainments;

- Extending access to parks and improving safety, e.g. removal of fences; provision of lighting; all-weather surfaces and shelters; improved supervision;

- Extending the diversity of park environments, e.g. planting of varied vegetation, including woodland and shrubs, to achieve a more 'natural' look;

- Extending the involvement of local communities in the design and management of parks, e.g. local people on management committees.

```
Fashions and          Costs rise faster      Park environments
expectations    →     than available     →   deteriorate
change                income                         ↓
   ↑                                                 ↓
Use declines and is   ←                       Parks become less attractive
restricted to certain groups                 and less safe
```

**Key issue:
how to prevent this process?**

Figure 2.42 Urban parks – the process of decline

2.6 Open space and the environment

One trend in the management of open spaces brings together leisure provision and concern for the environment. Many councils have carried out major tree planting and landscaping schemes, including the development of 'wild' or 'natural' areas, often in co-operation with local conservation groups. Their aim is to enhance the landscape's beauty and to broaden the range of habitats for wildlife. For example, Dudley Metropolitan Borough manages four such 'greenspaces' as nature reserves, totalling 250 hectares. The first of these, Saltwells, was declared a local nature reserve in 1981, under the Council of Europe's 'Campaign for Urban Renaissance' (Fig. 2.43). The project is overseen by the Blackbrook Valley Group, which consists of local people, interest groups, local council officers, and is chaired by the Borough's Leisure Services Department. Saltwells is one element in an overall open space strategy for Dudley Borough (Fig. 2.44).

A second aspect of some recent schemes is the linking together of open spaces by creating 'green ways' or 'green trails', allowing both people and wildlife to move more freely through the urban environment (Figs 2.45 and 2.46). The Nuneaton and Bedworth Borough Council (Warwickshire) has established a 'Your Green Track' project which is creating continuous green corridors as recreational and wildlife habitats. A key to its success was a grant of money from central government (Department of the Environment) after the Borough was made a Derelict Land Clearance Area in 1982 (a designation given because of the extent of derelict land, which qualifies the area for special government funds, e.g. Derelict Land Grant). This has allowed the reclamation of disused quarries and railway lines.

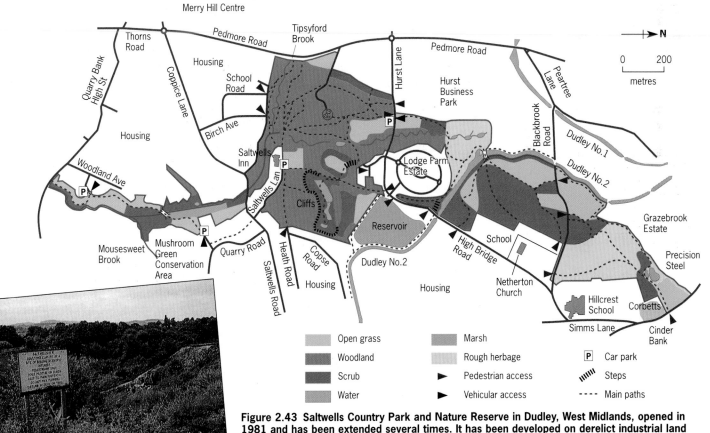

Figure 2.43 Saltwells Country Park and Nature Reserve in Dudley, West Midlands, opened in 1981 and has been extended several times. It has been developed on derelict industrial land in the heart of the Black Country. Part of the site is on old clay pits, which can be seen in this photo. Notice the balance between conservation and recreation values – the vegetation is being encouraged to allow the recovery to a woodland ecosystem while still permitting recreational access

Figure 2.44 Major green areas within the Dudley Open Space strategy (*Source:* Dudley Metropolitan Borough Council, 1993)

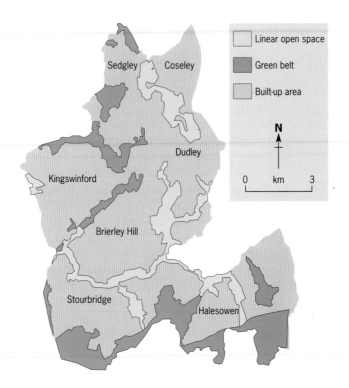

Figure 2.45 The proposed Green Chain for south-east London. This is a large-scale example of linking open spaces. It involves co-operation between several councils. Note the range of activities included

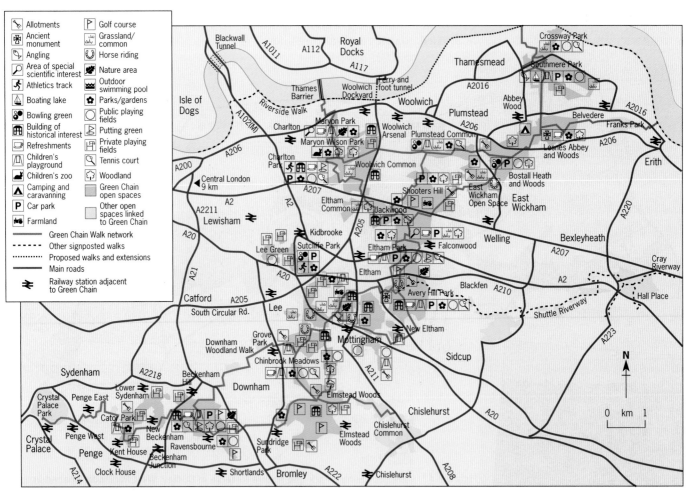

Figure 2.46 Aerial view of the Eltham area. The complexity of urban land-use patterns makes it difficult to link individual open spaces to form 'green corridors'

32 For a selected urban park, analyse its character in terms of safety, especially for women and children. Suggest ways in which safety could be improved.

33 Study Figure 2.46 and locate it on Figure 2.45. (Use a road atlas to help you pinpoint the major roads.)

34 Discuss the purpose and usefulness of the hierarchy concept in planning and provision for outdoor recreation in urban areas (Figs 2.37, 2.40, Table 2.5).

Summary

- Urban settlements concentrate both population and leisure facilities.
- Many types of leisure facility are spatially organised in a hierarchical structure.
- Leisure competes for urban space with other land uses.
- Individuals differ widely in their lifestyles and hence in their use of leisure facilities provided by the public and private sectors.
- Because of rising expectations and costs, leisure provision is increasingly an outcome of partnerships between the public and private (commercial and voluntary) sectors.
- Urban land values are one important reason for shifts in the location of leisure facilities.
- Constant changes in popularity and demand make investments in leisure risky.
- Local authorities vary in their policies and spending on leisure, but all are finding it increasingly difficult to fulfil the goal of social equity, i.e. equality of opportunity.

?

Study Table 3.1:

3 For each activity type in turn, write a brief descriptive participation profile. For example: '55 per cent of people taking part in "countryside and hillwalking" have done so within the last month. This is mainly a family activity (56 per cent), although walking with friends is quite popular (26 per cent). People travel 28 miles on average, and typically spend 6 hours on the journey and activity.'

4a For each activity, list the necessary or desirable resources, facilities and equipment. Think about those resources, etc. which are commonly available and accessible, and those which are widely spaced, might be far from population centres, or have special qualities. Remember, too, that golf is a very popular and readily available sport in Scotland.
b Rank each activity, from the most expensive to the cheapest.

5 For each of the four variables (a–d), describe the differences between the activities, and suggest possible reasons for them. (Your answers to Question 4 may help you.) For example – why do some activities involve longer travel and time commitments?

6 What do the figures *not* tell us about the participants?

7 Choose any one activity type from Table 3.1. What factors might cause the participation profile to change in one or more of the four variables (a–d)?

8 Describe each of the following in terms of the three categories in Figure 3.5:
a A family who drive out occasionally for picnics.
b A competitive orienteer.
c An angling club.
d Two friends who walk seriously most weekends.

Figure 3.4 Experts praise outdoor recreation as promoting mental and physical health, a sense of well-being, self-reliance, relaxation, companionship, challenge and heightened awareness of environmental values and issues

3.2 Participation: who uses the UK countryside?

Two key understandings which emerge from the discussion of leisure participation in Chapter 1 are (*a*) that there is a great variety of activities, and (*b*) that the percentage of the population which takes part in any one activity is relatively low. As around eight in every ten people use the countryside for recreation at some time – from rock concerts to rock climbing – their needs vary widely. Thus, *different activities require access to different resources and facilities.* Even the same activity can be enjoyed at many levels of skill, commitment and frequency (Fig. 3.4)

The diversity and resource demands are illustrated by the participation profiles, i.e. data about the people who take part, of the four activities in Table 3.1. Notice that the figures are percentages of those who took part, not of the total population. Remember, too, that the behaviour patterns shown in this and other participation surveys may reflect what opportunities were available, rather than the ideal, *preferred* patterns of the people surveyed.

Table 3.1 Results from a survey of outdoor recreation in Scotland (*Source:* TRRU, 1987)

Activity type	a How often? (% of participants taking part within the past 4 weeks)	b Who with?* (% of participants)				c How far? (Average distance travelled – miles)	d How long? (Average time spent away from home – hours)
		Alone	Family	Friends	Team/party		
Countryside and hill walking	55	18	56	26	7	28	6
Golf	62	14	23	64	2	13	5
Sailing	43	4	36	60	8	40	9
Mountaineering	25	10	24	34	35	104	17

*The percentages add up to more than 100% because some people responded in more than one category.

Classifying countryside users

It may seem impossible to make sense of the chaotic diversity of use. However, the Countryside Commission has used the results of its National Countryside Recreation Surveys to produce a classification of users. Its classification system is based on three variables: (*a*) *activity* types (Table 3.2); (*b*) *frequency* of participation; (*c*) *values* and *attitudes* (Fig. 3.5). This system is useful as a basis for making decisions about resource allocation and the

A Activity type

1 Walkers

About 40 per cent of the survey sample; most commonly middle-aged, employed, with above-average income and in social grade B; predominantly car owners and likely to be members of conservation and sporting organisations, e.g. National Trust and Ramblers Association; likely to have lived in or near the countryside for at least part of their lives.

2 Sports participants

Those who fish, ride, hunt, shoot, climb or take part in organised sports in the countryside, and who make up 10 per cent of the sample; have higher than average incomes, employment levels, and access to a car; more likely to be youngish, male and members of sports organisations. A distinct sub-group are the anglers, who are less likely to be affluent or to live in the countryside.

3 Informal recreationists

Approximately 50 per cent of the sample, whose use of the countryside is generally less strenuous than the other groups. Most popular activities are drives, picnics, strolls in the country and visits to historic buildings. Often known as the 'car-and-stroller' group, they are likely to live in larger cities, have lower incomes, be in social grades D–E, be relatively old and less likely to belong to conservation or sports organisations.

B Frequency of use

1 Frequent users

Visit the countryside at least once a week during the summer, are generally well informed about the countryside and tend to use familiar local territory; more likely to be in social grades A–C, be relatively affluent, employed, own a car and live in or near the countryside. Although they make up only 18 per cent of the population, they generate 68 per cent of all countryside recreation trips. Many walkers and sports participants fall into this category.

2 Occasional users

Use the countryside rarely in winter and perhaps twice a month during the summer; make up about 65 per cent of the population across a broad socio-economic spectrum and a wide range of interests.

3 Non-users

About 17 per cent of the population, and include those without interest as well as those for whom the countryside is inaccessible; more likely to be in social grades C–E, be unemployed, retired or housewives, live in larger cities and have low levels of car ownership.

C Values and attitudes

1 Aesthetic values

Place a high value on the countryside for its scenic beauty, tranquillity and unspoilt character. Such valued characteristics can be maintained only if access is in some way restricted, i.e. this category is essentially élitist and exclusionary, and includes some amenity and conservation groups.

2 Instrumental values

Those who see the countryside as resources to be used for their particular activities, and hence attempt to 'claim' resources for their own use, preferably exclusively. This exclusionary approach contains much potential for conflict through competition for the same resources.

3 Social values

Those who see the countryside as a place to be with their family and friends, or as an escape from urban environments. They tend to be more content with the more 'managed' sites such as country parks, and include the 'car-and-stroller' groups; they are not exclusionary and are generally tolerant of relatively high user densities.

Note: A guide to 'social grade':
A = Top management, executives, senior professionals
B = Middle management and professionals
C = Skilled industrial and clerical workers
D = Semi-skilled workers
E = Unskilled workers

Figure 3.5 Profiles of countryside users in the UK

9 Essay: With reference to Figure 3.5, outline how different values and attitudes towards the countryside can lead to conflicts between different users. Illustrate your answer by discussion of examples and suggest ways of reducing the conflicts.

10 You are a council planning officer. Your County Planning Committee has read the results of the *UK Day Visits Survey* (including Table 3.2) and has asked you to prepare answers to these questions for their next meeting:

• What types of leisure resources and facilities do visitors need?
• Where should we locate these recreation opportunities?
• What are the main problems we are likely to face?
• Why should countryside recreation be an important part of our plans?

Prepare your answers, using statistics where relevant.

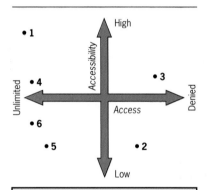

1 **High access/high accessibility.** All-year free access, e.g. common land and rights of way close to centres of population, for walking and informal recreation (see section 3.2)

2 **Highly restricted access and accessibility,** e.g. Ministry of Defence lands, including training ranges in Dartmoor and Northumberland National Parks

3 **Limited, event-specific access,** with accessibility controlled by entrance charge, e.g. open-air festivals and outdoor pursuits events on private land and water-space

4 **All-year or long-season access** with accessibility controlled by entrance charge, e.g. visits to National Trust properties

5 **Short-season access** with accessibility controlled by membership, e.g. hunting, shooting, fishing on private properties

6 **All-year free access** with accessibility constrained by remoteness, e.g. camping and walking in remote mountain areas

Figure 3.6 The access and accessibility spectrum

Table 3.2 Popular countryside activities (percentage of total visits) (*Source: UK Day Visits Survey*, 1996, Countryside Recreation Network, 1997)

General countryside		Forest woodland		Canal/River	
Walk/ramble	37	Walk/ramble	73	Walk/ramble	31
Eat/drink out	16	Drive/sightseeing	5	Pleasure boating/sightseeing	15
Outdoor sport	8	Cycling	5	Pursuing a hobby	8
Visit a leisure attraction	7	Countryside sport	4	Countryside sport	5

provision of recreational and sporting opportunities, and illustrates, too, how difficult making such decisions can be. For instance, not only do the user groups demand different resources, they also have differing attitudes and understandings about how the countryside environment should look and be used. As the old saying goes: 'You can't please all of the people all of the time'! Notice in particular that many interests are 'exclusionary' or even élitist: users try to claim preference and priority over desired resources. Thus, anglers try to exclude canoeists from stretches of river; walkers object to mountain-bikers on footpaths, etc.

3.3 Ownership, access and accessibility

Whether you can enjoy a relaxing picnic in a field, exhaust yourself orienteering through woods, pit your wits against a fish in a stream, or test your stamina at an open-air music festival, depends upon who owns the resources you need – field, forest, water, parkland. Of course, there are other factors such as your own interests, what money you have, how mobile you are, where you live, and so on. Yet ultimately you rely on owners making resources and facilities available to you. That is, you need access. However, the resources and facilities must also be accessible to you. It is important to distinguish between these related concepts of **access** and **accessibility** (Fig. 3.6)

The access you need depends upon what you want to do. Look again at the user types in Figure 3.5, this time in terms of access requirements: some demand access to a single location and a specific resource, e.g. climbing a particular rock face; others need access to a variety of resources and environmental settings, e.g. going for walks or pleasure drives.

Owners and attitudes

Land and water resources in the United Kingdom are owned by a wide variety of institutions, organisations and individuals. Over 80 per cent of the total area is privately owned. At least 35 per cent is under the control of owner–occupier farmers, with 300 titled families owning another 30 per cent. Major institutions own a further 10 per cent (see Table 3.3). These are the key 'gatekeepers' and decision-makers in the access game. In turn, they have a crucial influence on how conservation works in the British countryside, and hence upon the character and quality of the landscape in which we take our leisure.

Owners vary in their policies towards access across the dimensions of the spectrum of Figure 3.6: from optimising access and thereby reducing tensions, e.g. the National Trust, to denying access and so heightening the potential for tension and conflict, e.g. the Ministry of Defence (Fig. 3.7). Imagine the diagram in Figure 3.8 as an elastic sheet, with the four major 'actors' pulling at the corners; whoever has the most powerful pull dominates the availability of countryside resources. The relative pulling powers shift over time. For example, from 1945 to 1985, government planning policy gave strong priority to farming modernisation and productivity, and recreational developments were strictly controlled. Since 1985, however, the policy emphasis has been upon the diversification of rural economies, with a loosening of planning controls and encouragement of leisure developments (see Section 4.6, p.90).

Table 3.3 Major institutional owners of the countryside

Forestry Commission	1.1 million ha
National Trust (England,Wales,Scotland)	260,000 ha
Ministry of Defence	230,000 ha
Crown Estates and Duchy of Cornwall (Prince of Wales)	161,000 ha

11 Draw the graph axes of Figure 3.6 and locate the following: (*a*) private farmland close to a large city; (*b*) caravan site on a farm, open April–September, with an overnight fee of £10; (*c*) a sailing club on a water company reservoir; (*d*) a 'pay-as-you-play' golf course in the Green Belt.

12 Identify two other forms of recreational activity and setting: (*a*) describe them in terms of access and accessibility; (*b*) locate them on your graph.

13 You have found that in completing questions 11 and 12, the locations on your graph have been only approximate. Make a list of the variables for which you would need information in order to make your locations more precise. (Think about the difficulties you had in picking your locations, e.g. did you say, 'Ah, but it would depend on ...!'?)

14 Assess the usefulness of the access–accessibility model in terms of its strengths and weaknesses.

Smaller army needs more firing ranges

THE MINISTRY of Defence is poised to acquire more countryside and fire additional weapons in national parks, despite a 45,000 reduction in the strength of the armed forces.

The MoD owns more than 226,000 hectares of countryside but its need is increasing because of the loss of German training grounds and the return of 32,000 troops from Germany.

Another 450 hectares – a hectare equals 2.47 acres – was acquired last year for £3.8 million to extend the army's 37,000 hectares on Salisbury Plain in Wiltshire.

Figure 3.7 Newspaper report on the army acquiring more and more land in the countryside (*Source: Guardian*, 2 February 1993)

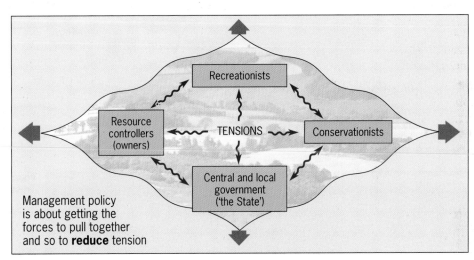

Figure 3.8 The tensions of access – 'Conflicts surrounding access frequently concern conflicting perceptions of the countryside and of what constitutes legitimate recreational and sporting activity' (Countryside Commission, 1986)

The Trossachs Trail, Scotland

Location
The Trossach Hills lie at the junction of the Scottish Highlands and the Central Lowlands. They are easily accessible to a regional population of 3 million, including Glasgow, and main routes to the Highlands pass through.

Environment
The attractive, varied scenery of mountains, forests, lochs and villages have made the Trossachs a popular visitor destination for more than a century. Visitors include both day-trippers and tourists.

The Trail
The Trossachs Trail is a 50km car touring loop linking a series of villages, visitor attractions and sites of interest. It is the central feature of a recreation and tourism plan covering 260sq.km.

The strategy
The project was set up in 1992 as the Trossachs Trail Tourism Management Programme (TTTMP). Although formally part of a sustainable tourism strategy for Scotland, the TTTMP area is an important recreational focus for the regional population. Over 1 million

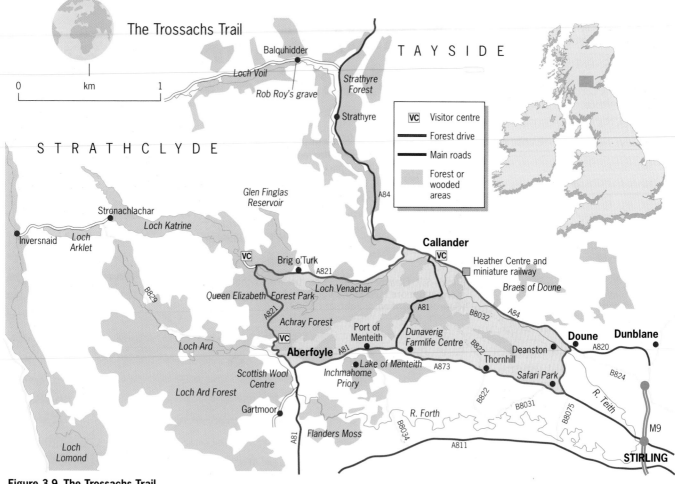

The Trossachs Trail

0   km   1

T A Y S I D E

S T R A T H C L Y D E

VC	Visitor centre
	Forest drive
	Main roads
	Forest or wooded areas

Balquhidder

Loch Voil

Rob Roy's grave

Strathyre Forest

Strathyre

A84

Stronachlachar

Loch Katrine

Glen Finglas Reservoir

Inversnaid

Loch Arklet

B829

Brig o'Turk

A821

Callander

VC

Heather Centre and miniature railway

Braes of Doune

Loch Venachar

Queen Elizabeth Forest Park

A821

Achray Forest

VC

Loch Ard

A81

Aberfoyle

Port of Menteith

Dunaverig Farmlife Centre

A81

Lake of Menteith

Inchmahome Priory

Scottish Wool Centre

Loch Ard Forest

Gartmoor

A81

Flanders Moss

R. Forth

B8034

A811

B822

B8032

A81

A873

Thornhill

Deanston

B822

Safari Park

B8031

B8075

Doune

A820

Dunblane

B824

R. Teith

M9

STIRLING

Figure 3.9 The Trossachs Trail

Figure 3.10 Typical Trossachs scenery

Figure 3.11 The 'Trossachs Trundler'

Over 10 000 visitors enjoyed Trundling through the Trossachs countryside on a 1953 Bedford bus during the summer of 1994, the second year of the service. The hugely popular 'Trossachs Trundler' – which is subsidised by Central Regional Council – also offers local people a better bus service. In 1994, a Glasgow link was established and over 40 000 leaflets were distributed to encourage even more people to travel back in time on the Trundler.

More than £350,000 has been spent on revitalising one of the most popular parts of the Trossachs Trail, Callander Meadows, which has suffered from flooding, poor maintenance and a lack of facilities. The TTTMP has:

• revamped the riverside walk;
• built an exciting new children's play area;
• provided 50 extra parking spaces;
• laid new footpaths with landscaping;
• developed links with the existing Callander–Strathyre cycleway.

This imaginative redevelopment of Callander Meadows has preserved the character of the beautiful riverside location and means it can welcome large numbers of visitors.

Figure 3.12 Callander Meadows

visitors pass through the Trossachs each year; two-thirds of them are day-trippers.

Objectives
• To protect and enhance the Trossachs environment.
• To improve the range and quality of visitor attractions, facilities and services.
• To improve visitor understandings and respect for local environments and communities.
• To encourage visitors to contribute more to the local community, economy and environment.

Examples of actions
• Repair work to eroded paths on Ben A'an and Ben Venue.
• Upgrading of car parks at Falls of Leny, Thornhill village.
• Completion of the section of the Central Highland Way cycleway within the TTTMP area.
• Establishment of the Trossachs Trundler bus service around the Trail.
• Farm Life Centre at Dunarerig, Thornhill (private-sector farm diversification).
• Creation of cycleways and forest walks at Brig o'Turk.
• Renewal of path and children's area, Callander Meadows.
• Improved signposting of attractions and footpaths.

The partnership
The TTTMP is run as a partnership between local, regional and national organisations. From 1991 to 1997 it contributed around £2 million to programme development.

The right to roam
Gaining public access to private land has been one of the longest, hardest-fought campaigns surrounding the use of the British countryside. The campaign involves both ensuring access to rights of way, e.g. footpaths (see Section 3.5), and acquiring unrestricted access to unenclosed land. This latter campaign has become known as 'the right to roam' – the right to walk freely across open moorland and mountain terrain. Landowners have resisted such open access. Their concerns have focused on invasion of privacy and economic factors such as damage to fences and walls, disturbance of breeding and grazing animals, and disruption of the management of game birds, animals and fish on commercial shooting and fishing estates. Some environmentalists, too, are worried about increased access and visitor impacts in often fragile environments (Fig. 3.14b). None the less, in 1999 the government finally agreed to bring in legislation to permit the right to roam across 1.62 million hectares of unenclosed land (Fig. 3.14a).

Figure 3.13 Roam is where the heart is … ramblers demanding the right to roam take part in an organised trespass across Pennine moorland in Yorkshire (*Source: Guardian*, 10 February 1999)

Delight at bill pledge over right to roam

The Government last night surprised and delighted ramblers and Labour backbenchers and infuriated landowners by promising a historic statutory right to roam across 4 million acres of open countryside in England and Wales.

Under the proposals, ministers expect 90 per cent of access arrangements to be made up of a cross-section of interest groups, but the Countryside Agency, launched next month, will be able to arbitrate in disputes and force landowners to open land.

The decision was welcomed by the Ramblers' Association as the vindication of 'a century-long struggle'.

The Country Landowners Association accused the Government of destroying the goodwill of the countryside.

The CLA president, Ian MacNicol, warned that the Government could not now cooperate in coming to voluntary agreements, and claimed that a statutory right of access, without appropriate compensation, would fail the European Convention on Human Rights, newly incorporated into UK law.

The new measures do not apply to developed land or to agricultural land other than that used for extensive grazing, and access rights are confined to people on foot. The package will be subject to mapping by the Countryside Agency and the Countryside Council for Wales, which will determine where the statutory right will apply, taking that decision out of the hands of landowners.

Legislation will give landowners discretion to close land or restrict access for a maximum of 28 days each year for land management reasons such as heather burning or shooting.

?

15 Read both articles of Figure 3.14 carefully. Summarise briefly (*a*) what the government legislation aims to do, and (*b*) the advantages and disadvantages of the proposals and for whom.

Figure 3.14 Right to roam issues
Left: Government proposals for the right to roam (*Source: Guardian*, 9 March 1999)
Right: Letter to the *Guardian*, 12 January 1999

Countryside more precious than right to roam through hamlet and dale

Which is more important, the Right to Roam or the environment? Is human recreation more important than the needs of ground-nesting birds, plants and animals? The high fells are their last refuge. Dogs run free but they can damage colonies of lapwings, skylarks and curlews.

Sponsored walks can bring up to 1,000 people a day trooping through farmyards here. Schools bring children all the year round. Hang gliders do not go well with conservation. It's not fat landowners who suffer, but wildlife and upland farmers are the ones currently leaving their farms.

Parking is a nightmare. In this hamlet we have a very rare flower growing just where mini-buses, coaches, army lorries and cars are parked. Other damage is widespread – hayfields spoilt, trees and plants destroyed, walls knocked down, erosion, wildlife disturbed, and much else. People should be decent but some are not.

Through our tiny Dales hamlet, the Countryside Commission seeks to put a bridleway for 12 000 plus bikes, walkers and horses (a 'motorway'). Cavers come every day of the year, motorbikes go off-road and the farmer next door has had a demand to let 4WD vehicles down the lane he uses for moving sheep and tractors.

Big money is behind much of this, so what can we do? The demands are relentless. Little communities cannot sustain it, and nature is rapidly being destroyed.
Hilary Fenten,
Horton-in-Ribblesdale,
N. Yorkshire

3.4 An origin–destination model of nodes and links

Any recreational trip consists of two main spatial components: *travel* and *on-site activity.*

The simplest spatial pattern produced is shown in Figure 3.15. We leave home (*origin*) and travel directly to a resource or facility (*destination*) – picnic site, country pub, beach, lake – enjoy the opportunities the attraction has to offer, then return home by the same route. The origin and destination (*nodes*) are connected by two direct travel *links*. In this basic model the travel component may not be seen as part of the leisure experience, but as a necessity to overcome what is called the *friction of distance*. Time, distance and perhaps cost become factors affecting accessibility and the likelihood of our participating. For instance, driving for an hour with your sailboard to get to a lake may influence your motivation: 'Oh heck, it's too far. I don't think I'll bother.' In turn, policies may aim to reduce this travel component by locating resources and facilities closer to demand, e.g. building climbing walls and dry ski-slopes in urban areas. In formal terms, such facilities become **demand-based** rather than **supply-** or **resource-based**.

However, over one-half of all informal recreation trips to the countryside include the element of 'driving for pleasure'. As Figure 3.15b shows, with such trips there may or may not be a primary destination, and the outward and return legs may take different routes (*links*). En-route stops (*nodes*) may include settlements as well as rural sites, e.g. stops in Ambleside or Keswick during a trip to the Lake District National Park. In other cases the travel may be the primary pleasure, e.g. 'going out for a drive', cycling.

We can see, therefore, that the origin–destination model, built with varying combinations of nodes and links, is a useful technique for analysing and planning countryside recreational experiences and behaviour. An excellent example is the Trossachs Trail in Scotland, planned and promoted for day excursions and touring holidays (see the Trossachs Trail case study, pp. 51–53).

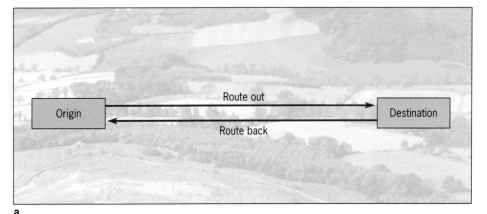

a

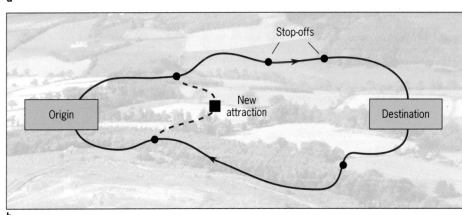

b

?

16 Use the Trossachs Trail example to illustrate the character and usefulness of the origin–destination model of recreation behaviour (Fig. 3.15).

17 Evaluate the Trossachs Trail project in terms of what it offers for the various user types identified by CoCo (Fig. 3.5).

18 Use the models in Figure 3.15 as a basis to draw the route and stops of a countryside trip you plan to take. Use an OS map of the area. Describe briefly the resources/ facilities you want to use and the activities you want to do at each stop. Who will provide them and on what terms will you be permitted access (e.g. free, entrance fee etc.)? Approximately how far will you travel, how long will the trip take and what proportion will be the 'travel' element.

Figure 3.15 Two countryside-trip models

3.5 Access and rights of way

The car has become a vital element in our enjoyment of the countryside, e.g. 90 per cent of visitors to National Parks arrive by car or coach. Yet surveys regularly show that the most popular recreational activity is *walking*, from a casual stroll to a three-week hike along the Pennine Way (Table 3.2, p.50). Whether the walk occurs directly from home or after a car drive, it is likely to include the use of rights of way.

Footpaths form the main part of the 240 000km of public rights of way in the UK, and have been called 'the linchpin of rural recreation' (Shoard, 1987). We take them for granted, yet no other country has such a network, and their value lies in how they enable us to penetrate the privately owned countryside. They are a unique and precious resource, but are under threat from development pressures, changing farming techniques and private landowners reacting to the increased numbers of people using those paths that still exist. A 1990 survey showed that 40 000km of paths were out of use, and in 1993 the Ramblers' Association claimed that five stretches of path were being removed each day (Fig. 3.16).

Conflicts continued through the early 1990s (Fig. 3.17), and in 1995, to stimulate progress, CoCo set a target to complete the national footpath network by the Millennium. Despite a variety of initiatives and funding support, the target was not achieved. The problem has become more complex as demands

Figure 3.16
Kimbolton, Cambridgeshire. This gate obstructs a footpath right of way. The gate is bolted shut and fringed with barbed wire

The battlefield and weapons: guns, barbed wire, bulls and dogs

There are 134,00 miles of footpaths and bridleways in Britain. Few people realise, though, that every footpath, however humble, is legally regarded as the Queen's Highway and that any farmer obstructing a path with barbed wire is as guilty of an offence as if he dug up a motorway to grow potatoes.

These facts I learn from Ken Ward, a passionate believer in the pleasures of exploring the country on foot, as we plod across a field of beans somewhere in Oxfordshire.

'The only way you'd know this is a footpath is from my map,' shouts Ken, up to the knees in beans and jabbing them with his walking stick. 'These are illegally-grown beans. It wouldn't take the farmer ten minutes to plough the path back through them. The 1990 Rights Of Way Act states that the path should be one metre wide and clearly marked. It will be impossible to walk across this field when the beans are up, and faint-hearted walkers won't dare because they'll mistakenly think they're trespassing.'

He consults his map, fiddles with his compass and we trudge on until we reach thick brambles, nettles and a fence topped with barbed wire.

'This is an obstruction,' roars Ken, whipping out some secateurs from a trouser-leg pocket and snipping at the brambles. 'By law there should be a stile here. But no. We'll have to risk permanent injury in order to follow the path.'

THE BATTLE to preserve the rights of walkers and ramblers is forever becoming more ferocious and vicious.

It can involve shotguns, barriers of barbed wire, fierce dogs and bulls and tractors used in fields to harass people.

In Ken Ward's years of wandering the countryside he has frequently met the wrath of landowners and farmers obstructing the public footpaths through their property although, by right, every pathway is the Queen's Highway.

'A few years ago I was on a footpath tour of the Cotswolds. We were following the footpath through a wood, but it vanished under bracken. There were no signposts, so we made our way the best we could. We came into a field and set out in the direction marked by our map.

'Suddenly, we heard a tractor tearing towards us, with the farmer at the wheel shouting and waving. We asked him to show us the footpath and public stile so that we could continue our walk; he did so by nudging us along with his roaring and revving tractor.

'I've even been threatened by a gun, though guns can sometimes be less intimidating than a ferocious-looking dog.

The Open Spaces Society is Britain's oldest national conservation body, and one of the most active campaigners for protecting the environment. One of its long-running battles is with the National Trust at its Hidcote Manor Gardens in Gloucestershire.

According to Kate Ashbrook, secretary of the Society, a footpath through the gardens is blocked by tall hedges and flower beds. The NT made an unofficial diversion taking walkers outside the gardens, but after further objections from the Society, the NT has been pushed to apply for official permission to the Cotswold District Council and is currently awaiting a public inquiry.

'You would expect the National Trust to be exemplary in their behaviour, but they only want people who pay to go through their gardens,' says Kate.

Multi-millionaire Peter Gabriel, former Genesis singer, has a 240ft stretch of footpath through his recording studios estate in Box, Wiltshire. But hordes of fans have been treading the public path hoping to catch a glimpse of the star. Now Gabriel, with the backing of the county council, is applying to the Environment Department for permission to re-route the footpath and regain his privacy.

Figure 3.17 Newspaper report on the fight for footpaths (*Source: Daily Mail*, 22 June 1991) © *Daily Mail/Solo*

Figure 3.18 Tension is often created when mountain-bikers and walkers use the same path

on rights of way have intensified. For instance, the growing popularity of active pursuits such as mountain-biking, trail-biking, orienteering and horse riding creates tensions and conflicts not only between landowners and recreationists, but between different groups of recreationists (Fig. 3.18).

Evolution of footpaths

The key understanding is that the footpath network developed to serve a quite different purpose from the way it is used today. Over hundreds of years, footpaths evolved to suit the *economic* activities of rural communities. It was part of everyday life for people to walk from their homes in villages or on farms, to the fields, woods, ponds, streams, commons and moors. Thus, footpaths became threaded through the rural landscape as part of a traditional economic and social system (Fig. 3.19).

Today, the role of footpaths is that of a resource for *recreation*. We use them to exercise the dog, to relax, to keep fit, to enjoy the beauties of the countryside, and so on. Keeping them accessible and usable is the responsibility of a County Council Highways Department, working through local parish councils (Fig 3.20). The central management issue arises from the fact that footpaths cross private land, and even run through farmyards and kitchen gardens.

We must remember, too, that footpaths are only one type of 'public right of way' and that 'rights' vary in their legal status (Table 3.4). Uncertainty arises from the long history of footpaths, and there may be a lack of formal documentation. The present-day legal basis for the categories in Table 3.4 lies in the National Parks and Access to the Countryside Act (1949), the Countryside

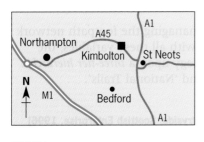

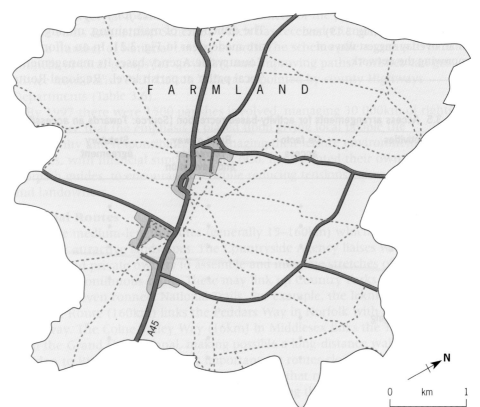

Figure 3.19 The footpath network of Kimbolton parish, Cambridgeshire. Notice how the footpaths radiate outwards from the nucleated settlement. A few link up with paths in neighbouring parishes (*Source:* definitive parish map)

Figure 3.22 Report on a community paths initiative by Staffordshire County Council (*Source: Enjoying the Countryside*, Spring 1992)

Staffs move yields path dividend

Staffordshire County Council operated a rights of way maintenance agreement whereby participating parish councils were paid a fixed sum per mile of path.

But the take-up was poor, says Staffordshire's rights of way project officer, Alice Coleman. So a new 'community paths initiative' was devised.

'We wanted to encourage those wanting to do more than just keeping the same paths clear,' says Alice Coleman. Parish councils, and local groups or individuals working in consultation with their parish council, were invited to apply for grants of up to £2000 to carry out a paths survey, produce a local walks leaflet, organise a refurbishing project or do anything else that benefited walking or riding in their area.

The scheme galvanised parishes into action, so that 21 different projects shared a total of £9000 in 1991/92.

Typical of those taking advantage is the Gnosall parish council. When parish councillor Bob Southern took over as Gnosall's local footpaths officer a year ago, the paths network around the village was mostly overgrown, blocked and inaccessible.

'The new scheme concentrated the minds of the parish council on the rights of way, and what we wanted to do to open up the local footpaths,' he says. He organised a local footpaths survey. This was followed up by with a programme of footpath clearance and renovation, based on creating circular walks around the most attractive routes.

These are advertised through leaflets available in local pubs (which are particularly popular with boaters using the nearby Shropshire Union canal), articles in the parish magazine and a central information board and map in the village community centre.

But by the end of 1992, the parish council hopes to have another four or five circular walks set up in the area. As well as making use of money from the community paths initiative, it is also involving an Employment Action team to clear paths and install stiles, bridges and waymarking, using kits and materials supplied by the county council.

National Trails

For more challenging experiences, longer, continuous routes are important. Long-distance footpaths were first proposed in the 1949 National Parks and Access to the Countryside Act, and given clear definition in the 1968 Countryside Act: routes where 'the public should be enabled to make extensive journeys on foot or on horseback or on a bicycle, not being a motor vehicle, and for which the whole or greater part of its length does not pass along roads mainly used by vehicles'. In 1988 their official title in England and Wales became 'National Trails'. In Scotland the term 'way' is retained, e.g. the West Highland Way; the Southern Upland Way.

The route of the first long-distance path, the Pennine Way, was proposed in 1951 but, because of complex negotiations with landowners and more than one hundred parish, district and county councils, was not opened until 1965. (see the Pennine Way case study, pp. 62–64). Attitudes of 'stakeholders' vary widely: those who benefit economically, such as publicans, shopkeepers, bed-and-breakfast owners etc., are likely to support a trail proposal. Other interest groups such as farmers, villagers, and even some conservationists, often oppose it strongly. It is not surprising, therefore, that it may take up to 20 years to negotiate completion of a lengthy National Trail!

Several paths were completed during the 1970s, including the South West Coast Path which, at 1000km, is the longest National Trail. Since 1996 it has been possible to walk the 300km length of the River Thames by following the Thames Path. In 1998, an extension to the Cotswold Way Regional Route was approved, to run between Bath and Chipping Campden, with upgrading to a

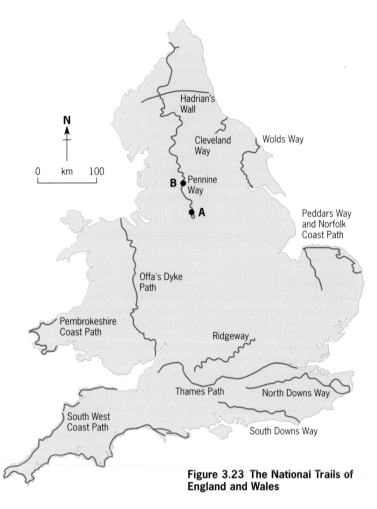

Figure 3.23 The National Trails of England and Wales

National Trail. By 1999 there were 12 National Trails (Fig. 3.23). At the Millennium, four major projects were under way which illustrate management responses to environmental pressures and recreation trends:

• From 1995: Sustrans (a civil engineering charity organisation) has a £42.5 million Lottery Fund grant to develop a 9000km National Cycle Network. This will include an integration of both urban and rural routes.

• 1998–2001: The construction of the Hadrian's Wall Path, running for 120km between Bowness-on-Solway to Wallsend, N.Tyneside. The cost will be at least £5 million, including a £1.35 million Heritage Lottery award. A primary concern is the restoration and conservation of Roman sites and sections of the Roman wall damaged by increasing visitor numbers.

• From 1999: The construction of the Pennine Bridleway National Trail. The main aim is to reduce conflicts and environmental impacts along the existing Pennine Way (Fig. 3.24).

• 1998–2001: The John Ellerman Foundation Charitable Trust has pledged £60,000 to the South East National Trails Wider Access Project. The money is to fund a project officer to improve access for 'the socially disadvantaged, disabled people and urban populations'.

Figure 3.24 The Pennine Bridleway National Trail (*Source: Countryside*, Winter 1998–99)

All set for England's biggest bridleway

The English Sports Council is giving the Countryside Commission £1,841,876 from the Lottery Sports Fund towards expenditure of £3,683,752 to develop the southern section of the Pennine Bridleway National Trail which runs from Middleton Top in Derbyshire to Long Preston in North Yorkshire.

The award means work can start on building the only national trail in the North of England catering for horse riders and cyclists as well as walkers. It will be readily accessible to the many thousands of horse and bike riders who live in the area.

Ideally, the surface will be vegetated, but where necessary it will be reinforced with locally derived stone. Some suitable sections will be developed for use by Riding for the Disabled groups.

When the trail is open, local economies will benefit from visitors using shops, pubs and cafés, as well as local accommodation including overnight stabling and grazing for horses.

The 231-kilometre section of the route

which will receive the funds runs from Derbyshire, through the Peak District and Manchester Pennine fringe, through Lancashire and up to the edge of the Yorkshire Dales National Park. It is on the doorstep of many towns and cities.

The route from Derbyshire to Kirby Stephen in Cumbria extends for 330km, but,

last month, the Countryside Commission launched formal consultation on a £2.3 million proposed northern extension which would run for a further 222km through Cumbria and into Northumberland, finishing at Byrness in the Kielder Park. This could be opened within five years of approval by the Secretary of State.

The Pennine Way

Opened in 1965, the Pennine Way was the first National Trail (then known as a 'long-distance route'). It runs north–south along the length of the Pennines for 402km from the Scottish Borders to Derbyshire (Fig. 3.23). It winds along mountain ridges, across open moors, through forests and river valleys, but the central idea is one of *challenge* (Fig. 3.27).

The Pennine Way is the best known and most used of all the National Trails, and there has been growing concern about erosion and crowding along some sections in the summer, especially in the south. However, this popularity also brings income and jobs to communities along and near to the Pennine Way. In order to find out who uses the path, how much they spend, and what they spend money on, a survey was carried out between April and October 1990 at a number of points along the route. The patterns of usage are summarised in Figure 3.25.

One important finding is that the trail is used in a variety of ways. Two main user groups are identified: long-distance walkers, and day walkers. Each of these groups is then divided into sub-groups.

This is useful information because each of the groups and sub-groups has distinct needs and motivations, makes different impacts and has different spending patterns. An equally important finding of the survey is that the levels of usage are distributed unevenly along the trail. This distribution is determined largely by the location of (*a*) access points and (*b*) key attractions such as waterfalls, viewpoints etc. From this finding it is possible to propose a general model which states that it is around these accessible and attractive **honeypots** that problems of management are most likely to occur (Fig. 3.26).

Impact and erosion

Levels of impact and erosion are not determined solely by numbers of walkers. It is true that along the Pennine Way the two most seriously eroded sections are also among the most popular: Edale to Kinder Scout (A in Figure 3.23) and across the flanks of Pen-y-Ghent (B in Figure 3.23). The crucial factor is, however, the fragile nature of the surface materials. These are peat bog areas, where the mat of surface

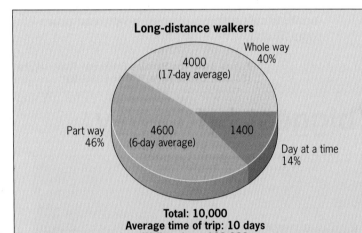

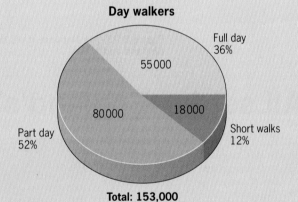

Long-distance walkers

Whole way 40%
4000 (17-day average)
Part way 46%
4600 (6-day average)
1400
Day at a time 14%

Total: 10,000
Average time of trip: 10 days
Walker days: 100,000

- 90% of those who walk the whole Way, walk from south to north.
- Part-way walkers start at more accessible points along the length of the Way. This helps to even out the numbers across the sections of the Way.
- 75% of the trips begin May–July.
- 71% are aged 17–44 and 78% are male.
- 77% have access to a car, and 78% are in white-collar jobs. (17% are students).
- Walkers come from throughout the UK: with 22% from South-East England; 17% from North-West England; 14% from Yorks–Humberside.
- Friendship groups of 2–3 people are the most common.
- 90% are experienced and regular users of the countryside.
- 55% use a car to get to and from the walk. Notice that trains and buses are an important means of access.
- 65% have walked all or part of the Way before.
- 35% of nights are spent in Youth Hostels; 38% in camp; 20% in hotels and bed-and-breakfast. 73% are on holiday.

Day walkers

Full day 36%
55000
Part day 52%
80000
18000
Short walks 12%

Total: 153,000

- 60% of day walkers begin walking towards the north.
- Starting-points and walks are spread evenly across the main sections of the Way. In each section these are popular, easily accessible starting-points.
- Evenly spread across the seasons.
- Broad age spread, 17–59 years, especially the 25–44 age group. 40% are female.
- Over 90% have access to a car and 75% in white-collar jobs (9% students).
- 54% come from the 3 northern regions: North; North-West; Yorks and Humberside, because of nearness to home.
- Family groups of 3–4 are the most common, often including children.
- 85% have some experience of walking in the countryside.
- 90% of day users arrive and depart by car. 50% travel less than 40km each way.
- 70% have been on the Way before, and 33% use it at least 5 times a year.
- 50% are on day trips from home; 27% on holiday and 23% on a short break.

Figure 3.25 Use of the Pennine Way, April–October 1990

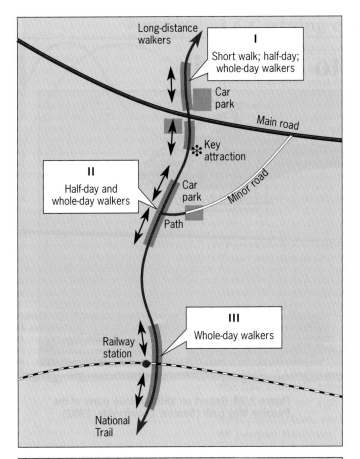

I A mingling of all walker types, and likelihood of greatest use and impacts. 'Car-and-stroller' visitors venture as far as the 'key attraction', stay a short while, perhaps picnic, then drive off. They use the locality differently from more serious walkers, who move through with only brief stops. Main user concentrations are within 1 km of the access point.

II Walkers must leave their vehicles some way from the trail and approach it on foot before fanning out for up to 10 km in either direction. Walker densities are lower and visitor types less varied than at access point I.

III These are full-day walkers, arriving by a morning train and leaving in the evening. The train times limit access and so the number and type of visitor. They are usually serious walkers who fan out at fairly low densities for up to 15 km, thus the impacts around the access point are not severe.

In general, impacts and potential conflicts decline from I to III.

Figure 3.26 **Model of usage patterns along a National Trail**

vegetation is easily broken up by walkers' boots. Once exposed, the soft peat is very susceptible to erosion during rainstorms and snowmelt periods. Walkers continue to churn up the peat, erosion accelerates, and as walkers detour around these quagmires they steadily expand the eroded, boggy surfaces, which can exceed 20 m in width. Along other stretches of the trail, where the surface is more resistant and resilient (i.e. able to recover from impact), the carrying capacity is much higher. Good examples are the better-drained areas

crossing limestone and sandstone without a peat blanket (e.g. over Cross Fell).

Controlling erosion
Both of the seriously eroded sections of the trail are in **National Parks** (Peak District and Yorkshire Dales), and since 1988 a series of projects, which will finally cost over £2 million, has been in progress over at least 60 km of the trail. Their aim is to control erosion and increase the carrying capacity of the eroded, intensively used sections of the trail. There is general agreement that this is a 'good thing', but much disagreement about how it should be done, especially inside National Parks. The ideal is to retain the 'naturalness' of the Pennine Way, and use natural materials such as local stone for the path surface, or perhaps wooden logs laid across the peat. However, because of their lower cost, ease of laying and durability, a variety of plastics and aggregates have been tried – even tarmac. Critics claim that such artificial surfaces lower both the quality of the environment and the experience of the walkers (Fig. 3.28).

A radical solution
Despite such efforts to reduce erosion, the pressures on the Pennine Way continue to mount, and it has become known, half-jokingly, as 'the M25' of National Trails! Not only do more walkers want to use it, but also pony trekkers, mountain-bikers and trail-bike enthusiasts. The most radical solution is the proposal for 'the second Pennine Way', to run roughly parallel to the existing trail as a bridleway usable by horses and two-wheeled vehicles, as well as walkers. In 1999, the route was approved and the project will be co-ordinated by the Countryside Agency (Fig. 3.24).

Figure 3.27 **'The Pennine Way was originally conceived as a challenging walk through fine upland scenery for all those suitably equipped to tackle it. The nature of the route has always demanded a reasonable degree of fitness, stamina and strong footwear'** (*Source*: Countryside Commission, 1992b)

Figure 3.32 The Ben Lawers National Reserve, Trossachs, Scotland. The car park at the Visitors Centre in the middle of this landscape has a design capacity of 30 vehicles. This restricts the number of visitors. The aims are to allow high-quality experiences for 'crowding-sensitive' visitors and to conserve the fragile moorland ecosystem

26 Define these types of recreational carrying capacity:
(*a*) physical or design;
(*b*) environmental;
(*c*) perceptual.

27 Look carefully at the 'honeypot' site shown in Figure 3.31. (Immediately to the right of the site is a car park for 15 vehicles, and a footpath leads from both ends of the stepping stones.)
a Describe the visitor types in terms of the CoCo classification of Figure 3.5.
b Write a brief report on the site in terms of the three types of recreational carrying capacity, e.g. evidence of capacity being exceeded.
c Suggest methods for increasing the recreational carrying capacity of this 'honeypot' by 50 per cent.

28 Explain what is meant by the statement that recreational carrying capacity is 'a relative not an absolute concept'.

29 Describe a recent outdoor recreation trip when the carrying capacity of the environment or facilities you were using were being exceeded (note which *aspects* of carrying capacity were being exceeded and how you became aware of this).

densities. Thus, carrying capacity is an important 'tool' used to balance **conservation** and development goals, and to match environmental settings with preferred recreation experiences, i.e. to provide for both 'crowding-sensitive' and 'crowding-tolerant' visitors; to protect areas of high conservation value while providing sites which can withstand high visitor densities.

Summary

- In the UK, eight out of ten people make some use of the countryside for leisure.

- There is a huge and growing demand for an ever-widening range of leisure activities, which is putting increasing pressure on countryside resources.

- Different user groups make different demands and impacts upon resources and facilities.

- The supply of leisure opportunities is the outcome of interactions between resource owners, developers, special-interest organisations and government agencies.

- Access and accessibility have an important influence upon leisure participation.

- Rights of way, especially footpaths, play a vital role in providing access to privately owned countryside, but are under threat from both overuse and development pressures.

- In order to achieve conservation objectives and to satisfy diverse recreation needs and expectations, National Park managers use techniques for visitor concentration and dispersion based on varied levels of recreational carrying capacity.

4 Managing recreation in the changing countryside

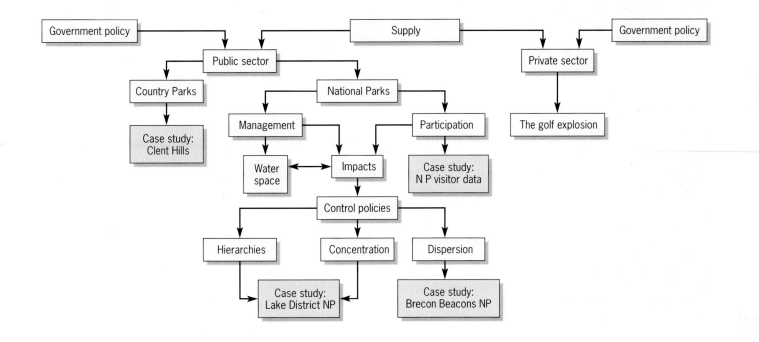

4.1 Introduction

In the countryside, as in cities, **recreation** must compete with other users for space and resources – farming, transport, industry, housing: e.g. the government forecasts that at least 2.5 million additional homes will be needed in the UK between 2000 and 2020, and that at least 50 per cent of them will be built in rural areas. This competition generates a constantly shifting balance between supply and demand, affecting all four 'Ps' of the leisure system: policy, planning, provision, participation (see p.5). **Management** of change involves the thoughtful allocation of resources according to selected criteria and priorities. Once again the concepts cascade of Figure 1.19 provides a useful framework for your study of this process.

As you follow the management processes and issues raised in this chapter you will find these recurring principles:

• The balancing of private and public rights and interests;

• The balancing of conservation and recreation priorities (Fig. 4.1);

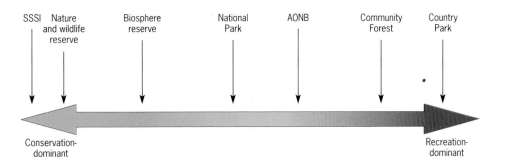

Figure 4.1 The conservation–recreation continuum

Figure 4.2 The Blencathra massif and the Greta valley, Lake District National Park. How can the attractive mix of farming, homes, woodland, open fell and roads be sustained for our enjoyment during the twenty-first century?

?

1 Define a 'Country Park' in terms of purpose, location and character.

2 Use examples to support the view that Country Parks are 'demand-based' rather than 'resource-based' facilities.

3 Illustrate the concepts of access and accessibility through an analysis of a Country Park by the following people (they all live in the same location, about 6km from the park): (*a*) a young, healthy couple with a car; (*b*) a group of teenage friends with mountain bikes; (*c*) a wheelchair-bound elderly woman who does not have regular access to a car (you may use one of the examples in the book, or an example with which you are familiar).

4 Describe the pattern of a typical visitors' trip (including who they are and what they do) revealed by the survey of Clent Hills Country Park (study the data of Figure 4.4 carefully).

• The management of resources for **multiple use** and **sustained yield**, i.e. meeting diverse and shifting demands without degrading the resource base over time (Fig. 4.2).

4.2 Finding space for leisure near cities: the example of Country Parks

Land-use surveys reveal that urban fringe zones, including Green Belts, are a rich source of recreational opportunities, provided by both private businesses and public agencies. Look around you as you leave a city: garden centres, 'working farms', picnic sites, pony stables, car parks at the start of footpaths, safari parks, paint-ball arenas, golf courses and driving ranges, fishing, sailing, water-skiing and windsurfing on lakes and reservoirs, go-kart tracks, and so on.

Inevitably, public access to open space has become an important element in planning policy in these urban fringe locations. One key result of this policy is the **Country Park**. Although open spaces for informal leisure – picnics, walks, rides etc. – within easy reach of cities have a long history, the formal category of Country Parks was not created until the Countryside Act 1968. Local authorities 'were given powers to provide Country Parks and picnic sites – places in country surroundings, not necessarily beauty spots, for the enjoyment of the countryside by the public' (Open University/Countryside Commission, 1985). Notice that they were 'given powers', but provision has not been compulsory. None the less, by 1998 there were more than 350 Country Parks scattered across every county in England and Wales. Most lie within 25km of cities and are between 10 and 1000 hectares in area. The key features are therefore, free **access** and easy **accessibility**, with the supply being located as close to demand as is practical (i.e. **demand-based** rather than **resource-based** locations).

Country Parks are **public-sector** facilities in that they are managed by city and county councils, with funding support and policy guidance from the Countryside Agency (Fig. 4.3). However, the land and water resources are often owned by the **voluntary sector** (e.g. the National Trust), other public bodies (e.g. the Forestry Commission), or private individuals. In some parks, the land may be leased back to a farmer who continues to graze animals. In other cases, the local authority acquires derelict land (e.g. disused gravel pits) from private businesses.

Figure 4.3 Guidelines given to local authorities on Country Parks. The photograph at the foot of page 68 shows Queenswood Country Park, Dinmore Hill, Herefordshire

Guidelines on Country Parks

1 To encourage the provision of Country Parks where the present facilities are inadequate. Indicators of need are:

a a deficiency of recreation areas within easy reach of large urban populations,

b pressures of use on existing facilities,

c growing traffic congestion and damage to the countryside environment, e.g. between Liverpool and Manchester.

2 To encourage the improvement of areas already in use for recreation which could be converted into Country Parks without too much expense, e.g. Lickey Hills and Clent Hills, West Midlands.

3 To encourage the development of Country Parks on land at present derelict or under-used, particularly where publicly owned. The use of high-quality agricultural land should be discouraged, e.g. Kingsbury Water Park, Warwickshire, and Pugnetts Park, Wakefield, have both been developed from disused gravel workings.

Two important objectives have been, first, to take pressure off **National Parks** by making opportunities available closer to the origins of demand, and second, to reduce the impacts of trespass and disturbance on farmers and residents in intensively used areas around cities. So, if you feel like a day or half-day out, you need not drive all the way to a National Park or risk trespassing. Country Parks vary widely in character, but share certain attributes: because they are relatively small and near large numbers of people, they must be managed for high-density use. Recreational carrying capacities will be high, and users must expect to encounter lots of people, especially at weekends.

Clent Hills and Kingsbury Water Park

The Clent Hills

The Clent Hills are an excellent example of all that Country Parks are meant to be – and of the impact problems associated with intensive use (Fig. 4.4). They lie along the south-west edge of the West Midlands conurbation and have been a popular 'green lung' for the urban population for at least 100 years. The built-up area extends to the foot of the hills, and main roads give easy access. The two elongated ridges that make up the park (Walton Hill and Adams Hill) provide contrasting views over the conurbation to the north and the Worcestershire countryside to the south. Although the ridge-tops are open and often crowded, the flanks are cut by thickly vegetated small valleys that create a sense of quiet and relaxation.

Clent Village, at the southern edge of the park, is the traditional entrance, but the park managers have attempted to disperse the impacts of visitors by developing two car parks and **facilities** on the northern edge of the park. Most of the land is owned by the National Trust (voluntary sector) but Worcestershire County Council (public sector) manages the park.

Kingsbury Water Park

Kingsbury Water Park represents the other extreme to Clent Hills – it is a new **recreational** resource created from derelict land for mainly water-based activities. Warwickshire County Council has taken control of extensive disused gravel workings which, as they lie in a flood-plain, had filled naturally with water. The designers have divided the area into two main **zones**. The first is a series of small lakes, each designated for a particular water-based activity, such as windsurfing, dinghies, remote-control model boats etc. (Fig. 4.5). Around the lakes, where there has been a regeneration of scrub and woodland, car parks, trails, picnic areas and children's activity areas for informal recreation have been laid out. The second zone is a wetland ecosystem that supports a variety of water birds. The motorway that runs through the site has been used as

Figure 4.4 Intensive use at Clent Hills Country Park

The two hills of the park are separated by a valley with a lane. Access is controlled by three peripheral car parks, and motor vehicles are banned within the park. A dense network of footpaths fans out from these access points. The visitor numbers have caused extensive impacts on vegetation and erosion, especially near car parks and along the ridge tops, where the bare surface sometimes extends to 50m. To reduce conflict and impacts, separate bridle paths for horses have been marked out. Mountain bikes are also causing concern.

A gently-graded path with hand-rails improves accessibility for people with disabilities. There is a permanent orienteering course.

Survey date: Sunday, 6 October 1991

Average length of stay 58min

Average journey (each way) 8km

Travel by car 82%

Regular visitors 71%

Activities observed:
Picnics; walking; jogging; cycling; horse-riding;sitting relaxing; orienteering; bird-watching; photography; model aircraft flying; exercising pets.

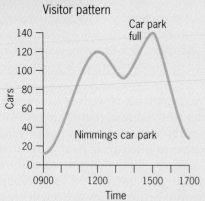

Visitor pattern

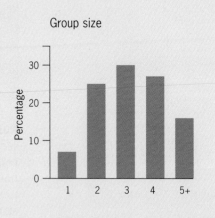

Group size

Figure 4.5 Kingsbury Water Park

the boundary between the zones: on one side, the medium-density zone for watersports and informal recreation; on the other the low-density zone for bird-watching and quiet walking. The main visitor centre has information, toilets, a shop and a teaching room.

Figure 4.6 The National Parks of England and Wales
(*Source:* **Countryside Commission**)

4.3 National Parks

National Parks make up the high-order tier of the park hierarchy. They are relatively large and widely though irregularly distributed across England and Wales (Fig. 4.6 and Table 4.1). Their boundaries enclose landscapes that are given protected status because of their high **conservation** value and because of their attractiveness for outdoor recreation (Fig. 4.7). Herein lies the central dilemma for park managers: how to conserve the precious landscape while providing high-quality recreation opportunities for very large numbers of visitors (see column d of Table 4.1).

World–UK comparisons

Throughout the world, National Parks are an important element in countries' policies for conservation, recreation and tourism (see Chapter 7). The world's first National Park was Yellowstone (USA), designated in 1872 ('designation' is the term used to mean the formal giving of the title and protected status). By the early twentieth century, countries such as Australia and New Zealand had National Parks, but Britain's first National Park, the Peak District, was not designated until 1951, as one of the outcomes of the National Parks and Access to the Countryside Act 1949. A further nine parks were designated during the 1950s, but the eleventh, the Broads, did not arrive until 1988. In 1999, the government approved the designation of two new National Parks: the South Downs and the New Forest. At the beginning of the twenty-first century, therefore, over 11 per cent of England and Wales lay inside National Park boundaries (see column a of Table 4.1).

5a Make a brief comparison between the location of National Parks (Fig. 4.6) and the population distribution of the UK (refer to an atlas).
b To what extent does the location of a National Park help to explain the volume of visitor use? (See Figure 4.6 and columns c and d of Table 4.1.)
c Suggest three factors other than location which may influence visitor usage of a National Park.
d What evidence is there in Figure 4.7 to support the claim that UK National Parks are multiple-use environments?

Table 4.1 UK National Parks – some key data (1996)

	a Area (sq. km)	b Resident population ('000)	c Population within 32km of park boundary ('000)	d No. of visitor days (mill)[1]	e Average spend, day visitors (£)	f Average spend per day, staying visitors (£)[2]
Brecon Beacons	1346	33	2000	3.7	7.00	10.10
Dartmoor	956	33	1100	4.0	7.30	18.50
Exmoor	693	11	260	1.5	8.00	12.00
Lake District	2292	43	600	15.0	13.50	15.50
North York Moors	1436	26	550	8.0	9.50	11.30
Northumberland	1030	2	200	1.5	8.00	5.60
Peak District	1438	39	1650	13.0	7.50	13.00
Pembrokeshire Coast	583	25	300	4.6	12.80	15.00
Snowdonia	2142	41	456	6.8	10.50	13.00
Yorkshire Dales	1773	19	2800	8.5	11.50	15.00
The Broads	303	6	360	5.3	10.70	13.30

1 These are estimates of the *minimum* number of visitor days. Some sources suggest that the Lake District and Peak District have at least 20 million visitor days a year, as surveys may not record walkers and others who enter the Parks by unusual routes, for example.

2 Totals *exclude* accommodation.

Figure 4.7 The Peak District National Park: a view from Mam Tor to Castleton and the Hope cement works. This landscape illustrates several key understandings about UK National Parks: they are multiple-use environments, where conservation and recreation values must be co-ordinated with economic activities and local populations

As yet, Scotland has no National Parks. The nearest protected area equivalents are Regional Parks and National Scenic Areas (NSAs), although there are Biosphere Reserves, e.g. Beinn Eighe. There have been vigorous campaigns for National Parks in Scotland, e.g. the Cairngorms (proposed as a World Heritage Site in 1999), and Marine Parks around the Inner and Outer Hebrides. Landowners and other economic interests have opposed such designations. However, in 1998 Scottish National Heritage (SNH) proposed: 'the establishment of National Parks in Loch Lomond and Trossachs [Fig. 4.9] and in the Cairngorms [Fig 4.10], each with an independent National Park Body with a majority of local representatives' (*National Parks for Scotland*, SNH, 1998). These proposals will be considered by the new Scottish Parliament.

Read the two definitions of Figure 4.8 carefully. They make it clear that there are crucial distinctions between UK National Parks and parks across the world:

• In most countries, greater primacy is given to conservation than in the UK.

• Although the UK definition stresses their wild and natural character, UK National Parks are, in reality, cultural and economic landscapes – the result of centuries of human settlement and land management. For instance, about 270 000 people live in our parks (see column b of Table 4.1).

UK definition of a National Park

'An extensive area of beautiful and relatively wild country in which, for the nation's benefit and by appropriate national decision and action [i.e. government policy], the characteristic landscape beauty is strictly preserved, access and facilities for public open-air enjoyment are amply provided, wildlife and buildings and places of architectural and historic interest are suitably protected, while established farming use is effectively maintained.'

(National Parks and Access to the Countryside Act 1949)

International definition of a National Park

'A relatively large area (1) where one or several ecosystems are not materially altered by human use and settlement; (2) where plant and animal species, geomorphological sites and habitats are of special scientific, educational and recreative interest, or which contains a natural landscape of great beauty; (3) where the government of the country has taken steps to prevent or eliminate, as soon as possible, use or settlement in the whole area and to enforce the respect of ecological, geomorphological or aesthetic features, which have led to its establishment; and (4) where visitors are allowed to enter under special conditions.'

(United Nations, 1977)

Figure 4.8 What is a National Park?

Figure 4.9 Proposals for the Loch Lomond and the Trossachs National Park

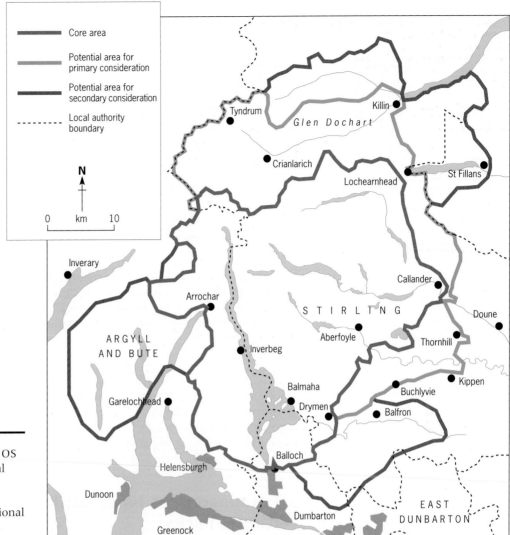

?

6 Use an atlas and, if possible, OS maps to describe environmental characteristics (physical and human) of the proposed Loch Lomond and the Trossachs National Park.

Figure 4.10 The Cairngorms and several other extensive, wild and remote areas of Scotland fit the definitions of National Parks more closely than perhaps any other parts of the UK

Table 4.2 Land ownership (%) in National Parks, 1990 (*Source:* National Park Authorities, in Edwards, 1992)

	Brecon Beacons	Broads	Dartmoor	Exmoor	Lake District	Northumber-land	North York Moors	Peak District	Pembrokeshire Coast	Snowdonia	Yorkshire Dales
Private	69.6	90.8	57.3	79.1	58.9	56.4	79.9	72.3	85.7	69.9	96.2
Forestry Commission	8.0	0.2	1.8	1.8	5.9	18.9	16.6	0.5	1.3	15.8	0.0
Ministry of Defence	0.1	0.0	14.0	0.0	0.2	22.6	0.5	0.3	4.6	0.0	0.3
Water companies	4.0	1.5	3.8	0.6	6.9	1.2	0.1	13.0	0.0	0.9	0.3
National Trust	3.5	3.0	3.7	10.1	24.2	0.7	1.2	9.6	4.2	8.9	2.5
Nature Conservancy Council	0.8	4.0	0.3	0.0	0.0	0.0	0.0	0.1	0.5	1.7	0.4
National Park Authority	13.0	0.5	1.4	4.4	3.9	0.2	0.6	4.2	2.3	1.2	0.1
Other	1.0	0.0	17.7	4.0	0.0	0.0	1.1	0.0	1.4	1.6	0.2

?

7 For each of the landowning groups shown in Table 4.2, suggest what their main objectives are (e.g. the main objective of water companies is to produce an ample supply of drinkable water at reasonable cost).

8 Look again at the UK definition for National Parks and identify those owners in Table 4.2 whose objectives:
a best fit the aims of a National Park;
b are most likely to clash with the park aims.

9 List the elements of the international definition of a National Park that would exclude any UK National Park. This is an important understanding because some 'world lists' of National Parks do not include the UK's 'National Parks'.

• UK parks do not 'belong' to the nation. As Table 4.2 makes clear, the land and water resources are mainly privately owned or owned by organisations whose priorities are not focused on public access and recreation, e.g. the Ministry of Defence. In contrast, parks in many countries are publicly owned through the national governments. For example, all but 1000 hectares of the 309 000 hectares of California's great Yosemite National Park are owned by the US Federal Government and administered by the National Park Service.

By some measures, therefore, UK National Parks are neither 'national' nor 'parks': notice how the international definition emphasises the absence of human impacts and focuses upon the removal of any such impacts where they presently exist. These impacts have major effects upon management priorities and policies for our parks.

4.4 Management issues and strategies in UK National Parks

The 1995 Environment Act sets out the principal goal for park managers: 'To conserve and enhance natural beauty, wildlife and cultural heritage, and to promote opportunities for the understanding of the special qualities of the parks by the public.'

If you reflect carefully on this statement, several issues emerge:

• What is meant by 'conserve and enhance' and is there a tension between them?
• What is meant by 'natural beauty' and who decides what is 'beautiful'?
• What is 'cultural heritage' and is it all of value?
• What does 'promote opportunities for the understanding' mean?
• How do we define 'special qualities'?

As you consider these questions, it becomes clear that National Parks are not simply 'the nation's playgrounds'!

Decision-making
The key decision-making body in each park is the National Park Authority (NPA). This administrative and planning board is funded by central government, with further support from the county councils within which a park lies. Each NPA is required to produce a Management Plan and Local Plans which set out the preferred strategy for the park. However, NPA decision-making is constrained in several ways (Fig. 4.11). In consequence, an NPA is a persuader and negotiator rather than an autonomous decision-maker, and must 'sell' its plans to a range of *'stakeholders'*.

Figure 4.11 Constraints on a National Park Authority
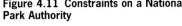

County Council
Although the 1995 Environment Act gave an NPA greater freedom and powers, it must still work with the local authorities. The NPA does not replace the county council planning committee within the park.

Central Government
The management plan for a park must be approved by central government, e.g. DOE, DNH.

NPA

Funding
NPA funds from central and local government are severely limited.

Ownership
The majority of the land and water resources in a park are not owned by the NPA.

?

10 Study Figure 4.7 and apply the following evaluation technique on the landscape shown.

The landscape evaluation technique sees the landscape as containing a set of items (e.g. trees, hills, buildings), and asks you to assess their value in terms of:

Impact on the landscape (I)	*Score*
Stands out very strongly	+2
Stands out	+1
Makes little impression	0

Contribution to the landscape (C)	*Score*
Excellent	+2
Good	+1
Neutral	0
Poor	−1
Very bad	−2

a Identify the main components in the landscape.
b Complete a copy of Table 4.3 for each item that is present. For instance, if you think the walls 'stand out' and make an 'excellent contribution to the landscape, the scores for this item would be: I = +1; C = +2; T (Total) = +3.
c Sum each section and overall total scores. (NB. The higher the total score the more 'valuable' is the landscape.)
d Discuss briefly your findings. How do they explain why the landscape has been designated as worthy of National Park status?

11 Group discussion. On page 74, five issues facing National Park managers are listed as questions. Discuss these questions and suggest some preliminary answers. (You should be able to improve on your answers when you have completed your study of National Parks.)

Management issues

Each NPA has four main tasks:

1 To conserve the valued natural, managed and built environmental features of the park.
2 To enable access and opportunity for a wide range of recreational activities and experiences.
3 To support the local economy, especially farming and visitor services.
4 To protect the quality of life of local communities.

These tasks demand that the resources of a park are used in quite different ways, so tensions and conflicts are inevitable. A fundamental purpose of park management plans is to resolve these issues. All plans are based upon the principles of *multiple use* and *sustained yield* – the resources of a park should be

Table 4.3 Landscape evaluation form

Section A: Natural features	I	C	T	Section D: Points	I	C	T
Cliff or crags				Settlements: traditional			
Hill, mountain peak				non-traditional			
Plateau				Car parks			
Valley, gorge, major gully				Caravan and camp sites			
Lake				Tips, quarries, mines			
River, stream				Industrial buildings			
Waterfall				Bridges			
Flat floodplain, marshy, estuary				Section sub-total			
Section sub-total							
Section B: Vegetation				**Section E: Networks**			
Moorland				Roads: major			
Scattered trees				minor			
Clumps of trees				Tracks and pathways			
Large woods or plantations				Railway track			
Reeds and marsh vegetation				Pylons, poles and wires			
Section sub-total				Section sub-total			
Section C: Farmed land				**Section F: Other items**			
Arable land				1			
Grassland				2			
Rough grazing				3			
Hedgerows				Section sub-total			
Walls							
Fences				Total			
Section sub-head							

Planners 'stifling' Brecon Beacons

By JOHN YOUNG

MORE than 10,000 people, about a quarter of the adult population of the Brecon Beacons national park, have signed a petition expressing no confidence in the park planning authority.

They claim that people wanting to start businesses, including farmers who are being encouraged by the government to diversify, are unable to do so due to excessively restrictive planning policies.

The petition calls for a referendum on whether some areas should be removed from the jurisdiction of the park committee, including the town of Brecon, where the council has passed a resolution supporting 'independence'.

The Brecon Beacons is one of the 11 national parks in England and Wales established under a 1949 Act of Parliament, and its dismemberment would be legally and practically almost impossible, but the petition organisers have asked Richard Livsey, SLD MP for Brecon and Radnor, to present the document to David Hunt, the Welsh secretary, in the hope that he will intervene in the dispute.

Ashford Price, who has won three Prince of Wales Awards for Enterprise, is a former farmer who now runs the Danyrogof Caves, said to be the largest complex in Western Europe and an important tourist attraction. He is anxious to expand his equestrian interests, including the breeding and training of shire horses, but has been unable to obtain planning permission.

'I have found no difficulty in working with other authorities like the Nature Conservancy Council and the Mid-Wales Development Board,' he said. 'But with the national park committee it is absolutely impossible.

'Farmers can't diversify. Many are selling up and their children are leaving the area. There must be changes which will allow people to earn a living or the place will end up as just one giant holiday home.

'What we are really concerned about is the off-hand attitude of planning officers. They are not really concerned about people and they seem to be keen on saying no to everything.'

Gwyn Gwillim, a member of the park committee and a Powys county councillor, claims that if everyone in the area had been approached the number of signatories could have been doubled.

'One of my complaints is that we are not consistent,' he said. 'We tend to put stricter controls on small individuals than on large bodies like British Coal, British Telecom and the electricity board, which is allowed to clutter up the countryside with pylons.

'We gave permission to the water board to put up a filtration plant, which is a real eyesore and looks horrible in a very sensitive area, yet ordinary people have to bother about whether they have the right coloured tiles or slates on the roof of their home.'

Martin Sitton, the newly appointed national park officer, said he was aware of the problems and recognised that communications in the past had been unsatisfactory. Since taking up the post at the beginning of this year he was determined to change things and intended to start planning 'surgeries' where people could come with complaints and had already attended a number of public meetings.

About 70 per cent of all planning applications were passed, which was in line with the national average, but some schemes would still have to be refused and that was the problem. Until now overall responsibility for the national parks had rested with the Countryside Commission, but from April the three parks in Wales will come under a new Welsh authority.

Figure 4.12 Objections to the Brecon Beacons National Park policies (*Source: The Times*, 16 February 1991) © Times Newspapers Ltd 1993

used for a variety of purposes in ways that will sustain their quality and quantity over time. These are ambitious aims, and it is not surprising that NPAs and even the idea of National Parks are not always popular! (Fig. 4.12.)

Pressures for development are unceasing, despite restrictive planning policies. During the 1980s the numbers of planning applications within the parks rose from 4500 to over 5500 a year (Fig. 4.13). Numbers fell during the economic recession of the early 1990s, but by 1997–8 applications were above 5500 once more. Remember – the continuing rise in recreation is only one cause of development pressures (Fig. 4.14).

Figure 4.13 A timeshare development at Langdale in the Lake District National Park. Planning permission was granted because: (*a*) it involves the reinstatement of a disused slate quarry; (*b*) the scale is appropriate for this sensitive environment; and (*c*) the development includes the use of local materials (stone and wood) and is well screened by trees to reduce visual impacts

Figure 4.14 Development pressures in National Parks

?

12 From Figure 4.12 give three reasons why there are tensions between local people and the Brecon Beacons NPA.

Use Figure 4.14 to answer questions 13–15.

13 Take each of the planning issues in turn, and build up a table, using the following headings:
Who applied?
What for?
Who opposed?
Why was the proposal rejected?

14 In order to examine impacts, draw a matrix like the one below. Assess each of the six proposals according to the four aspects listed, using these symbols in the matrix boxes:
Benefit +; Loss −; No effect 0.

	1	2	>
Leisure			
Conservation			
Local economy			
Local people			

15 Which of the planning issues involve leisure activities in the parks and which have both benefits *and* losses for leisure opportunity?

Snowdonia: A property developer applied to turn the disused gold mine at Clogau, near Dolgellau, into a 'living museum' providing up to 60 jobs and attracting ¼ million visitors a year, plus a cable car up the mountain. Although supported by the Snowdonia National Park Authority, it was opposed by the Countryside Commission, the Council for National Parks and the Snowdonia Society (the last two are voluntary action groups). At appeal the application was rejected as it would be 'undesirable and incongruous in the tranquil Mawddach estuary and would seriously affect the privacy of residents in the quiet village'. It was in conflict with the 'beauty, peace and quiet' which attracted so many visitors.

Northumberland: The National Park Committee has rejected an application by Tilcon to extend Harden Quarry on the southern edge of the Cheviot. It is a hard, decorative stone. The existing quarry has a 'life' of 39 years…. The extension would add 30 years and extend across four acres. The rejection was principally because of the 'unacceptable level of visual intrusion into the landscape'.

Pembrokeshire Coast: The Secretary of State for Wales has turned down a developer's proposal for 150 holiday cottages on a cliff-top site at Amroth, which would replace a static caravan park. The Inspector expressed concern at the precedent of converting caravans to permanent buildings and that 'the proposed buildings would be obtrusive and alien, spoiling the character of the locality'.

Dartmoor: A management agreement has been reached to avoid the ploughing of 300 acres on Hangar Down near Ivybridge. The permission to allow ploughing was given in 1987, but the National Park has paid a block sum and provided for 'no ploughing and for access in perpetuity'.

Peak District: The National Park Committee has turned down an application by a London development company to build a luxury hotel and timeshare holiday complex at Litton Mill in the Wye Valley. It contravened the Structure Plan and 'the scale and form of the development would have a seriously adverse effect on the appearance and cultural heritage of the mill, the local community, and the enjoyment of visitors'. Litton Mill is a Site of Special Scientific Interest (SSSI), and the development would impact on wildlife.

Brecon Beacons: Sun Valley Poultry Limited has opened a new turkey-processing plant at Abergavenny, just outside the National Park. This has led to several applications from farmers within the park for turkey-rearing units. Sun Valley says the plant needs 90 units, each 80m by 20m, for 7000 turkeys, plus traffic generation and soiled litter disposal. The National Park Authority feels such developments are incompatible with park objectives and policy.

It is clear, therefore, that UK National Parks face several key questions:

Access: Can and should the parks continue to permit free and unlimited access to growing numbers of visitors?
Activities: What types of recreational activities/experiences are appropriate?
Agreement: How can tensions and conflicts between different stakeholder groups be resolved?
Account: Who should pay for and manage the sustainable development for leisure – and how much are the parks worth?
Allocation: Do we need more National Parks and where should they be located?
Aims: Should the aims of the parks be modified?

Visitor usage of National Parks

Available data gives only approximate totals, but during the late 1990s the eleven UK National Parks were absorbing 70–80 million visitor days a year (see column d of Table 4.1). At least 75 per cent of this total occurred during the April–September period. The huge flow brings important economic benefits (columns e and f of Table 4.1). Yet in some ways the parks have become victims of their own success, with widespread evidence of congestion and overuse in some localities and sites, especially during summer weekends (Fig. 4.15). The figures in Table 4.1 also indicate that visitor presence varies widely – compare the Lake District and the Peak District with Exmoor and Northumberland (column d). Parks differ, too, in their location in relation to regional populations, but this does not necessarily determine visitor numbers (compare columns c and d in Table 4.1).

Figure 4.15 Traffic congestion at Castleton in the Peak District National Park

The Recreation in UK National Parks case study below extracts key data from the 1994 National Parks Visitor Survey (the most recent national survey). It illustrates (*a*) the broad contrasts between parks in terms of visitor numbers and types, and (*b*) visitor preferences for informal, social activities enjoyed in attractive, peaceful settings. These findings highlight important issues for managers.

Recreation in UK National Parks

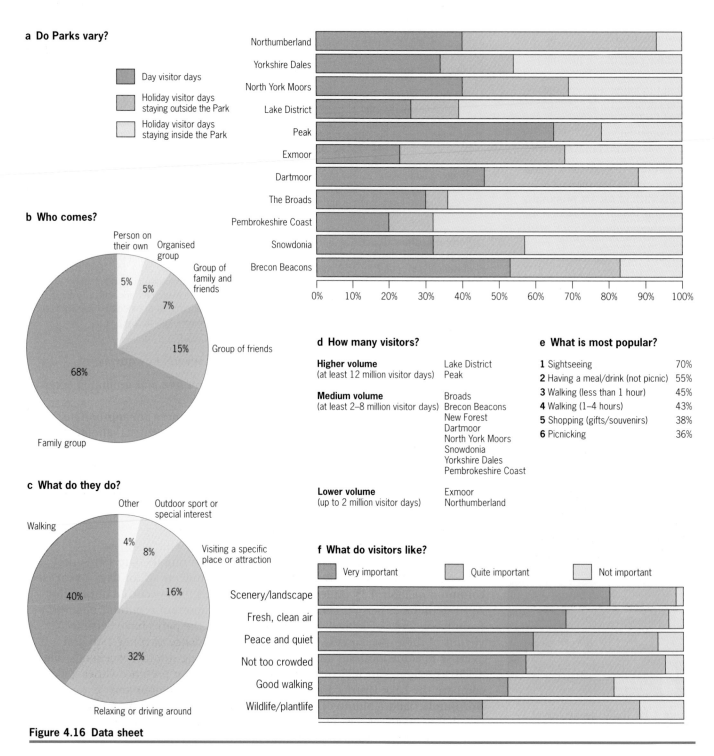

a Do Parks vary?

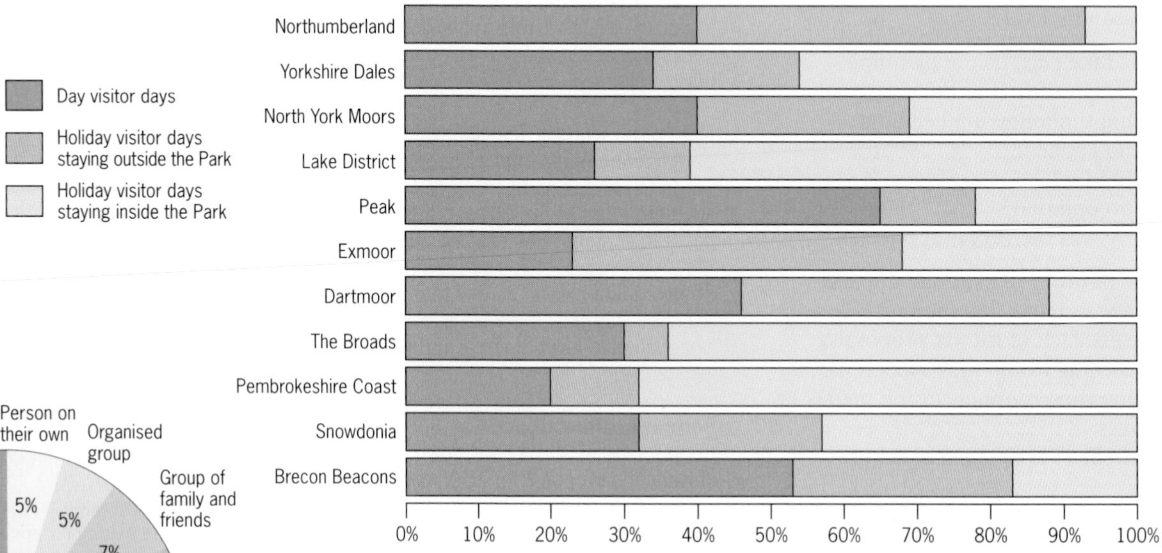
Day visitor days
Holiday visitor days staying outside the Park
Holiday visitor days staying inside the Park
Northumberland
Yorkshire Dales
North York Moors
Lake District
Peak
Exmoor
Dartmoor
The Broads
Pembrokeshire Coast
Snowdonia
Brecon Beacons
0%
10%
20%
30%
40%
50%
60%
70%
80%
90%
100%

b Who comes?

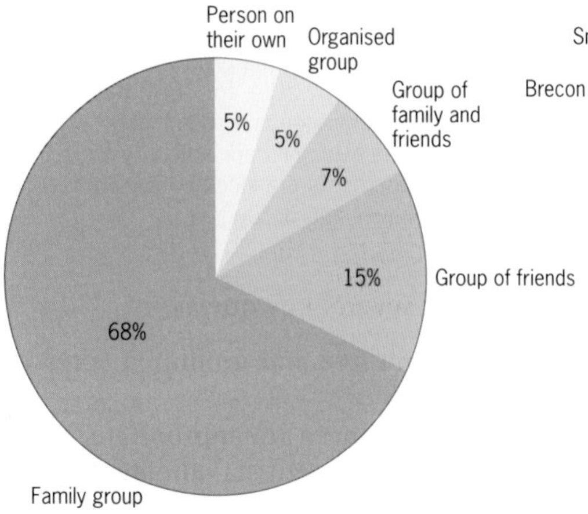
Person on their own
Organised group
Group of family and friends
Group of friends
Family group
5%
5%
7%
15%
68%

c What do they do?

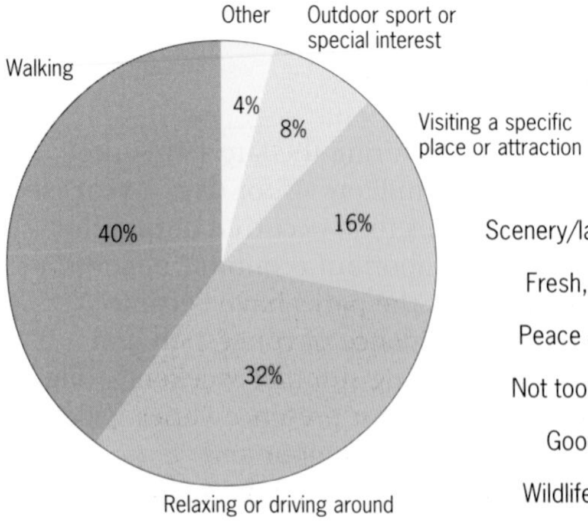
Other
Outdoor sport or special interest
Walking
Visiting a specific place or attraction
Relaxing or driving around
4%
8%
16%
40%
32%

d How many visitors?

Higher volume (at least 12 million visitor days)	Lake District Peak
Medium volume (at least 2–8 million visitor days)	Broads Brecon Beacons New Forest Dartmoor North York Moors Snowdonia Yorkshire Dales Pembrokeshire Coast
Lower volume (up to 2 million visitor days)	Exmoor Northumberland

e What is most popular?

1 Sightseeing	70%
2 Having a meal/drink (not picnic)	55%
3 Walking (less than 1 hour)	45%
4 Walking (1–4 hours)	43%
5 Shopping (gifts/souvenirs)	38%
6 Picnicking	36%

f What do visitors like?

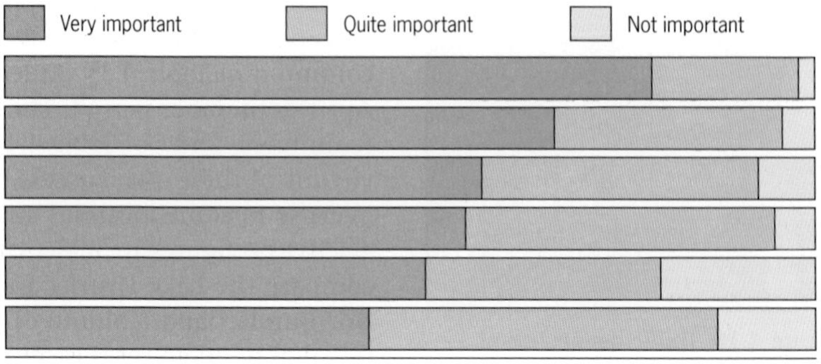
Very important
Quite important
Not important
Scenery/landscape
Fresh, clean air
Peace and quiet
Not too crowded
Good walking
Wildlife/plantlife

Figure 4.16 Data sheet

Figure 4.17 Waves of growth in National Parks

1950s
Continued growth in the popularity of 'traditional' outdoor activities for which the parks were originally intended, e.g. walking, climbing, camping, wildlife observation, etc.

1960s and 1970s
The surge in the arrivals of car-bound, less active visitors which enveloped the parks in a deluge of mass recreation and tourism, e.g. the 'car-and-stroller', the picnicker, the 'gift-shop browser', etc. Development pressure particularly for caravan parks, road improvements and parking.

1980s
Growth in the popularity of 'action sports' such as hang-gliding, water-skiing, sailboarding, orienteering, horse-riding, mountain-biking and other off-road vehicles, etc. As a National Park Officer said in 1990: 'A shift from passive to active – gawping to walking; from walking to riding – two feet to four; feet to wheels.' Development pressures for facilities and access permission for these activities.

1990s
Rapid growth in the private commercial leisure industry which has realised the development potential of the National Parks with their attractive environments and visitor popularity. This has resulted in a serious increase in planning applications for large-scale projects such as time-shares, hotels with golf, riding and sailing facilities, theme parks, health spas, etc.

?

16 Use the data of Table 4.1(p.71) to test these hypotheses and briefly discuss your findings.
a The bigger the park, the larger the number of visitors (columns a and d).
b Visitor volume increases as regional population increases (columns c and d).
c The larger the number of visitors, the greater the economic benefit to a park (columns d, e and f). Think carefully about the statistics you need to test this hypothesis.
Guideline: scattergraphs indicate the *direction* of relationships; correlation techniques indicate the *strength* of relationship between the pairs of variables. Use a software package if one is available.

17 Look carefully at Table 4.1.
a Suggest factors which help to account for the variations in visitor spending patterns between the parks (columns e and f).
b In which two parks are tensions between local people (column b) and visitors likely to be greatest? (Think about *all* the information in the table.)

It is not only the growth in visitor numbers that causes problems, but changes in the *type of visitor* and what they want to do. In Figure 4.17, these changes are summarised as four surges or waves that have swept over the parks during the past 50 years. Remember, each wave has not replaced the earlier one, rather it has been placed on top of it, resulting in the continuing growth of total numbers. Although similar waves of change have occurred across the countryside as a whole, they have been particularly intense within the National Parks because of their attractive resources and the relatively extensive access.

About 90 per cent of all visitors arrive by car, and transport issues loom large in all park plans, although visitor traffic is only one element in the overall problem (Fig. 4.18). However, once inside a park, visitor behaviour and hence resource demands and impacts vary enormously. It is this diversity that creates critical problems for park managers. For example, if you decide to go for a day's

Figure 4.18 Traffic types in the Snowdonia National Park

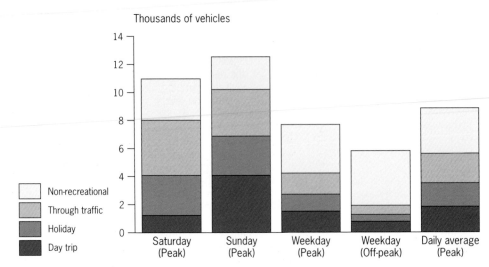

Thousands of vehicles

Legend:
- Non-recreational
- Through traffic
- Holiday
- Day trip

Note: This information relates to traffic on the six surveyed roads during a core 6-hour period on survey days in July and August (peak) and September (off-peak).

On the six surveyed roads (A4086, A470 North, A470 South, A493, A494, A5) recreational trips constituted an average of 64 per cent of the non-commercial traffic – 21 per cent were made by people on a day visit, 19 per cent by holidaymakers and 24 per cent by recreational through traffic.

Source: Snowdonia National Park Survey, Centre for Leisure Research, Edinburgh, 1995

?

18 From the case study data sheet (Fig. 4.16):
a Name the two parks with the greatest contrast between visitor patterns.
b Suggest three reasons why visitor patterns vary so widely and give examples of each. (An atlas may help you, e.g. population distribution, transport networks, holiday resorts etc.)
c The Lake District and Peak District National Parks are the two high visitor volume parks (see d).
(i) Describe the differences in their visitor patterns; (ii) Suggest reasons for this contrast; (iii) Outline how the patterns present different problems for the planners in each park, e.g. economic, social, environmental implications.

19 From Figure 4.18:
a Name two useful understandings about traffic in National Parks.
b Traffic management is a priority issue for planners in all parks. Use the information in the graphs to illustrate why solving traffic problems, including visitor traffic, is so difficult.

20 Essay: Is it true to say that the changes in leisure behaviour summarised in Figure 4.17 have meant that the management of National Parks has become increasingly difficult? Illustrate your answer with examples.

walking in the Yorkshire Dales National Park, you arrive by car or minibus and park all day at the access point for the paths or moorland you intend to use. Perhaps at the end of the day you may visit a café or pub. On the other hand, if you decide to 'go for a drive in the Dales', you may make use of several car parks, toilets, picnic spots, shops, cafés, pubs, themed sites (old woollen mills, steam railways etc.), short-walk opportunities, and so on. If your trip is to jet-ski or enjoy your mountain bike, however, your resource demands and impacts will be quite different (look again at the origin–destination models of Figure 3.15).

Management responses

When you examine a visitor and recreation management scheme at any scale, from a park as a whole to a picnic site, you will find that the park planners have asked, and attempted to answer, the following questions:

1 What is the character and value of the attractive resource? This involves a quantitative audit for various areas of the park, e.g. the length of road per sq.km, the area of trees, the number of bird species etc., and an evaluation of quality, using some form of landscape evaluation technique (Fig. 4.7 and Activity 9).
2 What should the carrying capacity of the resource be? For example, how many visitors and what types of activities can it absorb before the environment deteriorates and visitors begin to feel dissatisfied? How can carrying capacity be increased, and should it be?
3 How do visitors want to use the resource and how should they be permitted or enabled to use it, i.e. what is the appropriate use?
4 How can traffic and people be managed to fit the carrying capacity of the resource, i.e. how many vehicles and people, what range of activities, where, and when?

Recreational carrying capacity, as defined in the previous chapter (pp. 65–66), is therefore a central management concept – for instance, how much environmental impact and modification is acceptable to both managers and their objectives and to visitors and their expectations? Park planners and managers also base their proposals on three key principles:

Figure 4.19 Easy access to mountain tops in Switzerland, where a variety of trains, chair, and gondola lifts have a capacity to carry over 1 million people on to mountain tops in an hour! The photo shows the Rigi Mountain Railway above Weggis

Figure 4.20 Leaving your car outside: shuttle buses take visitors along the single road in Denali National Park, Alaska, USA

- The *Sandford principle* (from the Sandford Report on National Parks, 1974): that where conservation and recreation values are in conflict, conservation should be given priority.
- The *Edwards principle* (from the Edwards Report, *Fit for the Future*, 1991): that only those recreational activities that are appropriate for and compatible with the aims of National Parks should be allowed.
- The *Precautionary principle* (from the Environment Act 1995): that where there is significant uncertainty about the impacts of a proposal, decisions should be deferred until improved information is available.

Park managers use a variety of *positive* and *negative* techniques to control visitor numbers, distribution and behaviour. If we take the crucial example of traffic management, positive management inputs might include increasing car park capacities and upgrading roads. Throughput capacity can be increased by introducing time limits at car parks. A negative approach might include removing car parking space and excluding private vehicles from certain stretches of road. Many countries use a combination of positive and negative techniques. Thus, cars are excluded and are replaced by public transport systems (Figs 4.19, 4.20). In the UK, Dartmoor National Park indicates advisory routes for coaches; in the Peak District National Park cars are banned from the Upper Derwent Valley at peak periods, but there are cycle-hire facilities and an enlarged car park and picnic area at the entrance to the upper valley; in the Lake District National Park double yellow lines have been extended along the Buttermere–Crummock valley lane, but there is a Mountain Goat bus route from Keswick. In the UK, unfortunately, surveys reveal two major problems: first, people are very reluctant to leave their cars, and second, bus systems need heavy subsidies as they cannot charge economic prices.

Another option is to use *pricing* as a visitor control mechanism, e.g. entrance charges, car park fees. This has the advantage of bringing in income which can then be used for environmental management. Many countries do charge entrance fees (Fig. 4.21), and surveys in North America find that a majority of people are willing to pay, and indeed expect to pay, for the enjoyment of the parks. The charging of entrance fees at UK National Parks would be difficult because of the number of entrance points, the number of people who live in the parks and the volume of non-visitor traffic (Fig. 4.18).

Figure 4.21 Fee-charging in Long Key State Park, Florida, USA

21 Use the information of Figures 4.12 and 4.14 to illustrate the Sandford, Edwards and Precautionary principles.

22 What is meant by 'positive' and 'negative' management techniques? Give an example of each.

Visitor management – concentration and dispersion

All parks base their plans on the assumption that recreational carrying capacity will vary from place to place, i.e. that visitor densities and visitor expectations will vary from place to place. Although plans vary in detail, many adopt some form of **zoning** approach. Here are some examples:

- The Dartmoor National Park plan states its general aim for recreation as 'to encourage quiet, informal recreation use … and guide such use into those sites and areas best able to absorb it'. The plan identifies two key types of area – those managed to accommodate heavy use, and those with low recreational carrying capacity – and proposes a general zoning system (Fig. 4.22).
- The Peak District National Park, which experiences serious visitor pressures, has responded by developing a five-zone system, based on visitor densities and carrying capacity (Fig. 4.23).
- The Lake District National Park plan identifies 'quiet areas' and a hierarchy of lakes based on levels of recreational use (Fig. 4.24).
- The Pembrokeshire Coast National Park plan is based on a three-tier spatial hierarchy: low-impact areas; intermediate areas; intensive-use areas.

The technique of concentrating those visitors who are 'crowding tolerant' (see p.65) and allowing for the dispersion of 'crowding-sensitive' visitors at lower densities helps park managers to offer a wide range of recreational experiences while achieving their conservation objectives.

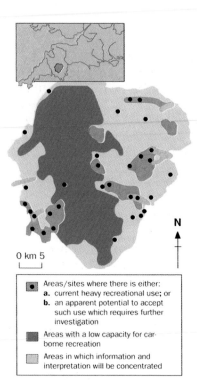

0 km 5

Areas/sites where there is either:
a. current heavy recreational use; or
b. an apparent potential to accept such use which requires further investigation

Areas with a low capacity for car-borne recreation

Areas in which information and interpretation will be concentrated

Figure 4.22 Planning for leisure: a proposal from the Dartmoor National Park Authority. The park is divided into two main zones, for conservation and recreation (*Source:* Dartmoor NPA, 1991)

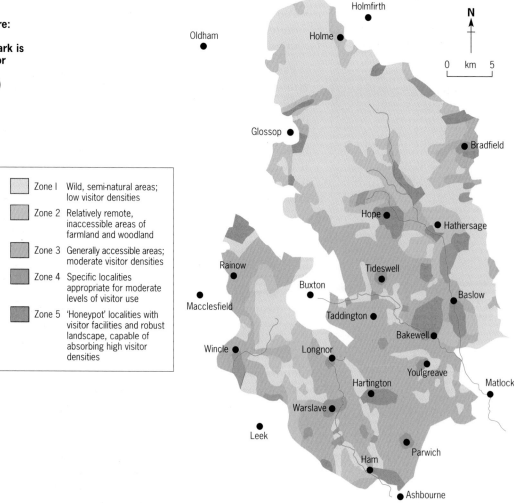

Zone 1   Wild, semi-natural areas; low visitor densities

Zone 2   Relatively remote, inaccessible areas of farmland and woodland

Zone 3   Generally accessible areas; moderate visitor densities

Zone 4   Specific localities appropriate for moderate levels of visitor use

Zone 5   'Honeypot' localities with visitor facilities and robust landscape, capable of absorbing high visitor densities

Figure 4.23 Management zones of the Peak District National Park

The Lake District National Park

The Lake District has to cope with at least 20 million visitor-days each year. Over 80 per cent arrive by car and coach, and three in every four come between April and September. Surveys show that the most attractive resources are the lakes, the uplands and mountains, and the traditional settlements such as Keswick and Hawkshead, as well as nineteenth-century resorts such as Ambleside. By far the largest number of visitors are car-bound, informal recreationists who make heavy use of the road network, parking and picnic sites, toilets, viewpoints, accessible short walks, and settlements for food, drink, shopping and browsing. However, because of the growing popularity of watersports and the widespread access rights for walkers and climbers, the lakes and the uplands are under considerable environmental pressure. Erosion, pollution and crowding have become increasingly common.

The response to visitor demand

Figure 4.24 shows how the park planners' response to this diverse demand has been based upon four key ideas:
(1) The setting aside of parts of the park as 'quiet areas'; (2) the concentration of high visitor densities into a small number of honeypots with high carrying capacities; (3) the protection of the central and northern uplands from penetration by vehicles – access

will, wherever possible, be based on the 'walk-in' principle; (4) the management of lakes according to a hierarchy of usage levels, from 'developed' to 'natural'.

The principal honeypots are focused along the two main entrance routes to the park, both leading from the M6: the Kendal–Ambleside axis in the south (B) and the Penrith–Keswick axis in the north (A).

The heavily used A591 road between the Ambleside and Keswick honeypots has been upgraded and provided with additional parking capacity to produce an efficient corridor through the heart of the park. In addition, HGVs are banned, except when they have business in the area. In these sections of the park, therefore, access, accessibility and carrying capacity have all been improved by positive management inputs.

The distribution of caravan sites in Figure 4.24 illustrates this policy clearly. As caravanning has grown in popularity, so farmers and landowners have made increasing numbers of planning applications for caravan sites. However, the National Park Special Planning Board has worked hard to contain the sites within the two main entrance axes and to restrict sites to a capacity of below 7000. This policy restricts traffic movements along the generally narrow, winding lanes, and limits the areas where clusters of caravans are highly visible in the landscape.

Controlling the lakes

The policy for the use of the lakes has been linked to the honeypot/quiet-area zoning principle. Lake Windermere, the largest lake, has the Ambleside-Windermere-Bowness honeypot along its north-east shore and has a long history of recreational boating use. The NPA has accepted this reality and permits a wide range of uses, including powered boats for waterskiing.

This is the only fully developed lake, yet even here a zoning system operates (e.g. waterskiers are restricted to a zone near their launching point at Lowwood).

On all the lakes the key controls are, first, that *all* boats must be registered and, second, a speed limit of 16km per hour must be observed. The only exception to this limit is the waterskiers' zone on Windermere. However, the NPA is trying to have all such powered boat activities removed from all the lakes, as it regards them as inappropriate in a National Park.

At the other extreme, the 'natural' lakes, on which no use of the water surface is allowed (except for lakeside owners), lie within the 'quiet areas' (e.g. Wastwater and Ennerdale Water in the west and Haweswater in the east). These are managed at low carrying capacities, to give low-density, quiet leisure experiences. In such areas, negative planning

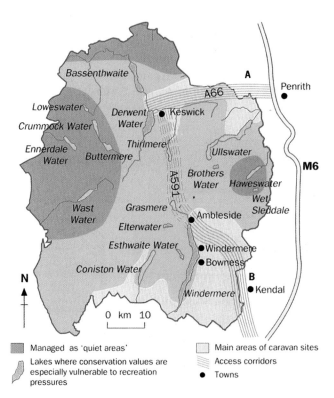

Figure 4.24 Balancing recreation and conservation: zoning of leisure in the Lake District National Park

The Lake District National Park

techniques are used to restrict accessibility and hence to control numbers of visitors (e.g. *not* upgrading the narrow, winding roads over the passes from the honeypots; *not* providing more parking spaces and facilities).

Between the two extremes are those lakes with moderate development levels (e.g. Lake Coniston), on which there is considerable activity, but the only powered vessels permitted are a few tiny hire boats and a cruise 'gondola' which provides trips

Figure 4.25 Watersports on Lake Coniston. Extensive public access to the lake-front makes the water-space accessible. Except for a commercial pleasure boat, and small rental boats, recreation is restricted to non-powered activities

along the length of the lake (Fig. 4.25). Coniston Village is a popular honeypot that has large caravan and camp sites, outdoor pursuits centres and stretches of free launching shore which benefit from the availability of the lake.

23 How have the managers of the Lake District National Park tried to provide for a range of high-quality recreational experiences, while conserving the quality of the environment? List as many measures as you can.

24 A watersports club in Manchester wants to persuade the Lake District planners to allow the use of a lakeside site and water space for jet-skiing in the National Park. Write two brief reports:
a In support of the proposal;
b In opposition to the proposal.

25 Essay: Describe the benefits and disbenefits of planners in National Parks such as the Lake District supporting a policy in favour of concentration of recreational activities rather than dispersal.

Getting away from it all

Two key objectives in all National Park plans are:

1 To conserve extensive areas of relatively wild, semi-natural landscape.
2 To provide opportunities for 'quiet enjoyment', 'tranquillity' and 'solitude'.

26 Use Figure 4.26 to explain how park managers attempt to fulfil both conservation and recreation objectives.

These objectives are clearly related. Managers set low recreational carrying capacities for areas of high conservation value, which in turn become attractive settings for 'crowding-sensitive' visitors (Fig. 4.26). However, as visitor numbers and mobility increase, and pressures for improved access intensify, achieving these objectives becomes more difficult, e.g. the serious reduction of 'tranquillity' revealed by the 1995 CPRE (Council for the Preservation of Rural England) Tranquil Areas Study (Fig. 4.27), even within National Parks.

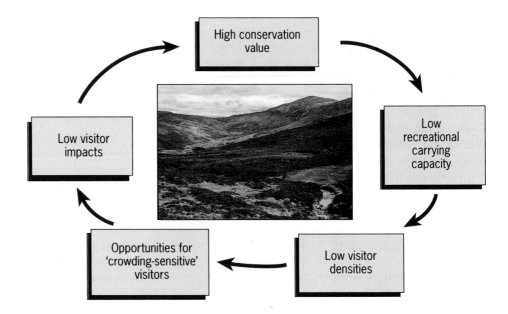

Figure 4.26 Conservation–recreation relationships

Figure 4.27 The erosion of tranquillity: the example of Cumbria, including the Lake District National Park

Early 1960s   Early 1990s

Tranquil areas

Urban and semi-tranquil areas

Vulnerable areas

Table 4.4: CPRE generalised criteria for the definition of 'tranquil areas' (*Source:* CPRE, 1995)

A 'tranquil area' lies:

- 4km from the largest power stations;
- 3km from the most highly trafficked roads; from large towns; and from major industrial areas;
- 2km from most other motorways and major trunk roads and from the edge of smaller towns;
- 1km from medium-disturbance roads and some main-line railways;
- A 'tranquil area' also lies beyond military and civil airfield noise lozenges and beyond very extensive opencast mining.

Common attributes used by park managers when locating and protecting areas attractive for people seeking 'peace and quiet' and the challenge of 'the great outdoors' are *naturalness* and *remoteness*. Thus, the built environment (buildings, roads, pylons etc.) is minimal, and semi-natural vegetation dominates. There is an absence of road access, with protection given by the need for 'the long walk in' and by limited waymarking to guide visitors. Low-impact and negative management techniques are given priority. Sets of criteria, therefore, can be used to identify appropriate areas (Table 4.4). The case study of the Brecon Beacons National Park introduces you to this approach.

A remote area in the Brecon Beacons National Park

The core of this park is the upland mass of the Brecon Beacons, which is a popular destination from the urban centres of South Wales and the West Midlands. The park plan is based on the understanding that there are 'differences in sensitivity, popularity and potential of the park' (BBNPA, 1995). From this basis, the plan identifies two types of problematic areas:

Pressure areas: 'Areas where an increase in recreational use is likely to make seriously worse existing problems such as physical erosion, traffic congestion, trespass or disturbance, or inconvenience to local communities.'

Vulnerable areas: 'Areas where wildlife habitats, archaeological features or qualities of remoteness are especially sensitive to local increases in visitor numbers or recreation activity. Their vulnerability arises from their being attractive and/or readily accessible to the general public, while lacking sufficient management and control of visitors to protect them.' (BBNPA, 1995)

The park managers have developed a 'remote area' policy which focuses upon the 'vulnerable areas' and especially upon the Carmarthen Black Mountain (Mynydd Du) (Fig. 4.28). The special qualities of this upland environment are 'the openness and expanse of the terrain, the relative absence of people and

Figure 4.28 Mynydd Du (the Black Mountain), Brecon Beacons

artefacts, the remoteness and exposure to the elements [which give] a sense of freedom and solitude, and an element of danger and challenge which is missing from everyday life, and which is less easy to find in busier parts of the park' (BBNPA, 1995).

Figure 4.38 A basic PAYP golf course, Bodenham, Herefordshire. This 9-hole course was opened in 1992 by a farmer, using two fields, and operates on an easy-access pay-as-you-play basis. Once planning permission for change of use has been obtained, the modifications are not expensive: mown fairways, small bunkers, tree landscaping, a simple clubhouse and car park, immediately beside a road for accessibility

?

31 A landowner intends turning part of her land into a golf course and sees two alternatives:
• To sell to a large commercial development company that wishes to build a full 18-hole course with clubhouse, hotel, landscaping etc., to be run as a members club.
• To retain ownership of the land and develop a low-cost 9-hole course and simple clubhouse to be run on a PAYP basis.

Write two persuasive statements:
a From a development company stating why she should support their proposal and sell.
b From a group of local residents and golfers who want her to go for the PAYP development.

32 Essay: Is golf development the most useful way of making more countryside resources available for outdoor recreation? Discuss.

Alternative courses

Criticism has been growing, too, over who has access to these space-consuming developments. Because of the high costs involved, most of the proposals have been from private-sector companies. They see their best chance of profits from high-quality, membership-only clubs. But this does not solve the problem of two million beginners and casual players who simply want to enjoy regular rounds with their friends, and are prepared to pay about £15 a round to do so. Local authorities have not had the money to increase the numbers of municipal pay-as-you-play (PAYP) courses, so a recent trend has been for farmers to set up very basic courses (Fig. 4.38). Planning committees have encouraged such initiatives by giving planning permission for change of use of farmland, unless it is Grade 1 quality or protected for conservation values. For example, the Six Hills Golf Club in Leicestershire began in 1986 when the farmer obtained planning permission to convert cattle pasture with a good meadow-grass cover to a 9-hole course. The fairways and greens were simply marked and mown across the meadows, and a portable cabin was bought cheaply to serve as a clubhouse and shop. The course operates on a PAYP basis and profits are put into improving the course and facilities. These PAYP facilities grew rapidly during the late 1990s.

A final aspect of concern is that some commercial developers submit a planning application for a golf course, but hidden within it there are 'ancillary developments' which are stated as vaguely as possible. These may be acceptable facilities such as a clubhouse, but they may also include conference centres, executive housing, hotels etc. The company submitting the application knows it would be unlikely to get planning permission for such profitable developments on their own, but hopes to slip them in under the 'golf umbrella'! Equally, planning committees may seek 'planning gain' by insisting upon improved landscaping, such as the setting-up of conservation areas, or improved roads, before giving permission. One response from county planning departments has been to set out clearer and firmer guidelines against which applications will be evaluated.

Summary

• Leisure must compete with other users for countryside resources.

• Countryside resources are managed for multiple use and sustained yield

• Country Parks have been located near urban populations to provide easily accessible opportunities for informal recreation.

• The land and water resources of UK National Parks are mainly under private ownership and are cultural, not natural, landscapes.

• National Parks are coming under severe pressure from increasing visitor numbers and an ever-widening range of recreational activities.

• Multiple ownership of resources in National Parks makes decision-making complex.

• The rapid growth in the demand for water-based activities has placed serious pressure upon the supply of water space.

• The shift in priorities for countryside management is providing new opportunities for recreation provision and for building up supply to meet demand for popular activities (e.g. the golf-course boom).

5 Travel and tourism in the United Kingdom

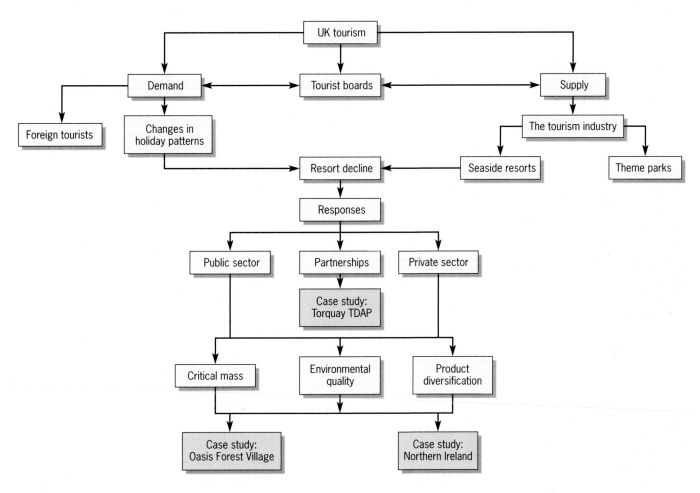

?

1 From Figure 5.1:
a estimate the proportion of total holidays that were taken within the UK in 1981, 1991 and 1998.
b summarise briefly the trends shown by the graphs and your estimates.

5.1 Introduction

During the past 25 years there has been a revolution in the way we spend our holidays (Fig. 5.1). In 1995 10 million fewer holidays were taken in the UK than in 1975. In 1989, for the first time, the UK population spent more on foreign holidays than on UK-based holidays (Fig. 5.2). By 1997 the gap had grown to £5 billion a year: £20 billion spent on foreign holidays, £15 billion

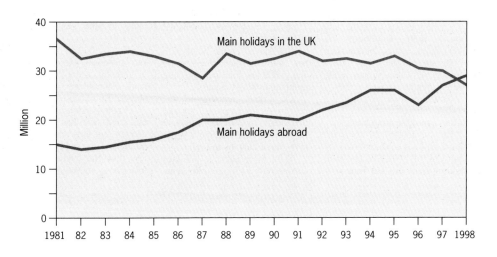

Figure 5.1 Holiday trends for UK residents, 1981–98 (million). The graph illustrates holidays of at least four nights, and omits 'short breaks' (*Source: Tourism Intelligence Quarterly*, BTA, April 1999)

Two weeks in Scarboro' v. Two weeks in Majorca

Tony and Carol soaked beside the sea

By Colin Wright in Scarborough

THE KENYON family huddled in a Scarborough sea-front café over a warming cup of hot chocolate and reflected on their decision to take a holiday in Britain instead of heading for warmer climes.

'Well, you can't complain, can you?' said Carol Kenyon. 'There's not much you can do about the weather and, anyway, the sun came out yesterday and it was beautiful.

'We all got out on the beach for the first time and I even managed to get my shoulders burned.'

This at the end of a week of virtually unremitting rain, wind and drizzle. The Kenyon family's resolve to enjoy themselves, come what may, was strangely touching.

They were sitting in the warmth of Paccitto's ice cream parlour and tea rooms watching fellow East Coast holidaymakers pass by swathed in plastic macs and clutching umbrellas.

Over the road on the sand the Kiddyland carousel was deserted. A large stack of deckchairs, tied down against the wind, told their own story.

Carol, 31, a mail order firm enquiries clerk, and her husband Tony, a 30-year-old van driver, had travelled with their children Kara-Rose, three, and Kyle, five, from their home in Plungington Road, Preston, Lancs, for a seven-day taste of the wonders of the Yorkshire coast.

They had been staying in a seven-berth caravan, which had cost them £220, savouring fish and chips, trying to keep dry and thoroughly enjoying themselves.

'The whole thing has been great. Nothing wrong at all. The scenery is beautiful, there is plenty to do at the camp where we are staying and we couldn't really have asked for anything more,' said Tony.

'All right, the weather hasn't been so great — but what do you expect on a holiday in Britain? You know before you come that it might rain and then you just have to get on with it.'

The Kenyons, eight years married, had been confirmed continental package tourists until the birth of their son: Ibiza, the South of France on a budget.

They say the delights of abroad now hold no great appeal. They feel the children are a bit too young for air travel (Kyle has sensitive skin anyway and does not like too much sun) and believe that Britain has plenty to offer.

For the past five years they have regularly taken two weekly holidays in resorts throughout Britain — one in June and the other September. Wales is next on the agenda.

It is said that when it rains and you have children in tow, the cost of a British holiday rockets — much to the benefit of amusement arcade owners.

Since they had not been on the beach due to the autumnal conditions, Mr Kenyon reckoned to have spent around £500 in seven days.

He was pleasantly surprised when he totted things up: £220 for the caravan (booked in January); £50 on petrol travelling to Whitby, Robin Hood's Bay and Filey; £60 on food for the four; £10 on amusements and rides; and £50 or £60 on drinks.

'That's not bad at all is it?' he said. 'It would cost more than that just to travel abroad.'

...as John and Sue soak up the sun

By John Harlow in Majorca

THE LOMBARDS may be the only people in Upper Elmers End Road with a suntan when they fly home from Majorca tomorrow to face the rigours of this soggy British summer.

This time last year the talk among their neighbours in Beckenham, south London, was of the greenhouse effect and a shortage of water, suntan lotion and ice cream.

Now it is of the prospect of a washed-out Wimbledon and further central heating bills.

But for another 24 hours the gloom will not be shared by John Lombard, his wife Sue and their children Kara, 10, and Tom, six.

The Lombards paid £1,600 for two weeks half-board at the Hotel Playa, Camp de Mar, a tiny resort on a white-sanded horseshoe bay. Their booking was made as soon as the 1990-91 Thomson brochure was published in October.

Sue stayed at the hotel with her mother-in-law three years ago, while her John was building up his plumbing business.

On Friday, relaxing in 86° heat by the Playa pool, John and Sue judged the £4,000 earmarked for the two weeks holiday a better investment than an umbrella.

With some package holidays costing only £150, the bill seems high, but the Lombards are unexceptional. Surveys show that Britons pay least for their basic package deal, but spend most on extras.

Sue said: 'I spent £1,000 on clothes and other things in the four months before the holiday, but much of it would have been spent anyway. We have brought about £1,500 spending money, and may go home with £200.'

About £700 of the pre-trip spree goes on the children, whose clothes fill two of the three suitcases. Both have six swimming costumes, four new bought at around £10-£15, four pairs of shoes at £3 to £18 and many T shirts. Underwear alone cost £40.

They will each use a bottle of sun-tan lotion, and drink a bottle of mineral water a day. Apart from a lunchtime snack, that is about it for extra spending.

A pair of sandals for John cost £60, and Sue has her evening dresses, but they spend only £50 on alcohol, probably 75 per cent less than the average youth 30 miles away in Magaluf.

There are a couple of 'extras' — car hire to visit John's brother on the other side of the island cost £18 a day, but cheaper than an around-the-island excursion selling for £80. The only one set-piece entertainment was a Pirates show which cost the four around £60.

The most expensive single items were gifts for their 'tribe', like a set of plates and salad bowl and locally made baby clothes together costing nearly £200. And there are gifts for themselves, like nougat or a bottle of 103 Black Label brandy or Tia Maria at £7 each.

Down in the market, negotiating a soft-leather handbag for £20, is where the Lombards notice the falling pound. In 1988, the exchange rate was 220 pesetas. Now it is 180. But the Lombards don't seem to mind.

Sue said: 'We have never found anywhere in England which could offer as much. I feel sorry for Scarborough — how can it compete?'

Figure 5.2 Comparing a family holiday in Scarborough with one in Majorca
(*Source: Daily Telegraph*, 24 June 1991) © The Telegraph plc, London, 1991

?

2 Write a newspaper article of not more than 200 words on the tourism revolution indicated by the graphs of Figure 5.1. (Guidelines: (i) Choose a 'punchy', eye-catching headline; (ii) write in a journalistic style; (iii) design and lay out your article by use of a software package if one is available.)

3 The family stories in Figure 5.2 illustrate the revolution in the 1990s.
a List three reasons (i) for choosing and (ii) for *not* choosing Scarborough for a holiday.
b Repeat the exercise for Majorca.
c Do the two stories remain accurate in the year 2000? If not, what are likely to be the differences?

4a As one of the Kenyon family, write to the Lombards, trying to persuade them to go to Scarborough.
b As one of the Lombard family, write to the Kenyons, explaining why you prefer Majorca.

spent in the UK. This chapter examines this revolution by focusing on three central questions:

• In what ways have our holidays changed?
• What factors have influenced the changes?
• What effects have the changes had on the UK tourism industry?

Answers to these questions are further developed in Chapters 6 and 7, which focus on global tourism.

5.2 The tourism industry in the UK

Two initial understandings are important. First, you become a **tourist** if you stay away from your usual home for at least one night. (In official figures, one 'tourist or visitor night' equals one night spent by one person away from home.) Otherwise, you are an 'excursionist' or 'day tripper'. None the less, with the exception of the accommodation element, both categories use the same set of resources and **facilities**. Second, the resources and facilities are enjoyed by both domestic tourists and foreign visitors to the UK. So the decline in 'main holidays' taken within the UK shown by Figure 5.1 does not necessarily mean a decline in the tourism industry. For instance, we are taking more varied holidays in the UK, including more 'short breaks', while the volume of foreign visitors has continued to increase.

During the 1980s the tourism industry was creating an average of 20 000 new jobs a year, although many were part time or seasonal. In 1991 the English Tourist Board was claiming that tourism had become 'the UK's most important industry', earning more than food manufacture, motor vehicles or aerospace (Fig. 5.3). Despite the economic recession of the early 1990s, tourism continued to grow. In 1997 the industry generated £40 billion, approximately 4 per cent of GDP, and employed 1.6 million people, 6.2 per cent of the total workforce. Each year UK residents take 120 million domestic tourist trips, spending £15 billion (see Table 5.1 for a breakdown of this travel). Official forecasts are that this domestic tourism will continue to grow at 3 per cent a year during the 2000–5 period.

In addition, there is the £12 billion from the more than 20 million foreign visitors each year, 30 per cent of whom are business travellers (see Section

Spending and employment, 1997

a Total spend: £32 billion

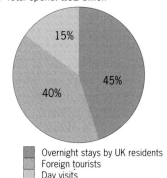

Overnight stays by UK residents
Foreign tourists
Day visits

b Total employed: 1.6 million

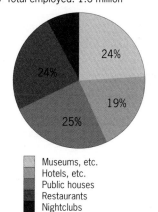

Museums, etc.
Hotels, etc.
Public houses
Restaurants
Nightclubs

Figure 5.3 The scale of UK tourism: spending and employment, 1997

Table 5.1 Regional distribution and economic impact of tourism, 1997

Region	Million visitor nights		Spending (£ million)	
	Domestic tourists	Overseas visitors	Domestic tourists	Overseas visitors
London	27.5	86.0	940	6600
West Country	76.0	14.0	2400	580
Heart of England	47.5	17.0	1400	720
East of England	50.0	16.0	1340	570
Southern	38.0	18.5	1110	820
South-East	33.0	19.0	810	800
North-West	30.0	10.0	1010	430
Yorkshire	30.0	9.0	1080	310
Northumbria	11.0	4.5	265	175
Cumbria	11.5	1.6	390	65
Scotland	45.0	21.0	1500	930
Wales	46.0	6.0	1200	220
N. Ireland	5.4	1.4	48	200

?

5 From Figure 5.3:
a Approximately how much did (i) UK residents and (ii) foreign tourists spend on staying holidays in 1997? As approximately 40 per cent of total spend goes on accommodation, what are the figures for this component?
b Why is it difficult to estimate from the available figures how many jobs are generated by *tourism*?

6 From Table 5.1:
a In what way is London different from all other regions in its tourism industry?
b Which region, outside London, is most dependent upon tourism?
c In which region is the balance between domestic and overseas tourism (i) most even and (ii) most different? Suggest reasons for this contrast.
d To what extent is it true to say that the scale and economic impact of tourism decrease with increasing distance from London?

7 For your own or a nearby town or city:
a Locate a TIC;
b Obtain a local tourist accommodation list (this may be available via a Web site);
c Analyse the list in of terms of *ownership* (e.g. national or international chains, family-run etc.), *size* (if number of rooms is given) and *location* (city centre, main routes inside urban limits, rural setting);
d Obtain four brochures of tourist attractions, and describe briefly the 'product' being offered.

5.6). In 1997, London alone attracted 7 million visitors from the rest of the UK, bringing in £2 billion, and over 10 million foreign visitors who spent at least £4 billion. Around 7 per cent of London's workforce is involved in the travel and tourism industry, although many jobs also serve the resident population (see Figure 5.3b). As capitals and historic cities, Edinburgh and Cardiff are also important tourist centres, but Belfast's potential has been restrained by 'the Troubles'.

The tourism industry which supplies this large and varied demand for touristic opportunities throughout the UK involves all three sectors – public, commercial and voluntary – often working in various forms of partnership.

The tourist boards

One of the primary roles of central government is to promote and facilitate tourism development, and it provides support of at least £50 million a year through national and regional agencies: the British Tourist Authority (BTA), and the English (ETB), Northern Ireland (NITB), Scottish (STB) and Welsh (WTB) Tourist Boards. Thus the BTA has an international role: 'In accordance with the Development of Tourism Act 1969, the BTA works to strengthen the performance of Britain's tourist industry in international markets by encouraging people to visit Britain and encouraging the improvements and provision of tourist amenities and facilities in Britain' (BTA, 1992).

The tourist boards support the tourism industry within their own parts of the UK through a regional structure (see Table 5.1). You will be most aware of their work through advertising, seeing promotional stands at exhibitions and shows, and in Tourist Information Centres (TICs). Most TICs are run by county and district councils with funding support from the tourist boards. They form a vital link between **supply** and **demand**, by holding accommodation lists, maps, brochures etc. Thus, if you run a guest house, falconry centre etc., you place your advertising material in the TIC for tourists to pick up.

This promotional and co-ordinating role is important because the tourism industry is very fragmented – at least 200 000 enterprises are involved. Thus, although **transnational** giants such as Forte, Granada and Grand Met dominate certain components (e.g. luxury hotels), a distinctive feature of the industry is the large number of small companies and family enterprises. Many such businesses have been given start-up support by government schemes that have seen the potential of the growing and diversifying tourism industry for economic development and rural diversification (e.g. bed and breakfast, craft industries, activity centres). Local councils, too, offer a range of amenities from deck-chair rental and putting greens to 'heritage experiences', and have active

Figure 5.4 A young family enjoying a UK beach holiday in the late 1990s

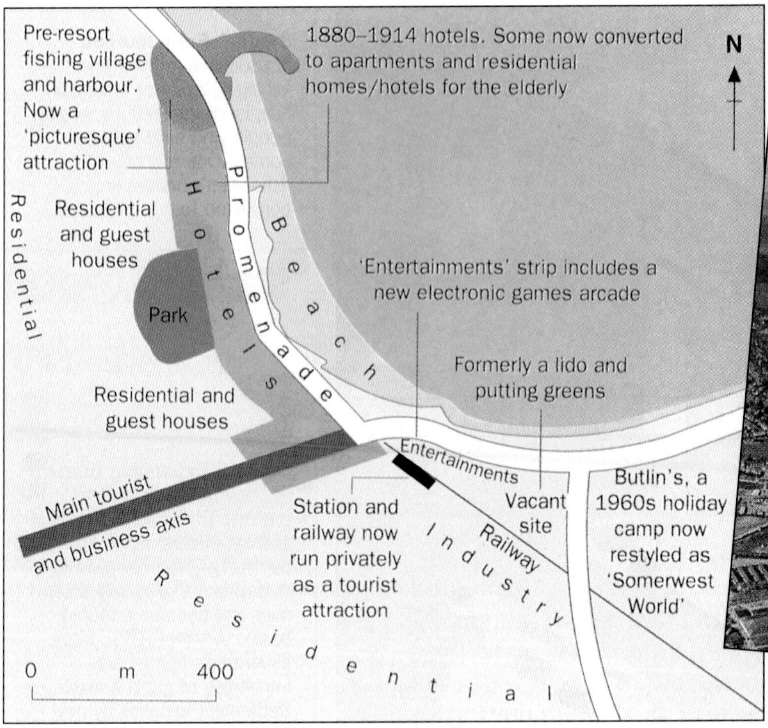

Pre-resort fishing village and harbour. Now a 'picturesque' attraction

1880–1914 hotels. Some now converted to apartments and residential homes/hotels for the elderly

N

Residential

Residential and guest houses

Park

Promenade

Hotels

Beach

'Entertainments' strip includes a new electronic games arcade

Residential and guest houses

Formerly a lido and putting greens

Main tourist and business axis

Entertainments

Station and railway now run privately as a tourist attraction

Railway

Industry

Vacant site

Butlin's, a 1960s holiday camp now restyled as 'Somerwest World'

Residential

0   m   400

Figure 5.6 A typical British seaside holiday resort – Minehead in 1989

Figure 5.5 Minehead – outline morphology of a 'bucket-and-spade resort'

tourism sections in their 'Leisure' departments. Government funding support was cut back during the 1990s, so such support and initiatives have increasingly been created through partnerships between the public and private sectors and by inputs from the National Lottery for specific projects.

5.3 The story of the British seaside resort

Despite all the changes in the ways we enjoy our holidays, two-thirds of all domestic holidays are still based at least in part beside the sea (Fig. 5.4). The traditional week or fortnight 'at the seaside' has produced a distinctive type of urban settlement – the **resort**. It is distinctive in its *location* – backing an accessible and attractive beach; in its main *function* – serving the accommodation, entertainment and activity needs of visitors; and in its *morphology* – a linear and crescent form giving maximum accessibility to the key attractive resources of beach and sea (Figs 5.5, 5.6).

Each resort has a unique location, morphology and degree of dependence upon its resort function (e.g. Great Yarmouth is a port and industrial town as well as a holiday resort). Many resorts, such as Blackpool, are towns created by tourism. Others have developed around existing settlements (e.g. Minehead was a fishing village). The model of Figure 5.7 illustrates the twin processes of *absorption* and *extension*. Some resorts show evidence of planning (e.g. older areas of Brighton), but most are towns which have grown piecemeal.

Within this diversity it is possible to identify certain characteristic land-use patterns in these traditional 'bucket-and-spade' seaside resorts which can be represented as a general model (Fig. 5.8a). The land-use pattern illustrated in the model can be explained in terms of the *bid-rent curve*: land values and hence rental values decline as one moves away from the location most accessible to the most attractive resources. Urban geographers call this location the 'peak land value intersection' (see Fig. 5.8a). In a seaside resort, land values are highest along the beach/sea frontage, with a peak where this frontage meets the main commercial area. Only those land uses and businesses which can afford the high land values and rentals will locate there.

?

8 Obtain a map of your area (e.g. an OS map, or one from a road atlas). On a tracing paper overlay, mark the places that you think are or could be tourist attractions. Classify them by type (e.g. historical site). Comment on your map.

9a Study the photograph of Minehead in Figure 5.6 and identify as many features on it as you can from the morphology map in Figure 5.5.
b How far does Minehead follow the model of a 'traditional seaside resort', shown in Figure 5.8a?

10 Outline briefly *three* factors which influenced the location and growth of traditional 'bucket-and-spade' resorts.

sprawls such as Peacehaven on the Sussex coast. Changing demand and, since the 1940s, planning restrictions have limited developments largely to specialist projects such as holiday camps, marinas and large caravan parks.

In many ways the period 1945–65 was the high point of 'the great British holiday'. Post-war enthusiasm, increasing prosperity, more holidays-with-pay entitlements, efficient and cheap rail and coach systems, a broader choice (from élite hotels, through boarding houses to the popular holiday camp packages of Butlin's and Pontin's) and improved marketing techniques all contributed to this boom. During the early 1960s, 80 per cent of all main holidays in the UK were seaside-based.

Post-1965 struggles

By the mid-1960s economic, social and technological changes were threatening the traditional resorts. Key factors included:

- Rapid expansion of car ownership;
- Industrial prosperity and longer holidays with pay;
- Introduction of jet passenger aircraft;
- Marketing of affordable foreign mass package holidays with a fresh image;
- Changing expectations and demands by holidaymakers;
- Many facilities and amenities in British resorts were becoming out of date.

In marketing terms, competition from an increasing range of new, fashionable products was making the existing British seaside product less attractive. The graphs of Fig 5.1 summarise the outcome. None the less, domestic tourism remains very important, but there have been fundamental changes in the character of these holidays (Fig. 5.11). Traditional resorts have been severely hit by these changes. Three examples illustrate the impacts:

Transport: The layout and morphology of the UK's seaside resorts (Fig. 5.8a) predate the dominance of the private motor vehicle. Road systems and parking capacity are inadequate (Fig. 5.10). For many resorts, day trippers are increasingly important (e.g. Blackpool has 11 million people living within 80km). They arrive by car or coach and want easy access to the beach and entertainment amenities. This has caused pressures for infrastructural adjustments (Fig. 5.8b). For many staying visitors the resort is a base from which to take car-based trips.

Figure 5.10 Street parking in Southport, Lancashire, causes considerable congestion in the peak holiday season

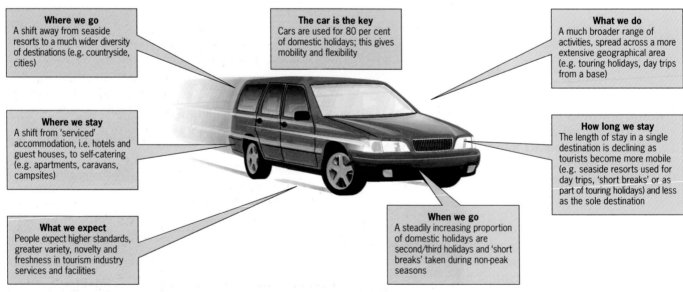

Where we go
A shift away from seaside resorts to a much wider diversity of destinations (e.g. countryside, cities)

The car is the key
Cars are used for 80 per cent of domestic holidays; this gives mobility and flexibility

What we do
A much broader range of activities, spread across a more extensive geographical area (e.g. touring holidays, day trips from a base)

Where we stay
A shift from 'serviced' accommodation, i.e. hotels and guest houses, to self-catering (e.g. apartments, caravans, campsites)

How long we stay
The length of stay in a single destination is declining as tourists become more mobile (e.g. seaside resorts used for day trips, 'short breaks' or as part of touring holidays) and less as the sole destination

What we expect
People expect higher standards, greater variety, novelty and freshness in tourism industry services and facilities

When we go
A steadily increasing proportion of domestic holidays are second/third holidays and 'short breaks' taken during non-peak seasons

Figure 5.11 Changes in UK holidays since 1965

Figure 5.12 Caravan holidays are becoming increasingly popular – they are inexpensive, they allow families to plan their own day, and they give access to beaches and countryside – but they take business away from local hotels and guest houses (though they do use local shops, restaurants, etc.) This photograph shows a static park and, in the background, a touring park near Barmouth, Wales

Accommodation: There has been a major shift away from 'serviced' accommodation ('serviced' = hotels, guest houses etc. where staff provide services including food) to self-catering, including the explosion in the use of touring and static caravans. Many apartments, campsites and caravan parks are attached to resorts and visitors may use the resort facilities and amenities, but do not fill the guest houses and hotels. In 1965, only 18 per cent of domestic holidays used self-catering accommodation. By 1995 this figure was 66 per cent. In 1997, 80 per cent of the accommodation capacity in Wales was self-catering (Fig. 5.12). Along the Skegness coast only 6 per cent of the capacity is in 'serviced' accommodation.

Expectations: A large proportion of hotels, guest houses, cafés, restaurants and entertainment occupy premises built before 1939. By the 1970s these buildings needed serious upgrading and redevelopment. For instance, visitors have increasingly demanded 'en suite' facilities, colour TV, central heating, car parking etc.; health and safety regulations have become more rigorous; tourists expect higher standards of entertainment such as indoor leisure complexes. Satisfying such expectations and requirements is expensive and has created severe financial problems for local authorities and businesses.

One major effect has been a polarisation process which divides Britain's seaside resorts into three broad classes:

1 *Large resorts:* Blackpool, Scarborough, Great Yarmouth, Brighton, Bournemouth, Torbay, Newquay. If the Isle of Wight is also regarded as a single resort destination, this class has at least 75 per cent of volume and revenue of seaside tourism. Blackpool alone attracts at least 4.5 million staying visitors who spend around £450 million. The resort has a capacity of 45 000 beds in over 2100 serviced units.

2 *Medium resorts:* Thirty-one resorts with more than 1000-room capacity (e.g. Weston-super-Mare, Bognor, Morecambe, Skegness, Weymouth). They have some capacity to invest, especially where the local authority is committed to enter partnerships with the private sector. Weston-super-Mare has approximately 300 000 staying visitors and 3 million day trippers a year, bringing £70 million to the local economy and supporting 4000 jobs. Between 1978 and 1987, the average length of stay fell from 7 nights to 4 nights.

3 *Small resorts:* Twenty-six resorts with less than 1000-room capacity and probably fewer than 40 000 staying guests a year (e.g. Cromer, Tenby, Bridlington). Resorts in this class have lost at least 50 per cent of their staying visitors since 1975.

The implications for the smaller resorts in particular are clear: they have a season of less than 20 weeks; have fewer than 2000 staying visitors a week; offer a narrow range of facilities and attractions; and are dominated by small businesses, often with poor entrepreneurial skills and hence limited potential for investment (e.g. a 1990 survey in Cornwall showed that only 10 per cent of small-business owners in the tourism sector had prior experience in tourism-related businesses). These factors make it difficult for such resorts to avoid a downward spiral (Fig. 5.13).

Figure 5.13 The vicious cycle for the small resort (*After:* Shaw and Williams, 1997)

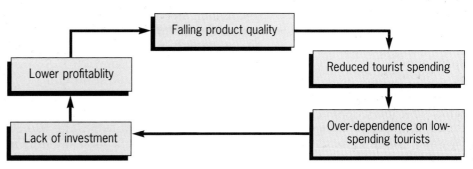

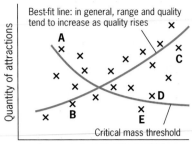

Figure 5.14 The critical mass concept of resorts

A High quantity, low range/quality – moderate attractive power, above the critical mass threshold but *struggling*

B Low quantity, low range/quality – weak attractive power, below the critical mass threshold – *declining*

C High quantity, high range/quality – strong attractive power, above critical mass threshold – *successful broad-based resort*

D Low quantity, high range/quality – strong attractive power, above the critical mass threshold – *fashionable, élite, specialist resort*

E Low quantity, high range/quality but too few to sustain critical mass as a specialist élite resort – *declining*

Figure 5.15 The opening of the refurbished Blackpool Tower (Source: Guardian, 15 May 1992)

11 Define what is meant by 'critical mass' and how this idea helps to explain the 'polarisation' process that has resulted in UK seaside resorts being grouped into three classes.

12 Suggest how you could measure the quantity and quality of tourist facilities, amenities and attractions in a resort in order to calculate its mass.

Critical mass

It is clear that too many resorts are chasing a declining market for domestic seaside tourism. An American, Donald Lundberg, has put forward the idea of **critical mass** (Fig. 5.14). He states that for a traditional resort to survive and thrive it must attain a certain mass. This 'mass' can be measured not only in the quantity of attractions but also by their range, character and quality (e.g. standard of hotels or restaurants, using measures such as 'star' or 'crown' ratings). Once this critical threshold of size, quality and range of product and image is achieved, then the resort's attractiveness in itself remains powerful enough for success and capable of attracting inward investment. Below the threshold, the magnet becomes steadily weaker. Resorts such as Blackpool seem to have achieved this critical mass (Fig. 5.15) while smaller and less high-profile resorts such as Minehead continue to struggle (Fig. 5.16).

Spruced up tower counters attraction of EuroDisney

ENGLAND'S riposte to EuroDisney officially opened yesterday with 10,000 perspiring school-children consumer-testing the £13 million refurbishment of Blackpool Tower.

The first part of a two-stage development ultimately costing £23 million, the investment is designed to secure the Lancashire town's position as Europe's most popular holiday destination.

Representatives of First Leisure Corporation, the owners of the 518ft 9in tower and a large slice of the rest of Blackpool's rumbustious attractions, refused to put the boot too heavily into their cross-channel rival.

'I am sure it will be extremely successful,' said Roy Page, divisional managing director, 'once it has overcome some inherent problems.'...

A PR company discreetly circulated statistics demonstrating that a family of four could have three holidays in Blackpool for the price of one Chez Mickey.

First Leisure's designers have been engaged in what Mr Page called a balancing act. Part of the £13 million has been spent in resurrecting the Victorian character of The Stick, as the hundred-year-old structure is known locally, part on luring punters less impressed by rococo carpets and aqua-marine tiling.

The principal white-knuckle rides will probably be the two high-speed lifts to the summit.

Last year a million people visited the tower, which also features a circus and a grade 1 listed ballroom. Mr Page hopes to boost that to 1.7 million.

5.4 Resorts respond to change

Resorts have fought hard to adapt to demand and so remain attractive and competitive. Policies vary and so when you visit a British seaside resort, look for the signs listed in Table 5.2. As you run through the items, two central understandings emerge: first, carrying out change is expensive; second, for any resort, selecting the most appropriate options is crucial. For example, one of the classic elements in a 'bucket-and-spade' resort is the pier (see Fig. 5.8a). Most piers were built before 1914 and today those that remain are either derelict or extremely costly to maintain: the dilemma for a resort is whether continued investment is worthwhile. These realities tend to reinforce the polarisation process and support the critical mass idea. Larger resorts can invest more and take up several options; smaller resorts attract less investment and have few options. In these smaller resorts, support from the local authorities in subsidising projects is essential (e.g. Swanage council has largely funded the renovation of the pier and seafront, Fig. 5.17). Even in the largest resorts, public-sector funding is vital. For example, in Blackpool, where the Pleasure Beach and Tower attract 7 million visitors a year, several million pounds of public-sector money has helped the refurbishment of the Winter Gardens as a conference centre and the local authority runs the Sandcastle all-weather centre which attracts over 1 million visitors a year.

Table 5.2 Resort responses to change

- Improve and upgrade 'serviced' accommodation.
- Rising costs and the popularity of self-catering accommodation have brought extensive conversion of hotels to apartments (e.g. Minehead).
- Extensive caravan parks and campsites on the peripheries, to cater for the boom in 'do-it-yourself' holidays and the spread in car ownership (e.g. Great Yarmouth).
- Indoor leisure and entertainment complexes to combat the erratic British weather (e.g. Rhyl).
- Replacement of outdoor swimming pools ('lidos') by elaborate leisure pool complexes (e.g. Blackpool).
- Upgrading and refurbishment of the physical environment, especially the promenade (e.g. Weston-super-Mare) and pier (e.g. Swanage) and including shopping parades, eating places, parks and beach management, in response to higher expectations by visitors.
- Infrastructure improvements: road improvement, traffic control and parking schemes which allow car-bound visitor access while protecting pedestrians. This car–pedestrian conflict is particularly intense along the promenade or esplanade. Where the railway has closed the vacated land may provide valuable access and parking space (e.g. Blackpool, with access road and large car park close to the Pleasure Beach). Elsewhere, the railway and station have become a tourist attraction (e.g. Minehead, Figure 5.16).
- Improved signposting and information.
- New facilities and amenities to modernise and diversify the product and to attract new markets (e.g. development of marinas, golf courses etc.).
- Conversion of buildings to alternative uses such as retirement and nursing homes, language schools etc. (e.g. Brighton). Seaside resorts are popular retirement locations and offer attractive environments and spacious buildings for educational institutions.
- Strategies for lengthening the tourist season, such as off-season festivals, special events, 'weekend breaks'. The classic is, of course, the Blackpool Illuminations which run through October.
- Diversification by development of business and conference centres which can attract in all seasons and which draw relatively high-spending visitors (e.g. Bournemouth).
- Marketing strategies to establish a 'brand image' (e.g. the promoting of a group of Devon resorts as 'The English Riviera'), and introduction of special-interest holidays.

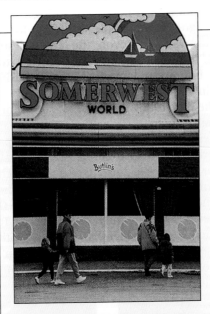

Reviving the seafront. The wide promenade remains with only minor changes, but the older seafront buildings are struggling to survive. The old building with the spire remains as an amusement arcade, but in Spring 1993 was adjoined by a row of empty commercial premises. Part of this pre-1914 strip has been redeveloped as the 'Carousel', a hall given over to electronic games, as an attempt to attract young people.

Butlin's: Built as a typical 'Hi-de-Hi' holiday camp in 1960, this has suffered from the changes in holiday fashions. Like other Butlin centres, it has been restyled and marketed as a 'World', in this case 'Somerwest World' with a western/cowboy theme. It is a self-contained resort accommodating 9000 holidaymekrs, many self-catering, plus day visitors, and employs 1300 people. It is of major economic significance to the Minehead district.

The original resort owed its growth to the coming of the railway in the 1880s. This provided access from Bristol and the industrial towns of the Midlands. The station stands at the heart of the resort, at the junction of the promenade and the main commercial street, a sign that when it was built the settlement was very small. The line was closed in the 1960s but has reopened as a private leisure venture, running excursions almost to Taunton. The old steam engines, rolling stock and station fittings are an important tourist attraction.

Figure 5.16 The changing face of Minehead

Planning the site

The site is to be visually contained with a buffer zone of mounds and trees 40–100 metres wide.

The site is likely to include existing woodland. This will be modified to enhance diversity of habitats and scenic attractiveness.

The accommodation is to be laid out to ensure privacy and contact with nature.

Service infrastructure (e.g. roads) will be carefully located in order to minimise impact.

The central all-weather complex is located and designed to reduce its intrusiveness and to be easily accessible.

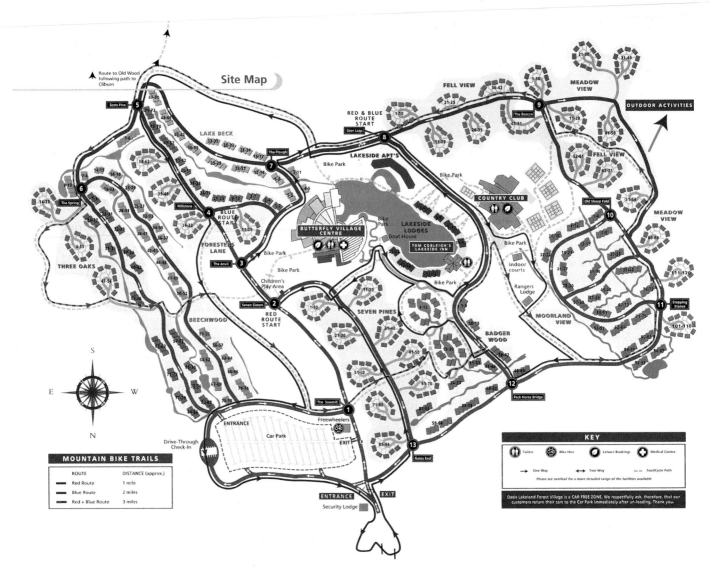

Figure 5.23 The plan of the Oasis Forest Village

Recreational pressures are to be managed through carefully planned footpaths and cycleways, and sports and leisure facilities will be in harmony with the natural habitats.

New water areas, wetlands and streams are to be created to further diversify habitats and add recreational facilities.

The development is designed to minimise energy consumption and pollution (e.g. visitors are encouraged to walk and cycle and not to use their cars during their stay).

There is a long-term forest management plan in co-operation with surrounding landowners, including the development of nature-oriented activity programmes run by the forest ranger service.

a What attracts people?
(% first choice among visitors)

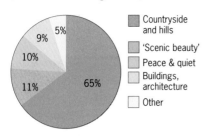

- Countryside and hills
- 'Scenic beauty'
- Peace & quiet
- Buildings, architecture
- Other

b Who comes? (% of total)

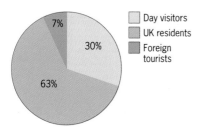

- Day visitors
- UK residents
- Foreign tourists

c Why do they come? (% of total)

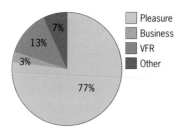

- Pleasure
- Business
- VFR
- Other

d Where do they stay? (% of total)

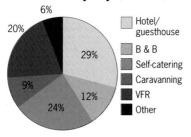

- Hotel/ guesthouse
- B & B
- Self-catering
- Caravanning
- VFR
- Other

Figure 5.24 Tourism in Herefordshire

Rural tourism and heritage tourism

Two factors that are helping to sustain the UK's domestic tourism market are (*a*) a reduced dependence upon the traditional seaside resort and (*b*) the introduction of new tourist products and experiences. As more people become more mobile, even though they may use a resort as a base for accommodation, they spend significant parts of their holiday touring surrounding settlements and countryside. In response, the private and public sectors are offering an ever-widening range of opportunities which in turn encourages visitors to explore their destination region further.

Rural tourism and **heritage tourism** are two good examples of this expansion of demand and supply (the Center Parcs and Oasis Holiday Villages use countryside images strongly in their advertising). They are closely related, and a set of principles or guidelines have been suggested for their successful development (Fig. 5.25). At least 50 per cent of all domestic holidays now make use of countryside and heritage resources and attractions, and all counties have a tourism strategy within their Structure Plan. For example, Herefordshire has had its Rural Tourism Strategy since 1993, which involves a partnership between the Heart of England Tourist Board (central government), the County Council (local government), the Association for the Promotion of Herefordshire (private-sector businesses) and organisations such as the National Trust (voluntary sector). Such projects are based upon identifying and making effective use of attractive resources (Figs 5.26, 5.27).

Principles of rural tourism

a The promotion of tourist enjoyment of the countryside should be primarily aimed at those activities which draw on the character of the countryside itself, its beauty, culture, history and wildlife.

b Tourism development in the countryside should assist conservation and recreation, by bringing new uses to historic buildings, supplementing the income of farmers and aiding the reclamation of derelict land.

c The planning, design, siting and management of new tourist developments should be in keeping with the landscape and, wherever possible, seek to enhance it.

d Investment in tourism should support the rural economy while encouraging a wider geographical and temporal spread so as to avoid problems of congestion and damage through overuse.

e Those who benefit from rural tourism should contribute to the conservation and enhancement of the countryside.

f The tourist industry itself should seek to develop the public's understanding and concern for the countryside and of environmental issues generally.

Figure 5.25 Principles of rural tourism (*Source:* Ryan, 1991)

Northern Ireland

'Different places, different perceptions: in Britain, the whole of Northern Ireland is seen as dangerous; on the north coast, the city of Belfast is regarded with alarm; in Belfast centre, it is West Belfast the citizens regard as a virtual no-go area' (Fred Mawer, *The Independent*, 12 June 1993).

Outsiders' perceptions of a place strongly affect its potential for attracting tourists. The low point for tourism was in the early 1970s, when 'the Troubles' began. Since then, the number of people visiting the province has been on the increase, slowly but surely. In the early 1990s, Northern Ireland received about 250 000 visitors a year.

Figure 5.26 The rural beauty of Northern Ireland: the High Mournes, Co. Down

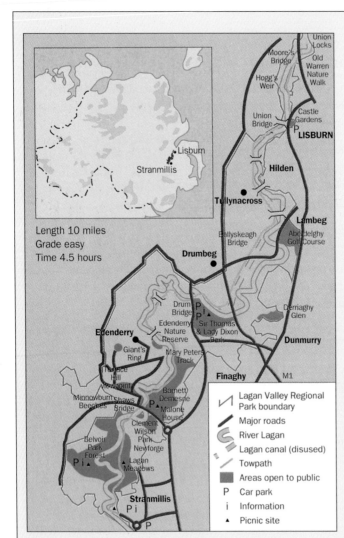

Length 10 miles
Grade easy
Time 4.5 hours

Lagan Valley Regional Park boundary
Major roads
River Lagan
Lagan canal (disused)
Towpath
Areas open to public
P Car park
i Information
▲ Picnic site

Lagan Valley Regional Park Towpath – Lisburn to Belfast

In Lisburn, join the towpath at Moore's Bridge. On the opposite side of the River Lagan you can see a site of industrial archaeological importance, known as Union Locks. This impressive feature consisted of four locks that lifted the barges a height of over 26 feet within a distance of less than 100 years. During the canal era this area included the canal manager's residence, a lock-keeper's house, repair workshops and stables.

From here you head towards the centre of Lisburn, passing under Moore's Bridge built in 1825 and on to Hogg's Lock. Here you will find mallard, little grebes and swans dabbling for food.

Turn right and cross Union Bridge, Castle Gardens, high up on your left, is all that remains of what was known as Lisburn Castle, destroyed in the great fire that ravaged the town in 1707. Keep a sharp eye out for the shy and elusive otters that frequent the Hilden area. This stretch includes the remains of Hilden Lock and the large premises of Barbour-Campbell Threads Limited.

On then towards Lambeg where it is said that the Northern Ireland linen industry was born, and certainly as early as 1626 a bleach green was already in existence. Even by the time the Huguenots arrived in 1685 the industry was firmly established, although these settlers did bring new methods and ideas the river Lagan and Canal played an important part in the development of the linen industry throughout the Lagan valley area, with nearly all of the merchants operating a private quay.

As you head towards Ballyskeagh, Lambeg Village and church sit on your left. Further along as you round a corner you will find the red sandstone arches of Ballyskeagh High Bridge. It is rumoured that the last man to hang, for the offence of stealing sheep, did so from this bridge.

Cross the river via a small footbridge. Sir Thomas and Lady Dixon Park on your left and St Patrick's Church, set back on your right, are both well worth a visit. In addition, from the towpath, you can see the restored lock-keeper's house at Drum Bridge.

Our journey towards Shaw's Bridge passes through one of the most scenic areas of the Park. Mature trees and woodland, together with a variety of wild flowers, provide an array of colour during the changing seasons. Soon you reach Eel Weir Picnic Site, whilst the small secluded village of Edenderry and former mill, that grew out of the linen industry, are visible on your right. Access to the Village, Edenderry Nature Reserve, Minnowburn Beeches, Terrace Hill viewpoint and the Giant's Ring is provided via the Gilchrist Bridge. Malone House, built in the early 19the century, is visible on the horizon.

Turn right and cross Shaw's Bridge, the famous old bridge that was built in 1709. Beyond this point, on the opposite side of the river, lies Clement Wilson Park. The path then follows a dry section of the old canal to as far as No. 3 lock and lock-house. Pedestrian access to Belvoir Park Forest is provided on your right. Shortly you will reach the Red bridge that enables the towpath to cross the river. The trees overhanging the river on your right are part of Belvoir Park Forest. Further along on your left you will find a number of access points to Lagan meadows. Your journey finishes at Stranmillis car park. You are now less than 2 miles from the commercial heart of the city of Belfast.

Figure 5.27 Part of a brochure advertising walking and cycling routes in 'The Linen Homelands' of Northern Ireland

But compared with Scotland, which received over 10 million tourists, the numbers are still very low.

How can it attract more tourists? The reputation that Northern Ireland has for bad weather, along with the ever-present threat of terrorist activity, undoubtedly continue to depress visitor numbers. One of the few attractions that remains comparatively busy throughout the year is the Giant's Causeway on the north coast. Not surprisingly, it is the isolated rural beauty of the countryside that the tourist brochures emphasise – the quiet, empty beaches and the remote landscapes (Fig. 5.26); they make no mention of 'the Troubles', but promote the image of peaceful, rural heritage, craft industries and friendly people (Fig. 5.27). The peace accord of November 1999 may well herald the rejuvenation of Ulster's tourism industry.

?

16 Jot down five words that describe the image you have of Northern Ireland. Compare your list with those of other students. Divide the list into words that are 'negative', 'neutral' and 'positive'. Comment on the image or images that come out of your list.

17 Use Figure 5.26 to write a paragraph for a tourist brochure to attract visitors to the area.

18 The material in Figure 5.27 is part of the 'Walking and Cycling Guide' to 'The Linen Homelands' in Northern Ireland. The brochure is one of a series produced by three local councils – Banbridge, Craigavon and Lisburn – with funding from the EU Marketing Development Support Scheme. Make a list of the attractive resources and tourist opportunities being promoted. Identify separately:
a natural heritage attractions;
b human heritage attractions.

?

19 Use the data of Figure 5.28 to describe the supply of activity holidays – e.g. activity types; resources and facilities needed; who supplies them.

20 For your local region, choose *either* two contrasting heritage attractions *or* two activity centres and discuss:
a who has developed the attraction;
b what they are offering;
c what resources they are using;
d what type of visitors are likely to be attracted.

The growth and character of this form of tourism can be illustrated by an analysis of *holiday cottage rentals* and *activity holidays*. In 1996, 4.5 million holidays were taken in rented holiday cottages in the UK, about 7 per cent of all holidays, and with spending of over £1.1 billion. There were some 150 rental agencies, including tourism giants such as Thomson which had bought up three smaller agencies. It is estimated that approximately 60 000 cottages are available for holiday rental, varying widely in size and standard: 40 per cent at the seaside, 44 per cent in the countryside and 16 per cent in towns. Devon and Cornwall have 35 per cent of the total. A key problem is seasonality. Only between May and September are more than 60 per cent of the properties filled.

Activity holidays are defined as 'holidays where an activity or special interest forms the main purpose'. In 1996 there were 13 million activity holidays, about 20 per cent of all holiday trips, with spending of £2 billion. A broad range of activities are included that vary according to what the destination environments offer (Fig. 5.28). Because of the environmental resources they use, many activity holidays are based in areas of high conservation value (e.g. National Parks, lakes, mountains and woodlands), and in some locations there is concern over environmental impacts (e.g. the level of pony trekking and watersports in the Llangorse area of the Brecon Beacons National Park).

Heritage tourism includes a broad spectrum of experiences and hence

a What do we do in Scotland? Most popular activities (% of participants)

Hiking/rambling	48
Watersports	27
Golf	18
Climbing/caving	13
Fishing	10
Heritage/history	9
Mountain biking	8

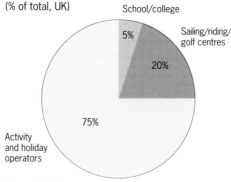

b Who provides?
(% of total, UK)

School/college 5%
Sailing/riding/golf centres 20%
Activity and holiday operators 75%

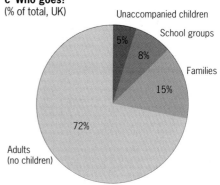

c Who goes?
(% of total, UK)

Unaccompanied children 5%
School groups 8%
Families 15%
Adults (no children) 72%

Figure 5.28 Characteristics of activity holidays, 1996

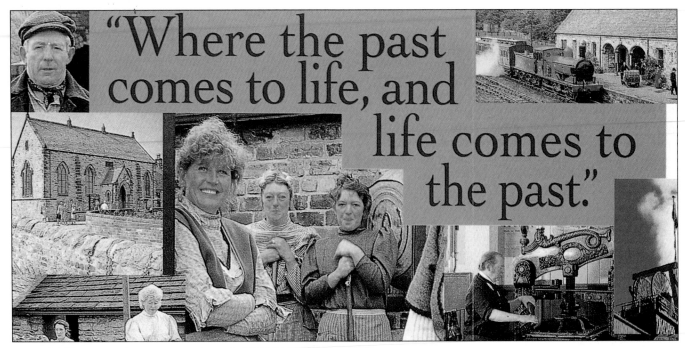

Figure 5.29 Heritage tourism: an advert for the Beamish Heritage Museum

destinations. This form of tourism is all about 'theming'. Thus we have the very high-quality Ironbridge (Shropshire) and Beamish (Northumbria) Museums with their industrial heritage themes (Fig. 5.29); there is a long-running controversy about how Stonehenge will be 'themed' and presented to represent our distant past; historic cities such as Edinburgh and York are promoted with a particular historical identity.

5.6 The theme-park boom

'Themed' attractions are not a new phenomenon (e.g. zoos and safari parks use the 'wildlife' theme). However, fashions change, people show greater concern about the enclosure of wild creatures, and the costs of meeting expectations rise. As a result, Windsor Safari Park, for example, closed in the 1990s. In contrast, the wave of modern **theme-park** developments has been one of the success stories of the past 20 years (e.g. the Windsor Safari Park site is now the home of Legoland, which attracts 1.5 million visitors a year).

What is a theme park?
'To qualify for theme-park status ... a park must be built around one or more fantasy or historical themes, charge some form of all-inclusive entry fee, and offer a broad-enough range of facilities and attractions to occupy a family for the whole day (rides, playgrounds, scenic displays, some indoor entertainment, shopping and catering)' (Tucker, 1991). By this definition, although the UK has literally thousands of 'themed' attractions, at most a dozen qualify for full theme-park status (Table 5.4). By definition, theme parks are expensive to develop and maintain, and in consequence are mostly owned by large corporations (e.g. the Tussaud's group owns Alton Towers).

Of course, the majority of visitors to theme parks are excursionists rather than tourists, but market researchers believe that the tourist component is essential for the long-term success, i.e. economic profitability, of the larger parks. Although the first theme park in the UK, Thorpe Park, did not open until 1969, by 1997 total attendance was approaching 10 million, with average admission charges exceeding £12.

Table 5.4 Major theme parks in the UK, 1997 (million visitors)

Alton Towers	2.75
Chessington World of Adventures	1.70
Legoland	1.42
Frontierland, Morecambe	1.30
Flamingo Land Theme Park, Kirby Misperton	1.16
Thorpe Park	1.14
Drayton Manor	0.94

Figure 5.30 The Thunder Looper, Alton Towers: opened in 1990, this 'death-defying' ride reaches 97km/h in 2.8 seconds, loops a 23m looper twice and suspends passengers at 37m

Figure 5.31 Disneyland Paris Resort: the scale of large theme parks

21 Project: Select one theme park, collect information (check Web sites) and analyse the park under these headings: *a* theme and attractions; *b* location and setting; *c* ownership; *d* cost; *e* market segment; *f* local economic and environmental impacts.

More quality, more excitement, more expense

During the 1990s, growth rates slowed down. To remain competitive and retain market share, owners have constantly to add more quality, more excitement and more originality: bigger and more terrifying 'white-knuckle' rides mean huge investments (Fig. 5.30). The upgrading of Chessington cost Tussaud's £10 million in 1987; in the mid-1990s, it was planning to invest £50 million in a scheme for Woburn Abbey. The transnational MCA Corporation fought environmentalist opposition for much of the 1990s to obtain planning permission for a £2.6 billion 'film studios' project on Rainham Marshes in Essex, but recent uncertainties about future growth have deferred the project. It is not surprising, therefore, that this is one area of tourism that is controlled by a small number of huge companies and where a location with access to large markets is vital.

Disneyland Paris ® Resort

The 'benchmark' for all UK theme-park developers is, of course, the Disneyland Paris Resort, opened in 1992 (Fig. 5.31). The Walt Disney Corporation evaluated sites in several countries (including the UK) before choosing France. As their intended catchment area is the whole of western Europe, they made accessibility in relation to transport networks and to centres of population very important in their locational decision.

To attract the millions of visitors necessary to be profitable, these mega-developments must have associated hotels, restaurants etc. which make them fully **integrated resorts**. The sheer scale of a project such as the Disneyland Paris Resort brings sub-regional economic benefits, but inevitable environmental impacts, and the Disney Corporation has made great efforts at landscaping and environmental enhancement in the surrounding districts. For instance, the traffic generated by the combination of more than 10 000 employees, service vehicles and the cars and coaches of the visitors, puts enormous strain upon the existing transport infrastructure. It also affects the quality of life of communities over a wide area. In recognition of this, to subdue local opposition and to protect the company 'image', the Walt Disney Corporation has jointly funded, with the French authorities, large-scale improvements to the regional road and rail networks. Despite all the investment, the careful planning and the Disney brand image, the resort lost money for the first few years. One response was to change the original name of 'Euro Disney' to 'Disneyland Paris' to suggest the combined attraction of 'Paris' and 'Disney'. One explanation for the early failure to reach target numbers of visitors was the high cost of visits, and especially of the accommodation in the Disney-owned hotels. Since 1996, prices have been cut, and visitor numbers have climbed: lower profits per visitor, but more visitors! In 1999, the Disney Corporation revealed plans to develop a second huge park nearby, based on a 'film studios' theme.

The statistics lead some market researchers to calculate that a small and crowded country such as the UK, with high land prices and restrictive planning policies, can support only one Disney-scale theme-park project. Remember, too, that developers require accessible locations (e.g. 20 million people live within a 2-hour drive of Alton Towers) and large sites of at least 300 hectares. One answer is to develop a theme park within an existing facility (e.g. Woburn or Beaulieu), or to develop derelict land (e.g. Thorpe Park was built on disused sand and gravel workings).

The crucial threshold that changes an attraction from a large theme park mainly for excursionists to an integrated resort that draws large numbers of tourists is the addition of accommodation and other entertainment facilities. In the UK, Alton Towers has been the first theme park to cross this threshold. This puts it ahead of its competitors and perhaps on the path to become the first fully integrated resort.

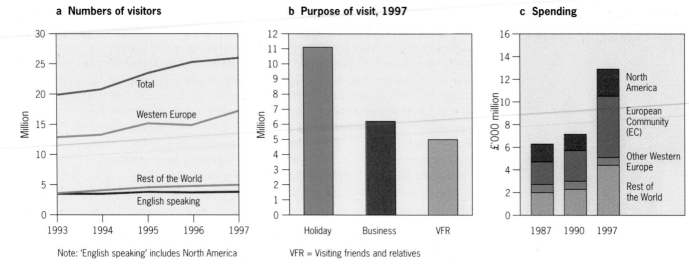

Note: 'English speaking' includes North America

VFR = Visiting friends and relatives

Figure 5.32 Foreign tourists in the UK
(*Source:* BTA, 1998)

Table 5.5 Origins of foreign tourists: the top four, 1997

France	3.8m
USA	3.1m
Germany	3.1m
Irish Republic	2.1m

5.7 Foreign tourists in the UK

In 1997 approximately 25.3 million foreign visitors arrived in the UK, and spent almost £12.4 billion. This compares with 15 million and £6.2 billion in 1987. These figures and the graphs of Figure 5.32 show very clearly the scale and importance of foreign visitors. Approximately 70 per cent come from continental Europe, reflecting proximity, accessibility and economic connections as influential factors (Table 5.5). The overall trend is for continued growth, with forecasts of 31 million arrivals by 2003. However, dips in the graphs illustrate how political and economic factors can affect tourist flows. For instance, the fall-off of arrivals in 1986 was caused mainly by the drop in numbers of Americans travelling abroad as a result of terrorist attacks upon US airlines and citizens. The dip in the early 1990s was caused by an economic recession, with cut-backs in both holiday and business travel. Reduced numbers result in reduced spending, with a knock-on effect on employment (e.g. numbers of jobs in the leisure industry fell in 1992 and 1993 for the first time in a decade).

Once in the UK, foreign visitors differ markedly from domestic tourists in where they go, what they do and what they spend. In 1997 they stayed an average of nine days, spending an average of £57 per day. The purpose of the visit affects both length of stay and spending: business travellers stay an average of six days and spend most per day; holiday tourists stay ten days on average; VFR(visiting family and relations) tourists stay fifteen days on average but spend least per day.

Where do they go?

Approximately 40 per cent of all bed-nights are spent in London, where most trips begin and end. A further 50 per cent are spent in the rest of England, leaving 10 per cent spread through Northern Ireland, Scotland and Wales. At least 80 per cent of foreign visitors arrive through the airports, ferry terminals and the Channel Tunnel in south-east England. Once the holiday tourists leave London they tend to follow touring itineraries. These may be organised coach tours or independent trips by rental car or public transport. Such tourists use mainly urban accommodation but the majority are unlikely to visit or stay in seaside resorts. In particular, they focus heavily upon a small number of internationally known honeypots: Stratford-upon-Avon, Oxford, Windsor, York, Edinburgh, the English Lake District, the Scottish Highlands.

Despite the economic benefits, the resulting impacts of this visitor concentration cause tensions and environmental problems in these honeypot destinations (Fig. 5.33). In order to combat these problems, tourist boards are

Figure 5.33 Newspaper report on tourism pressures on Stratford (*Source: Guardian*, 2 August 1990)

Overwhelming enthusiasm as four-hour culture hunters land in Bard's honeypot

The super-comfort land-liner with dark glass windows slides gently to a halt, touching down like an alien spaceship. Inside, its cargo yawn as they struggle off Pringle cashmere sweaters and put on 'Shakespeare Lovers' baseball caps.

Bailing out of their air conditioning, they arrive into the warmth of morning in Stratford-Upon-Avon, and minutes later are heading in an orderly crocodile for breakfast at McDonald's.

Within the hour, the citizens of Osaka shuffle reverentially around the half-timbered house in Henley Street where, 426 years ago, the world's most famous dramatist and most consistent tourist attraction was born.

Four hours later, these Shakespeare enthusiasts are back on the road, this time their objective being to go to 'Edinburgh, Scotland'.

Stratford tourism is a bit like that: a short, concerted invasion; then an orderly retreat,

But business people of Stratford do not complain, when the tourist trade accounts for around a quarter of their local economy. Stratford's experts would like more encouragement given to their tourists, rather than them being sent to alternative attractions.

The tourist trade recognises places like Stratford as 'honeypot' locations.

Roger Thompson, managing director of a town-tour company, Guide Friday, is concerned about the ideas being discussed, including the fear that Stratford, like so many other 'honeypots', is in danger of being environmentally overwhelmed by tourist hordes.

Mr Thompson, who is chairman of the Shakespeare Country Association of Tourist Attractions, is anxious that the trade is not seen as anti-green. But in a letter to Alan Howarth, Stratford's MP, he warned of the possible damage that dispersing tourism away from Stratford and similar attractions could cause.

August in Stratford's busiest month, when the pressure of visitors, that each year adds up to $2\frac{1}{2}$ million tourists, is at its peak.

?

22 For your own city, or one with which you are familiar:

a Identify three features attractive to foreign visitors.

b Collect and analyse tourist policy and information material, and suggest what 'image' the city is promoting – i.e. 'place marketing' (check Web sites).

encouraging tour operators and independent tourists to adopt more diversified itineraries and to include less-well-known attractions, such as the rural beauty and heritage of Northern Ireland, urban and industrial heritage attractions such as Wigan Pier and the Beamish Museum (Fig. 5.29) and 'Big Pit' in South Wales. Such tourism promotion is often an element in economic regeneration policies for declining or less-prosperous regions. Many cities have 'place marketing' policies that aim to promote their image as attractive, distinctive business and pleasure destinations for both domestic and foreign tourists.

Summary

- Patterns of British tourism have changed greatly as domestic holidaymaking has declined and foreign holidays have increased.

- Tourism is the UK's most important industry, involving the commercial, voluntary and public sectors.

- Resorts, located mainly along the coast, are a distinctive category of urban settlement whose main function is the provision of tourist services and facilities.

- Seaside resorts have been forced to adapt and change as tourist demands have changed. Government policies and tourist boards are encouraging and assisting this adjustment.

- Survival of traditional resorts depends upon the achievement of a 'critical mass' in terms of quantity and quality of attractiveness.

- The tourism product in the UK is becoming increasingly diversified and more widely dispersed as a growing range of attractions competes for the market.

- Themed attractions are a major growth area, but full-scale theme parks require massive investments and have severe environmental impacts.

- Foreign visitors and business travellers make up an important component of UK tourism and have patterns of behaviour distinct from domestic tourists.

6 The global explosion of tourism

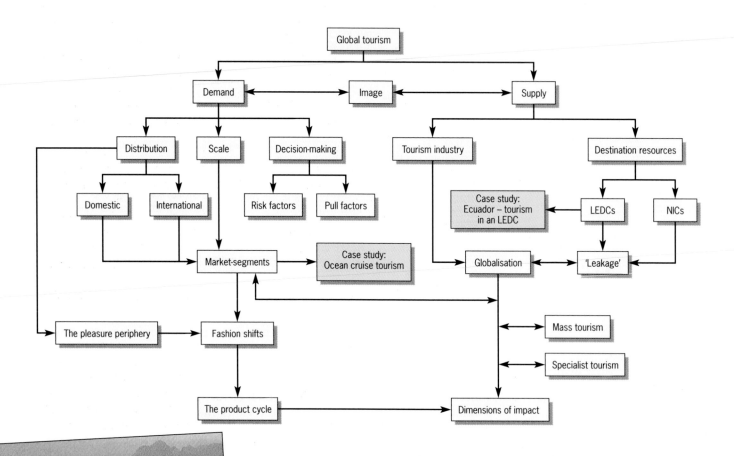

6.1 Introduction

Over the past 30 years tourism has expanded rapidly to become a global phenomenon, and a major influence upon the lives of people worldwide. Yet it is in danger of falling victim to its own success, and today stands at a critical stage in its evolution: can it continue to improve the quality of life for increasing millions of people (Fig. 6.1), or must it become yet another global environmental problem? This chapter and Chapter 7 will help you to explore this broad issue by considering a series of more specific questions:

1 Why do people travel?

2 How, where and why is tourism growing and changing?

3 How are **demand** and **supply** organised through the tourism industry?

4 Who controls resources and makes decisions about tourism opportunities?

5 What are the positive and negative impacts of tourism, and for whom?

6 Can tourism be developed as a 'sustainable' rather than an 'exploitative' option?

At its most elemental: *is tourism a good thing – and if so, for whom?*

Dear Bob,
Here's a card to add to your tourism resources. Mass tourism is at its best here in Thailand. This village is near the River Kwai and we're going on up to more remote places near the Burmese border. Interesting comparing tourism in China (just opening up) to Thailand (well established). Hong Kong was fantastic.
Annette

PAR AVION
BY AIR MAIL

DR. R. PROSSER
C/O CLAREMONT HOUSE
ORLETOM
LUDLOW
SHROPSHIRE
ENGLAND

A caravan of raft houses gather in the front of Kanchanaburi's city on Khwae Yai River.

Figure 6.1 Greetings from a student

Figure 6.2 Holidays as relaxation and for getting a tan

Figure 6.3 Tourism as the new global religion – people of all faiths share a belief in the importance of travelling to see famous 'sights'. Tourists from India recording their visit to the Bangkok temples

6.2 Making travel decisions

This chapter is being written in a *gîte* (rented cottage) in Brittany, France. My family and I have come here for our summer holiday. We hope to enjoy our time together, but each has his or her own motives and expectations. My wife wants to relax, read novels under the trees and eat in local restaurants. Our daughter and her friend intend to get a tan on the beach, swim, attract the attention of young Frenchmen and get invited to discos. Our son would prefer to be on a Greyhound bus trek around the USA but cannot afford it, so he has rented a bike and has disappeared into the countryside to sketch. I want to improve my windsurfing, observe holidaymakers 'at play' as tourism is my research interest – and finish writing this chapter! So, each one of us has different hopes for the holiday (Fig. 6.2).

The above is just one of millions of holiday 'portraits' which could be 'painted' all over the world, as increasing numbers of people respond to the urge to travel. Indeed, it has been claimed that travel has become the new global religion (Fig. 6.3), with holidays as 'pilgrimages' to 'holy' places. Many holidays do improve our spiritual as well as physical well-being. There is no doubt, too, that for many people the planning, taking and reflecting on a holiday are important events. But *why* do we go – what are the motives and factors that influence our decisions? What are our expectations? Look again at the family 'portrait' – one family, one holiday, yet so many motivations and expectations! This is why understanding and forecasting demand is so complex.

Why go on holiday?

A holiday can be defined as a pleasure trip that involves staying away from your normal place of residence for at least one night. (Some official definitions suggest a minimum of four nights; day trippers are classified separately as *excursionists*.) So, there is always the underlying motive of 'change' or 'getting away'. This can be seen in terms of **push factors** (getting away *from*) and **pull factors** (getting away *to*). Beyond this, however, people go on holiday for many reasons, and each of us has different motives at different times (Fig. 6.4). This may explain the '*why*' of travel, but decisions are affected by other elements – *Where to? When? How much? How long? Who with?*

This diversity, when combined with the huge and growing volume of tourism, means that enormous demands are made on resources, natural and

'We always go there – it's just so comfortable and peaceful'

'I'm going to get a great tan'

'The kids will love the beach and the warm sea'

'It's cheap and easy to get to'

'We want to learn about new places and new people'

'We're going to visit relatives'

'I'm going to improve my skills at skiing' (sailing, climbing, etc.)

'I'm going on business but then will stay on and take a trip'

'It'll be a new challenge'

'We just need a change'

'I need some excitement in my life'

'I just need a rest'

'We won it in a competition'

'We'll be the first of our friends to go there'

'I want to go there before it gets spoilt'

'I want to meet some new people'

Figure 6.4 Why go on holiday?

Figure 6.8 Travel agencies in Guilin, a Chinese provincial city, 1997. The travel potential of China's 1 billion population is enormous

Table 6.3 Origin of tourists, 1995 – 12 popular tourist destinations and the main countries of origin of visitors (percentage of total arrivals) (*Source:* WTO, 1997)

Spain	%	Mauritius	%	Belize	%	Barbados	%
France	23	France	27	Guatemala	38	UK	29
Portugal	17	East Africa	24	USA	29	USA	26
Germany	16	Germany	11	Mexico	13	Canada	12
UK	15	South Africa	10	Europe (not UK)	8	Caribbean	12
Italy	5	UK	8	UK	3	Germany	7
Total arrivals 64.0 mill			440,000		400,000		430,000
Greece	**%**	**Iceland**	**%**	**Mexico**	**%**	**Bermuda**	**%**
Germany	23	Germany	19	USA	93	USA	82
UK	23	USA	14	South America	3	Canada	9
Italy	7	Denmark	12	Canada	1.5	UK	4
France	6	Sweden	11				
Netherlands	5	UK	10				
Total arrivals 9.5 mill			192,000		17.5 mill		420,000
Botswana	**%**	**Hong Kong**	**%**	**Cook Islands**	**%**	**Thailand**	**%**
South Africa	50	China	21	New Zealand	26	Malaysia	15
Zimbabwe	34	Taiwan	18	USA	14	Japan	11
UK	4	Japan	15	Australia	9	Singapore	6.2
Europe (not UK)	4	USA	8	Canada	7	South Korea	6.0
Zambia	3	UK	4			Germany	5.5
Total arrivals 930,000			9.7 mill		62,000		6.3 mill

6 Using the information in Table 6.3 (and an atlas), give examples that illustrate the following statements:
a Visitors arrive mostly from neighbouring countries;
b Some destinations are dominated by visitors from one other country;
c For some destinations, visitor origins vary widely;
d Visitor origins are influenced by cultural and economic linkages;
e Ease of access is an important factor influencing where visitors come from;
f Some destinations act as 'hubs' or 'stopovers' on long-haul journeys;
g Some destinations are connected strongly with tour operators in specific countries.

7 From the information and data in Section 6.3, compare and contrast the tourism patterns and trends of Spain and Botswana and suggest reasons for any similarities and contrasts you find.

The reasons behind the explosive growth rates shown by the figures for all regions of the world are based upon, first, more people in more countries having more time, more money, greater awareness and increased mobility, i.e. increased effective *demand*; second, the globalisation of economic activity facilitated by the revolution in communications and transport technology (Fig. 6.7); third, the expansion of the travel and tourism industry, i.e. increased *supply*.

All forecasts suggest that global tourism will continue to expand. In 1997, 612 million international visitors, up by 75 per cent since 1987, spent US$448 billion. The World Travel and Tourism Council (WTTC), the organisation which represents the industry, claims that tourism has become the world's largest industry, employing 80 million directly and another 150 million indirectly. It generates 11–12 per cent of global GDP, a total of US$4.4 trillion. Yet forecasts indicate that international tourists could reach 1 billion by the year 2010, and that by 2020 some 100 million Chinese may be travelling abroad each year (Fig. 6.8).

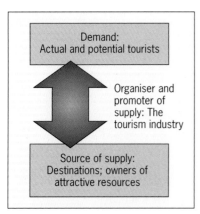

Figure 6.9 The tourism system

Figure 6.10 Making use of your 'gap' year. Mount Bromo, Indonesia

Figure 6.11 The tourism environment

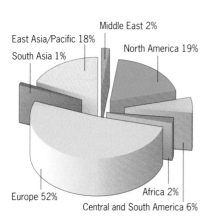

Figure 6.12 Regional market share of international tourism receipts, 1995 (*Source:* WTO, 1997)

6.4 Who decides what holidays are available? The supply of tourism

The model in Figure 6.9 presents tourism in its simplest form as a three-component system, the three components interacting to create a functioning whole. The crucial organisational role of the industry is to provide *access* and *accessibility* by bringing demand and supply together. The power of this industry in the decision-making process is enormous. It influences your experience as a traveller and the extent to which destinations are permitted to control and develop their own attractive resources. For instance, as a student you may think of yourself as an 'independent traveller' rather than a 'package tourist'. But to gain access to a Lapp community, an Indonesian volcano etc., you interact almost inevitably with the industry: information, transport, food, perhaps accommodation (Fig. 6.10). Equally, any potential destination wishing to market its attractions as a tourist product can do so only through the network of the industry: advertising, booking, transport, etc.

The all-embracing influence of the industry can be appreciated by closer analysis of the system (Fig. 6.11). A further key understanding emerges from a study of Figure 6.11: in reality, tourism involves a set of quite distinct industries – transport, marketing, construction, hospitality, entertainment and so on. It is a broad sector of economic activity, and it is for convenience only that we use the umbrella term 'tourism industry'.

Less economically developed countries (LEDCs)
Over 60 per cent of all international travel is still between countries of the developed North (more economically developed countries, or MEDCs), with over 70 per cent of all tourism spending occurring in Europe and North America (Fig. 6.12). However, the highest proportional growth rates are found in regions which contain a number of less economically developed countries, or LEDCs (see Table 6.2). Yet one of the key problems faced by many LEDCs has been that of connecting with the global network of the tourism industry. Governments seeking economic development have, understandably, realised the attractiveness of their resources for tourism – beaches, warm and sunny climates, forests, deserts, mountains, wildlife, 'exotic' cultures, antiquities and so on – and their potential for income, jobs and development. To organise and

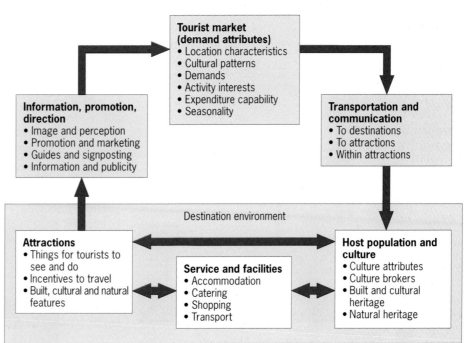

Ecuador – tourism in an LEDC

Data sheet

Tourism statistics
Population: 11.5 million (1996)
Area: 283 560 sq. km
Income from tourism: US$253 million
Tourism income as percentage of GDP: 1.6
Jobs in tourism: 50 000
Tourism jobs as percentage of total employment: 1.5
Importance: ranked fourth after oil, bananas and ships

Main tourist segments etc

a Colombians and Peruvians attracted by beach holidays and low prices;
b Affluent, well-educated North Americans and Europeans mainly attracted by Galapagos wildlife and Andean culture;
c Young 'backpackers', mostly from North America and Europe, who travel cheaply across all parts of the country.

Key findings from a 1997 survey

- A range of attractive resources, especially the Galapagos Islands World Heritage Site.
- Size and rate of growth is much less than in the main rivals, Peru and Costa Rica.
- Failure of government to give priority to tourism policy, hence difficulty of attracting internal and international investment.
- Lack of a tourism infrastructure capable of handling a large flow of tourists (e.g. airports, roads, railways).
- Lack of effective policy partnership between private and public sectors.
- Poor data availability makes forecasting and planning difficult.

Mode of arrival (%)

Air 63; Land 34; Sea 3

Purpose of visit (%)

Pleasure 75; VFR 15; Business 10

Environment and tourism

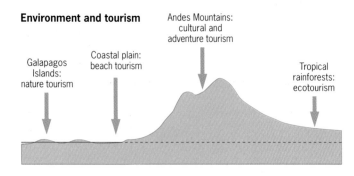

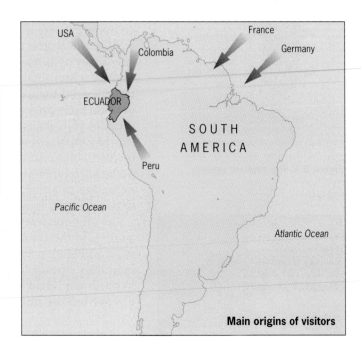

Main origins of visitors

Tourism growth, 1991–6

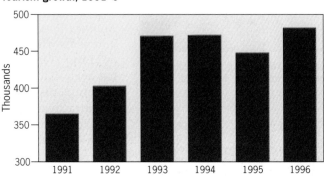

Hotels
Accommodation (no. of bedspaces)
Total: 85 000
First class: 33%
Medium grade: 30%
Simple: 37%

Employment
Total: 50 000
Hotels: 30%; Restaurants etc.: 52%
Travel agencies: 8%; Transport: 3%
Other: 7%

1991–6 growth: +40%

Figure 6.13 Expensive resort complex, British Virgin Islands, developed and run by a multinational company

Figure 6.14 The Tanjung Aru Hotel, Kota Kinabalu, Sabah, Malaysia. This luxurious resort hotel was originally a government project, but has been sold to a transnational company because of the costs involved (right)

market these resources and products, they have frequently been forced to rely on international structures already in existence. Such structures are mostly controlled by **transnational corporations** based in economically advanced countries of the developed North. For example, the eight largest hotel chains in the world are all US-based companies; virtually all major airlines are based in the USA and Europe. Indeed, one interpretation of the international tourism industry sees it as *'economic colonialism'*: the countries of the South have become politically independent, but remain economically dependent as their resources are still exploited by the economically dominant countries of the North (Fig.6.13).

Newly industrialising countries

The group of countries known as NICs (**newly industrialising countries**) have managed to weaken their dependency ties to MEDCs and transnational corporations. They have been increasingly able to raise money internally, to invest it, and organise and run their own industries. This progress has been typified by countries in South-East Asia such as Malaysia, Singapore and Thailand where, between 1985 and 1995, economic growth rates were 6–9 per cent a year. They have been able to raise large sums of investment capital, and tourism development has been a significant part of this investment and of government policy (e.g. between 1991 and 1996 the volume of tourist accommodation in South-East Asia increased by 50 per cent; international arrivals in Thailand grew from 5 million to 7.5 million).

National policies involve partnerships between the government (*public sector*) and commercial investment (*private sector*), although the role of the public

Figure 6.15 Morning rush hour at the Bangkok temples. Each morning, fleets of minibuses bring tourists from their hotels to the entrances of the temple complexes

sector varies. Private enterprise is a combination of internal and external money, and many companies (e.g. international hotel chains such as Hilton and Sheraton) have joint investments with internal developers in major cities such as Bangkok and Kuala Lumpur. A primary government role may be tourism promotion and marketing. For example, the Malaysian government is directly involved in tourism development, and declared 1991 a 'Year of Tourism'. One initiative was the organisation of promotional events throughout the UK and Western Europe. Displays emphasised Malaysian culture and natural attractions, while Malaysian and European tour operators advertised their 'products'. None the less, the level of capital investment and management skills required continue to cause problems for countries trying to control their development (Fig. 6.14).

Figure 6.16 Hot spots: factors likely to reduce tourist flows to a destination

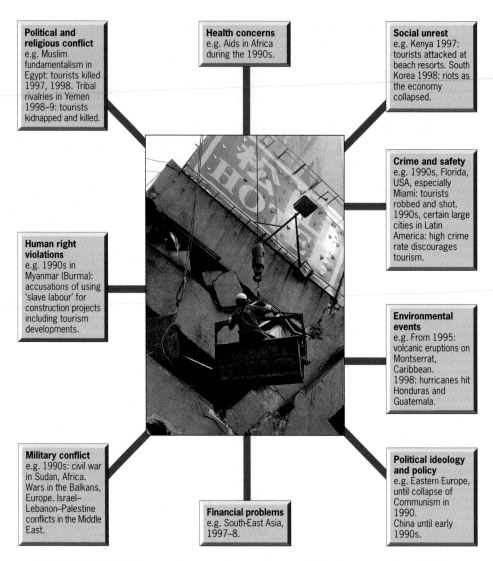

Political and religious conflict
e.g. Muslim fundamentalism in Egypt: tourists killed 1997, 1998. Tribal rivalries in Yemen 1998–9: tourists kidnapped and killed.

Health concerns
e.g. Aids in Africa during the 1990s.

Social unrest
e.g. Kenya 1997: tourists attacked at beach resorts. South Korea 1998: riots as the economy collapsed.

Crime and safety
e.g. 1990s, Florida, USA, especially Miami: tourists robbed and shot. 1990s, certain large cities in Latin America: high crime rate discourages tourism.

Human right violations
e.g. 1990s in Myanmar (Burma): accusations of using 'slave labour' for construction projects including tourism developments.

Environmental events
e.g. From 1995: volcanic eruptions on Montserrat, Caribbean. 1998: hurricanes hit Honduras and Guatemala.

Military conflict
e.g. 1990s: civil war in Sudan, Africa. Wars in the Balkans, Europe. Israel–Lebanon–Palestine conflicts in the Middle East.

Financial problems
e.g. South-East Asia, 1997–8.

Political ideology and policy
e.g. Eastern Europe, until collapse of Communism in 1990. China until early 1990s.

Hurricane holiday boom

HONDURAS is hoping to lure tourists with a taste for destruction by inviting them to see the aftermath of Hurricane Mitch.

The minister of tourism, Norman Garcia, said yesterday that the country would capitalise on a surge in visitors who have come to witness the effects of October's deadly storm which killed more than 5000 people in Honduras alone. The ministry wants to offer a 15-day tour which includes the chance to see the destruction, to help with reconstruction and to visit standard tourist attractions.

Figure 6.17 Making an attraction out of a disaster (*Source: Guardian*, 12 January 1999)

Since 1992 the Thai government, in a country with a large tourism industry led by the private sector (Fig. 6.15), has run campaigns to diversify its product and improve its image away from the 'sex and beach' tourism of Bangkok, Pattaya and Phuket. Apart from broadening and enlarging the market, the goal has been to disperse the distribution and benefits from tourism more widely through the country (e.g. government-owned Thai International Airlines has offered special deals involving visits to the system of National Parks, i.e. this was a public-sector initiative). One indicator of the success of this policy has been the rapid growth of trekking holidays in northern Thailand, centred upon the town of Chiang Mai. However, there is evidence of negative impacts upon local communities and the environment as this form of adventure tourism has grown in scale. This issue is examined in Chapter 7.

The vulnerability of NICs and LEDCs and their dependency on the financial and business structures of the MEDCs was demonstrated in 1997–8 when the currencies of a number of countries, especially in South-East Asia, collapsed. This led to economic decline, rapid inflation and, in several countries, riots and social unrest. Despite offers of special discounts, tourism arrivals declined seriously (e.g. on the island of Bali, Indonesia, the occupancy rates in hotels during May 1998 were below 50 per cent compared with over 90 per cent the previous year). This illustrates an important characteristic of tourism: it is sensitive to economic, social and environmental events which may or may not be under the control of the affected destination (Fig. 6.16). Yet some countries are very creative in marketing even disasters as tourist attractions! (Fig. 6.17).

Table 6.4 Top six European leisure–travel groups, 1997 (*Source: Travel and Tourism Analyst*, No.3, 1998)

Group	Country	Turnover (billion Deutschmarks)
TUI	Germany	8511
C+N Touristic	Germany	7300
DER	Germany	6552
Airtours	UK	6175
Thomson Travel	UK	5056
Kuoni	Switzerland	5030

Figure 6.18 UK tourism giants: Airtours and Thomson

?

8 Explain what is meant by 'economic colonialism' and why LEDCs that use tourism to assist their development may remain dependent upon the rich countries of the developed world (MEDCs).

9 Give examples of the part played by governments in tourism development in LEDCs and NICs.

10 By analysis of the images in Figures 6.10, 6.13, 6.14, 6.15 and 6.19, outline why LEDCs are attracted by tourism and the problems they may face in developing a successful tourism industry.

11 Discuss briefly the structure and character of the tourism industry.

Mass tourism and globalisation

Global mass tourism is big business: scale grows, competition intensifies, communication systems accelerate, capital investment multiplies. During the 1990s, pressures to reduce unit costs by economies of scale and to increase market share produced two major trends. First, the increasing dominance of a small number of multinational companies, achieved in part by mergers and takeovers. The twin goals have been to achieve the *critical mass* of supply and customer income necessary to sustain the huge capital investments and to reduce competition. Second, the adoption of the *vertical integration* model of organisation, where a single corporate group is a full or part owner of several stages and components in the travel and tourism system: airline operations, tour operations, travel agencies, accommodation.

The structure of the European industry is an excellent example of these processes at work. During the 1990s a few large corporations gained increasing control of the tourism system (Table 6.4). Germany is Europe's largest tourist market, which helps to explain the size of German companies. However, all these top-ranked corporations own and run businesses in several countries (Fig. 6.18).

Airtours

- Most of its business is in the UK, where it is vertically integrated – its own airline, the Going Places travel agency chain, tour operations.
- 1997: 15 per cent of UK summer-holiday package market.
- Niche brands: Late Escapes; Aspro; Tradewinds; Eurosites.
- 1995: First went transnational when it bought the Ving travel agent chain and resort hotels in Scandinavia.
- 1996: Bought the Danish Spies/Tjaereborg group.
- 1996: Went into partnership with Carnival Cruise Lines.
- 1997: With Carnival Lines, bought out Costa Crociere, an Italian cruise line.
- 1998: Bought Belgium's Sun International, including tour operators, a travel agent chain, a small airline, and UK short-break operators Bridge Travel and Cresta Holidays.
- 1998: Bought a majority share of the large German company Frosch Touristik, with a diversity of products – long haul, language holidays, cruises.

Thomson Travel Group

- The slowest of the major European companies to go transnational.
- 1997: 21 per cent of UK summer-holiday package market.
- 1997: Took over Austravel, a long-haul ticketing specialist.
- 1998: Bought Fritidressor, the second-largest leisure group in Scandinavia, including a charter airline and holiday villages.
- 1998: increasing vertical integration – charter airline (Britannia); the Lunn-Poly travel agency chain (800 outlets); Holiday Cottages, the largest UK domestic holiday accommodation rental business; increased foreign accommodation holdings.

A role for small businesses

As you read through the preceding section you may have said, 'Hey, wait a minute! It's not all like this.' If this was your reaction, you were quite correct. The supply of mass tourism is controlled by 'big business', but the tourism system supports and is supported by a vast substructure of small businesses: guest houses in Blackpool, tavernas in Greece, beach bars in the Caribbean, camel rides in Australia (Fig. 6.19). The owners may be local people or incomers, but they are all generally families, individuals or partners and, although start-up conditions are easy, the risks and failure rates are high. These enterprises possess a number of typical features: relatively low capital

Figure 6.19 A bus taxi in the British Virgin Islands: a local business enterprise

12 Suggest two reasons why the list in Table 6.5a is dominated by MEDCs.

13 Using Table 6.5b and c, list those countries that are:
a Net earners (earnings greater than spending);
b Net spenders (spending greater than earnings).

14 Comment on your lists (NB: If a country appears in only one column of the tables then, clearly, that is the greater element).

Table 6.6 The 'leakage' of tourism income (*Source:* Cooper et al., 1993)

Fiji: the balance sheet – the impact of $1000 tourist expenditure on Fiji's balance of payments

		$
Tourist expenditure (+)		1000.0
Import requirements (–)		
Direct	120.8	
Indirect	115.3	236.1
Net effect on balance of payments	763.9	
Induced imports (–)	326.3	326.3
Net impact after induced effects		437.6

Using the national economy of Fiji as an example, the table shows that, for each additional $1000 of tourist expenditure, $120.8 immediately leaks out of the economy as imports required throughout the Fiji economy in order to support this additional level of tourist activity, leaving a net inflow of foreign exchange equivalent to $763.9.

However, the resulting increase in income levels in Fiji will generate further imports as a portion of this additional income is respent. Some of this responding of income will be on goods and services that are produced by firms and individuals located outside Fiji's national boundaries, resulting in an increase in imports of $326.3, leaving a net inflow of foreign exchange of $437.6.

requirements, personal control and commitment, business skills and lots of hard work, low 'leakage', significant use of local resources and products. Tourism also supports an extensive informal or 'black' economy, from beggars to unlicensed street traders.

Equally importantly, tourism at all scales of business creates lots of jobs, i.e. it is labour-intensive (e.g. some top-class hotels have more staff than guests, one Boeing 747 'Jumbo' aircraft in full service supports 400 jobs). Many are part-time, seasonal, involve anti-social hours and are low-paid, but they are jobs.

6.5 The tourism industry and controlling income

International tourism behaves as an export industry. The 'product' of services and goods is sold and paid for in foreign currency (e.g. over £12 billion a year is brought into the UK from foreign visitors – see Chapter 5). But this product is 'exported' in a peculiar way in that the buyers consume their purchases, i.e. their travel experiences, at the point of production and supply. Thus, countries such as Malaysia and Thailand sell you tourist experiences to gain British currency, create jobs, raise national image etc., like any other export industry, and then you travel to these countries to consume your purchases – and to spend more money. For this reason, foreign exchange earnings from tourism appear in official figures as 'invisible' exports. As Table 6.5 shows, among the world's top earners, the gross totals are huge. However, receipts from tourism are impressive in all regions of the world, especially in LEDCs with a limited capacity for earning foreign currency (Fig. 6.12).

Table 6.5 Tourism: The world's 'top ten', 1995 – international totals, including business travel (*Source:* WTO, 1997)

Rank	a Arrivals (millions)		b Earnings (US$ billions)		c Spending (US$ billions)	
1	France	63	USA	62	USA	45
2	USA	47	France	26	Germany	44
3	Spain	45	Italy	25	Japan	33
4	Italy	29	Spain	23	UK	24
5	Hungary	24	UK	16	France	15
6	China	23	Austria	14	Italy	14
7	UK	22	Germany	12	Netherlands	12
8	Poland	19	Hong Kong	9	Canada	11
9	Austria	18	Switzerland	8	Austria	10
10	Mexico	17	China	8	Belgium	8

Problems of keeping tourism income

The economic benefits arising from this foreign currency have been one of the principal driving forces behind many tourism development policies in countries as diverse as Britain, Brazil, Botswana and Bangladesh. Not only can the money be invested internally – it can also be used to buy imported materials, equipment and other goods needed for development programmes.

Unfortunately, things are not always this straightforward. First, spending by nationals of a country on international travel takes money out of that country. Thus, the gross income must be set against this expenditure to obtain the net balance (Table 6.5). Furthermore, many destinations, especially smaller LEDCs in the Caribbean, the Pacific and Africa, have found that at least 50 per cent of the money earned 'leaks' away (Table 6.6).

Leakage
Leakage is defined as the proportion of the income that is lost from the destination country and from which it therefore does not benefit (Fig. 6.20).

Figure 6.20 The leakage concept

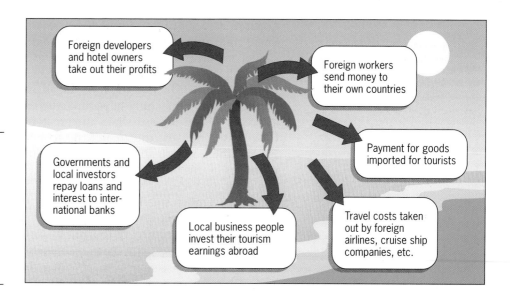

Table 6.7 Economics – who benefits? Cost beakdown for a British example of a foreign package holiday: percentage of total cost (*After*: Ryan, 1991)

Retained by tourist-generating country:	
Transport cost	40
Agent commission	10
Publicity	8
Administration	6
Gross profit margin	3
Received by the destination country:	
Hotelier	30
Local services	3

15 Give three reasons why a tourism destination is more likely to have a higher degree of control over small-scale projects than over large-scale projects.

16 Write a brief report for a Minister of Tourism, suggesting options for reducing 'leakage' of tourism income, including the problems of applying each option. (Structure your report from the list of factors which affect 'leakage'.)

17 From Figure 6.21:
a Which destinations have maintained their 3-star rating since 1993?
b Which destinations have faded seriously, and why?
c Which destinations would you add to the 3-star list, and why? (You will find the Travel sections and supplements of newspapers and magazines as well as TV programmes and Web sites useful in discerning the 'in' destinations.)

For instance, if you buy a T-shirt in Spain, which has been made in Taiwan, some of your purchase price will not stay in Spain, but 'leaks' to Taiwan to pay for the import of the garment. In addition, foreign investors and transnational companies (e.g. hotel chains) may take their profits out of the country.

This leakage process in turn reduces the potential **multiplier effect** – the benefits from the money circulating through the destination country. For example, if the T-shirt was made in Spain, then Spanish workers will have earned extra wages which they then spend, which passes the money on through the economy and so on (i.e. it multiplies the benefit of your original spending as the money passes through the Spanish economy). If the money 'leaks', however, there is no such multiplier effect.

Table 6.7 illustrates how a fully inclusive foreign 'package' holiday from the UK may have limited benefit to the destination country. Only one-third of the cost of your holiday price actually reaches the country you visit, and remember, some of the 30 per cent the hotelier receives may then leak to pay for imports etc. Two further points are worth noting: first, the figures exclude your spending while in the country, which may add 20 per cent to the income; second, the 40 per cent taken as the travel component helps to explain why so many countries are keen to develop their own airlines. For example, if you fly to Kenya on Kenya Airways rather than British Airways, the economic benefit to Kenya is increased, although airlines are notoriously expensive to run.

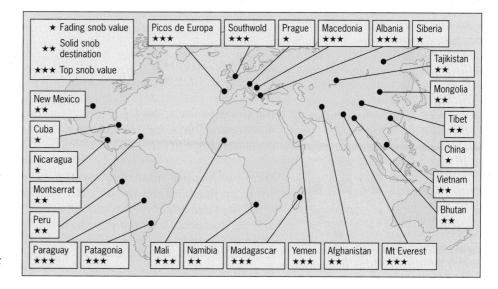

Figure 6.21 Worldwide snob holiday destinations (*Source: The Independent on Sunday*, 31 January 1993)

Control

Small countries with narrow economic bases (i.e. few industries), limited capital and lack of a skilled workforce find that they have to borrow capital and use foreign companies to build and manage their developments, especially in the early stages. Much of the food, drink and entertainment also has to be imported. Thus, they only have limited control over their tourism industry. This issue of control is crucial – the greater the control of and involvement in the tourism industry, the greater the economic benefit is likely to be. Tonga, Fiji and the Cook Islands, all tropical destinations in the Pacific, are good examples of this principle: Fiji has the largest tourism industry of the three, but has the lowest level of local ownership, and loses 60 per cent via leakage; Tonga has a much smaller industry but local people control most of it, so the leakage is only 8 per cent. The 50 per cent leakage from the Cook Islands is due largely to the control of tourism by New Zealand.

6.6 The impact of fashion

Figure 6.22 Marketing an image. Advert promoting marriage in exotic locations

A further fundamental characteristic of tourism is that it is a fashion industry. Status, image and prestige are powerful motivations for travel to particular destinations. For instance, it is not simply getting a tan that is important, but where you acquire it: Margate and even Marbella are 'out'; at the moment, Mauritius and the Maldives are 'in'. Where will fashionable suntans come from in ten years' time? (Or as skin cancer scares take hold, will natural skin tones become fashionable?) The fickleness of fashion is evident from Figure 6.21: these were the 'snob' destinations of 1993. A map produced today would look very different!

Weddings & Honeymoons on Tropical Islands

There has always been an irresistible appeal to getting married on a tropical island, and it is now easier than ever to turn this dream into reality. The Tropics were made for people in love. What could be more romantic than to marry the one you love on a palm-fringed beach with the sunshine sparkling on turquoise waters, or amidst spectacular tropical gardens, the air heavy with the scent of bougainvillaea, hibiscus and orchid.

Tourism marketing plays heavily on the power of this characteristic (Fig. 6.22). Fashion trends influence not only choice of destinations (look again at the problems being faced by British holiday resorts) but also expectations, experiences, types of environment, activity etc. Skiing, for example, has boomed, but downhill skiing is losing some of its glamour to cross-country skiing and heliskiing. An analysis of British tourism shows a significant decline in the popularity of package holidays as fashion shifts to greater independence of travel (Fig. 6.23). In 1997, British holidaymakers bought 8 per cent fewer inclusive tours than in 1996, while independent travel grew by 2 per cent, and VFR and business travel were each up by 8 per cent. Furthermore, long-haul holidays grew from 4 per cent of inclusive packages in 1987 to 18 per cent in 1997, as package tours to Europe became less fashionable.

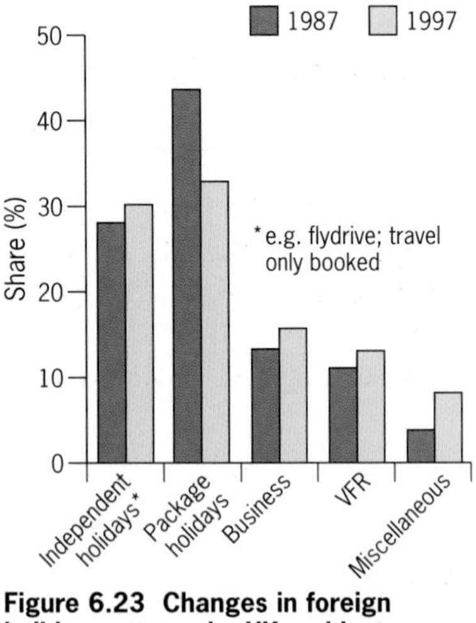

Demand–supply relationships: the example of ocean cruise tourism

No sector demonstrates the dynamic character of tourism better than ocean cruise package holidays. Traditionally, ocean cruises have occupied a niche as an élite, high-cost sector of the tourism market. Indeed, by the early 1980s, cruises seemed in decline as jet aircraft gave ready access to new, high-fashion destinations worldwide. Yet during the 1990s cruise holidays became one of the fastest growing and profitable sectors of the tourism industry (Fig. 6.24).

Figure 6.23 Changes in foreign holiday patterns by UK residents, 1987–97

* e.g. flydrive; travel only booked

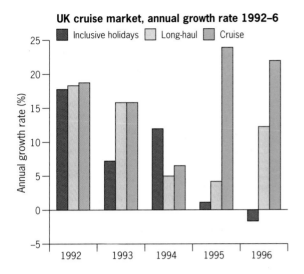

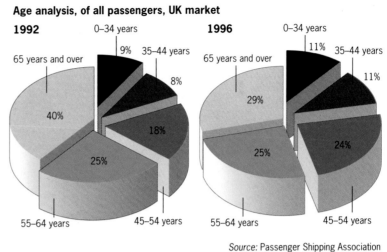

Source: Passenger Shipping Association

Figure 6.24 Sailing into the sunset (*Source: Guardian*, 17 October 1997)

This emergence as a form of mass tourism has been encouraged by several shifts in demand, supply and the relationship between them (Fig. 6.25). These shifts illustrate several fundamental attributes of tourism processes:

• the importance of fashion, status, prestige and new experiences;
• progressive market penetration from a trend-setting élite;
• increasing dominance of transnational corporations;
• the use of economies of scale to reduce unit costs and so broaden the potential market;
• an increased range of options around a core format;
• demand and supply are dominated by MEDCs – two-thirds of world demand and cruise origins come from North America (see the North American ocean cruise market case study on page 131), although cruise itineraries are global (e.g. the Caribbean and the Mediterranean are the main spheres of influence but cruise ships now touch the north and south polar regions).

In other ways, cruise tourism has certain distinctive characteristics. For example, it is very capital intensive: in 1998 some 39 new ships costing US$12 billion were due for delivery by 2003 to the North American market alone. Many new orders are 'mega-ships' of over 100 000 tonnes, capable of carrying

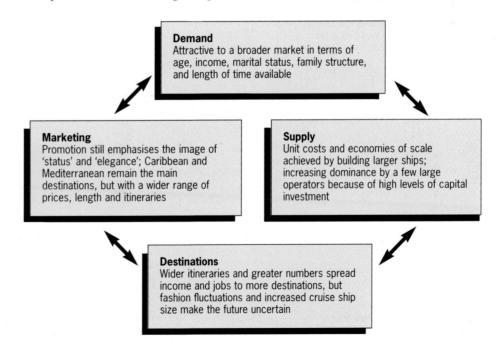

Figure 6.25 The changing world of ocean cruise tourism

Figure 6.26 The size of ships to come – cruise ships get bigger and bigger (*Source: Guardian*, 21 October 1997)

Cruise colossus breaks records

IT WILL have a population of 5,000, an area of nearly four acres, a chapel, a television station and a conference centre.

Eagle ships are so large they may just as well count as 'land'. At 1,019ft long, they outstretch three football pitches, at 157.5ft wide they are twice as broad as Broadway in New York. And at 206.5ft tall, they will look down on 20-storey buildings.

Nor is this vast unnamed floating mini-city – twice the tonnage of the QE2 – a crazed one-off. Royal Caribbean, the mid market American cruise line, has ordered a second.

Figure 6.27 Cruise ships moored at Road Town, Tortola, British Virgin Islands. Passenger spending, harbour fees and provisioning are a valuable source of income. This harbour is much too small to accommodate very large cruise ships, however, and the government cannot afford the cost of new facilities, though in 1999 a UK government loan helped to extend the dock facility

several thousand passengers (Fig. 6.26). These are huge floating resorts rather than comfortable hotels. Furthermore, they require costly, specialised onshore docking and maintenance facilities that are available in only a few ports, which strengthens the reason for the 'hub' system used by cruise ship companies (Fig. 6.28).

The ever-growing size of cruise ships has serious implications for the second distinctive characteristic, namely the impact of cruise tourism on destination ports. A typical cruise itinerary includes brief stops at a series of ports, during which passengers may shop or take optional trips to beaches, temples, 'native' villages etc. (Fig. 6.27). The visitors eat and sleep on board, so the impact on the local people and environment is less than with residential tourism. In turn, the economic benefits are limited to the day-trip expenditure and the harbour fees. None the less, for many islands and LEDCs this is a valuable source of income and seasonal jobs. Few such ports of call will be able to accommodate the mega-ships, however, which may have serious implications for the impacts of future developments (Fig. 6.29).

Airlines and cruise lines operate the 'hub' system – collecting customers into a few major terminals and then redistributing them. Miami is an excellent example: a major hub for the North and South American airline networks and highly accessible for the Caribbean tourist destinations, with easy transfer from airport to liner terminal.

The cruises visit a variety of islands, with stopovers ranging from a few hours to two days to allow shore visits, shopping and excursions. Accommodation and most meals are taken aboard the ships. Cruise itineraries have considerable flexibility, and companies can alter routes and stopovers from year to year according to popularity and fashion.

Figure 6.28 Cruising – the hub system

The North American ocean cruise market

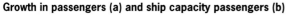

Growth in passengers (a) and ship capacity passengers (b)

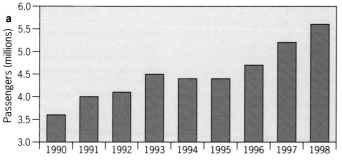

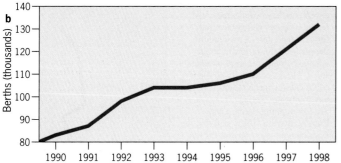

Top cruise companies

	Passenger capacity	
	1998	**2002**
Carnival Cruises	24420	83446
Royal Caribbean	23006	33446
Princess Cruises	15250	22400
Norwegian Cruise Line	10927	10331
Holland American Cruises	10290	14550
Celebrity Cruises	8382	16182

Scale of business, 1997

Example: Carnival cruises

Passenger days:*	12 million
Total revenue:	US$2.5 billion
Net income:	US$0.7 billion
Revenue per passenger day:	US$206
Net income per passenger day:	US$52

*One passenger on a 7-day cruise = 7 passenger days

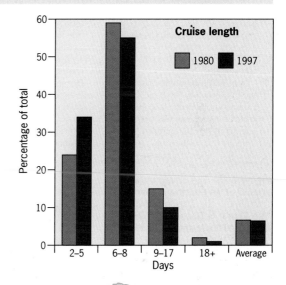

Passenger characteristics

Annual income

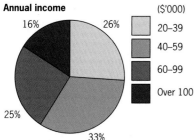

($'000)
- 20–39
- 40–59
- 60–99
- Over 100

Status (% of total)

Married 75%
Single 25%

Children at home: 32%
Of this 32%, 54% brought children on the cruise.

No children at home: 49%

Age

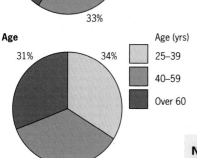

Age (yrs)
- 25–39
- 40–59
- Over 60

New ships on order for North American cruises 1999–2002

No. of passengers	No. of ships
Over 3000	3
2000–3000	17
1000–2000	10
Less than 1000	12

Total cost: US$11 billion
Total number of extra passengers: 72500

Ships on order

For delivery 1999–2002: 42
26 of these are over 75000 tonnnes
20 will carry over 2000 passengers
Total cost: US$11 billion

Main departure ports, 1997

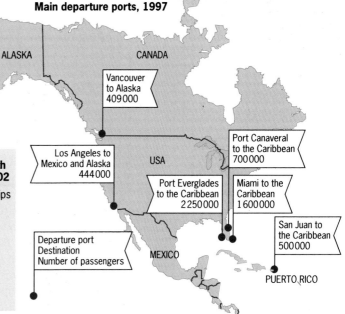

Port threatens wildlife haven

A VAST PORT, able to take 660 cruise liners and 16 million tourists a year, is being planned in a wildlife haven on the British Caribbean islands of Turks and Caicos.

The plan, made for an uninhabited, unspoilt island in the group, has triggered outrage among conservationists.

They fear that the scheme, backed by a Canadian property developer, will lead to nearly half of the island of East Caicos going under the bulldozer to develop the docks, roads and a network of leisure centres, shops, golf courses, hotels and luxury flats for wealthy North American and European visitors.

The project calls for the building of an eight-mile main road and bridge to link East Caicos with the smaller island of South Caicos. This will be used to bring in low-paid staff and workers to the port and complex.

Dr Mike Pienkowski, chairman of the UK Overseas Territories Conservation Forum, said that the scale of the scheme was outrageous and out of step with modern thinking on eco-tourism.

This was 'a proposal for one of the largest cruise liner ports in the world: it would destroy most of East Caicos, including its many natural lakes and marshes, as well as having a devastating effect on superb mangroves and coral reefs and fisheries'.

The project could also trigger serious social problems. 'The population of East Caicos is zero and the population of South Caicos is 1200. But there will be 6000 to 7000 service jobs required. There is no grinding poverty in the Turks and Caicos. They will be importing all of the labour from Haiti and the Dominican Republic along with all the social problems,' he said.

A report by the developers, Pagebrook, says the scheme, covering 8500 of East Caicos's 17 500 acres, will be able to accept two cruise liners a day, leading to 660 ships a year, with an estimated 1.6 million passengers.

'That number of passengers arriving is larger than any other Caribbean island and about the same as the Bahamas. But this one will be at a single site, whereas in the Bahamas passengers disembark

at several sites,' said Dr Pienkowski.

Conservationists say that, unless the project is blocked, an area of internationally important wetland, home to breeding birds such as the roseate flamingo, Kirtland's warbler and the West Indies whistling duck, will be damaged and destroyed. Other threatened species include rare cacti, rock iguanas and loggerhead, green, hawsbill and leatherhead sea turtles.

Ethlyn Gibb-Williams, executive director of the Turks and Caicos National Trust, said: 'The developers have conducted some public hearings which have put forward their side. a rosy picture. People need the full truth about what is coming and need to take a stand. This is potentially so big it could cause considerable environmental damage.'

In London, the Foreign and Commonwealth Office said that the development was a matter for the Turks and Caicos Government, even though the islands are a dependent territory.

The company appears to have

won support in the islands. In a statement, Nigel Taylor, assistant to John Kelly, the Governor, defended the cruise-liner port scheme, saying that it would help to distribute the growth in tourism across the islands.

Mr Taylor said that economic and social impact assessments had been made. He made no mention of any environmental impact assessment.

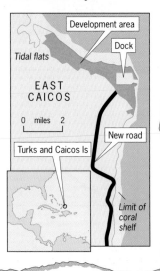

Figure 6.29 The environmental impact of an enormous tourist complex in the Caribbean (*Source: The Times***, 5 December 1998) © Times Newspapers Ltd 1998**

18 Use the information and data on cruise ship tourism, including the case study, to illustrate the six 'fundamental attributes of tourism processes' listed on page 129.

19a Define the term 'pleasure periphery'.
b Give three reasons for its outward spread during the twentieth century.

20 Figure 6.31 shows an extract from a 1993 holiday advertisement. Suggest three likely motivations that would attract people to such a holiday.

21 As an environmentalist, give three reasons why tourism should not be developed in Antartica.

The pleasure periphery

The idea of tourism as a fashion industry, constantly seeking new experiences, helps to explain the concept of the **pleasure periphery**. This depicts the boundaries of tourism as a tidal wave surging ever outwards across planet earth from major tourist-generating regions (Fig. 6.30). At the outer edge of this surge, in 1992 around 6000 tourists visited Antarctica, and by 1998 this figure had reached 15 000. Each spent an average of £5000 on the trip, indicating the strong motivations driving people 'to the ends of the earth' (Fig. 6.31).

6.7 The product cycle

The understanding of travel and tourism as constantly seeking fresh resources leads to the claim that it is an essentially *exploitative* industry. It exploits the resources of a region while they remain in demand, before moving on to new source regions. A crucial outcome of this process is that any specific destination may experience a **product cycle**, comparable to that in primary extractive industries such as mining and forestry. Figure 6.32a outlines this product cycle over time for a single tourist destination.

It is also possible to locate different destinations upon the model at a particular time, as in Figure 6.32b. The examples given in Figure 6.33A–D illustrate the situation in the mid-1990s. In the early twentieth-first century we can expect destinations such as Alaska to move into the 'growth' stage (B), with some parts of regions such as North Queensland approaching 'saturation' (C). Into the 'emergent' stage (A) will come remote regions such as Kamchatka (North-East Asia) and Kazakhstan (Central Asia).

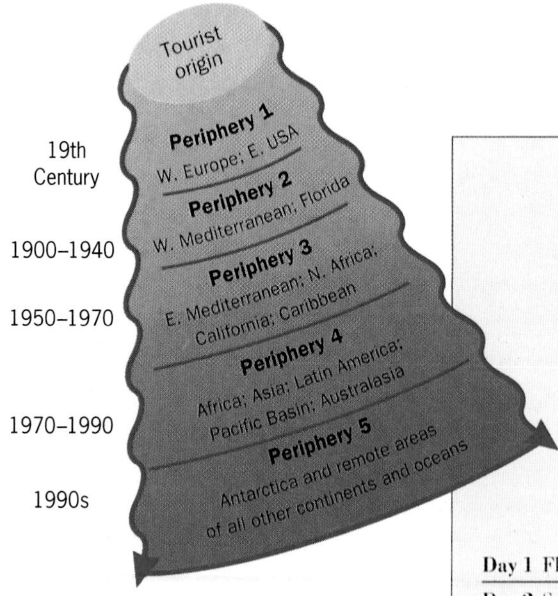

19th
Century

1900–1940

1950–1970

1970–1990

1990s

Tourist
origin

Periphery 1
W. Europe; E. USA

Periphery 2
W. Mediterranean; Florida

Periphery 3
E. Mediterranean; N. Africa;
California; Caribbean

Periphery 4
Africa; Asia; Latin America;
Pacific Basin; Australasia

Periphery 5
Antarctica and remote areas
of all other continents and oceans

Figure 6.30 The pleasure periphery

Figure 6.31 At the outer edge of the pleasure periphery. Advertising a 'voyage of discovery' to Antarctica (*Source:* Noble Caledonia Ltd)

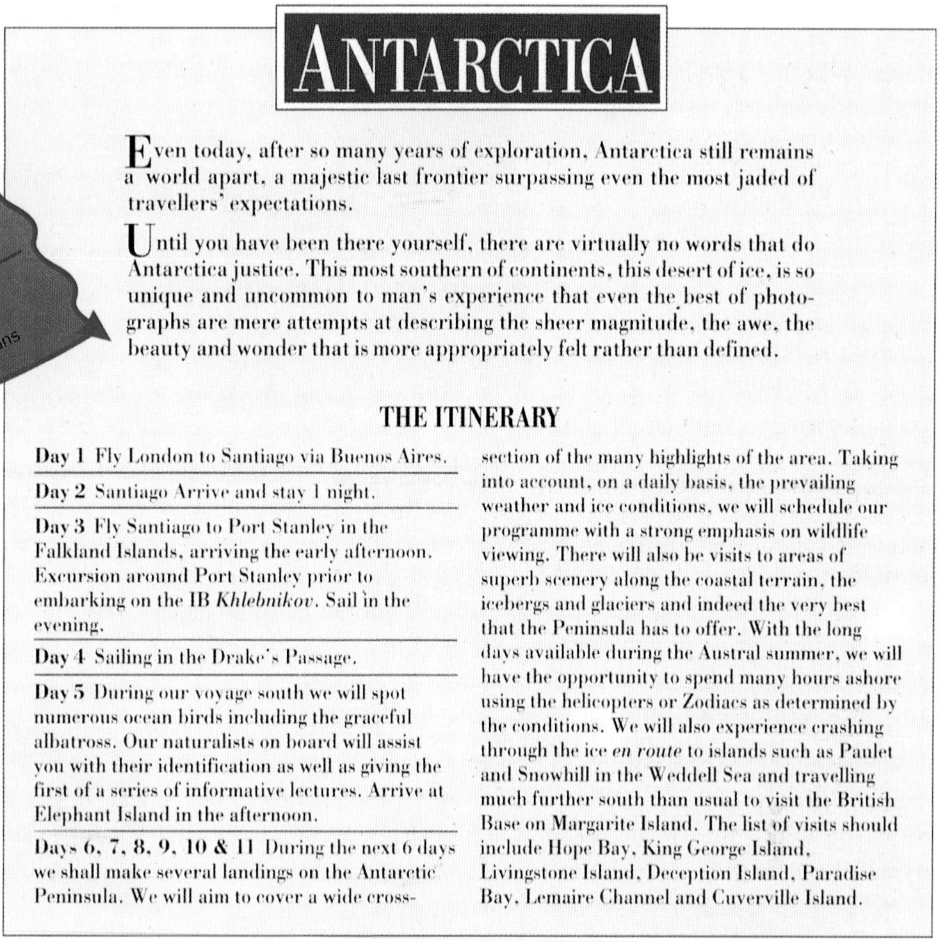

ANTARCTICA

Even today, after so many years of exploration, Antarctica still remains a world apart, a majestic last frontier surpassing even the most jaded of travellers' expectations.

Until you have been there yourself, there are virtually no words that do Antarctica justice. This most southern of continents, this desert of ice, is so unique and uncommon to man's experience that even the best of photographs are mere attempts at describing the sheer magnitude, the awe, the beauty and wonder that is more appropriately felt rather than defined.

THE ITINERARY

Day 1 Fly London to Santiago via Buenos Aires.

Day 2 Santiago Arrive and stay 1 night.

Day 3 Fly Santiago to Port Stanley in the Falkland Islands, arriving the early afternoon. Excursion around Port Stanley prior to embarking on the IB *Khlebnikov*. Sail in the evening.

Day 4 Sailing in the Drake's Passage.

Day 5 During our voyage south we will spot numerous ocean birds including the graceful albatross. Our naturalists on board will assist you with their identification as well as giving the first of a series of informative lectures. Arrive at Elephant Island in the afternoon.

Days 6, 7, 8, 9, 10 & 11 During the next 6 days we shall make several landings on the Antarctic Peninsula. We will aim to cover a wide cross-section of the many highlights of the area. Taking into account, on a daily basis, the prevailing weather and ice conditions, we will schedule our programme with a strong emphasis on wildlife viewing. There will also be visits to areas of superb scenery along the coastal terrain, the icebergs and glaciers and indeed the very best that the Peninsula has to offer. With the long days available during the Austral summer, we will have the opportunity to spend many hours ashore using the helicopters or Zodiacs as determined by the conditions. We will also experience crashing through the ice *en route* to islands such as Paulet and Snowhill in the Weddell Sea and travelling much further south than usual to visit the British Base on Margarite Island. The list of visits should include Hope Bay, King George Island, Livingstone Island, Deception Island, Paradise Bay, Lemaire Channel and Cuverville Island.

As a resort or destination region passes through the product cycle, so all aspects of the tourism system change – the destination, the tourists, the organisation of tourism, the impacts. Figure 6.34 follows this transformation from the time a few adventurers 'discover' an area, to the time when mass tourism dominates the economic, social and physical environment. It is important to remember that the product life cycle model may not be applicable to all destinations. It does not apply, for example, to modern, integrated resorts which are planned and built in their entirety, such as 'The Big Six' resorts of southern France, built in the 1970s as part of France's regional planning policy (Fig. 7.14, p.144); Cancun, Mexico, with a capacity of 30 000 bedspaces, developed since 1975; the Center Parcs and Oasis Villages complexes in

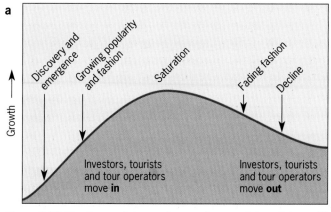

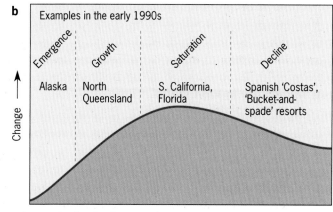

Figure 6.32 Tourism and the product cycle, a useful model on which to place a destination for a tourism case-study analysis

22 For a resort or destination region you have visited, place it on
a the product cycle model (Fig. 6.32);
b the evolutionary model of Figure 6.33.

23 For any two of the life cycles depicted on the graphs of Figure 6.35, describe that cycle and suggest reasons for the shape of the graph. Can you give examples for your selected destination types?

24 Essay: Outline the concept of the product cycle and assess its usefulness for the study of tourism in a destination region. Use examples to illustrate your answer. (You may wish to refer back to Chapter 5 and include UK examples.)

A

Figure 6.33 The tourism product cycle in the 1990s

C

A Emergent: Alaska. While cruises to the southern coasts of Alaska and visits to Denali National Park are well established, the tourism potential of the wild, remote resources of this vast state are just emerging. Glaciers, wetlands and forests are being opened up by both the public-sector (National Park and National Forest Services) and private-sector specialist tour operators (hunting, wildlife watching, photography, backpacking).

B Growth: North Queensland. The tourism industry and the tourists have discovered the wonderful assembly of high-quality natural resources along the hundreds of kilometres of the North Queensland fringe: sun, sea, sand, rainforests, coral reefs. All are marketed as 'unspoilt' and 'uncrowded', but are experiencing the explosive growth of tourism. Cairns Airport has been upgraded to take jumbo jet aircraft. In 1996, along a 40km stretch of coast near the Whitsunday Islands, there were developments being built and planning applications for resorts worth at least A$60 million. Japanese investors and tour operators have been applying the greatest pressure.

C Saturation: Southern California and Florida.
They remain powerful magnets for millions of American 'snowbirds' who flee the harsh North American winters, as well as international tourists. But you can drive the 300km from north of Los Angeles to the Mexican border south of San Diego, and the only open stretches of coast are military bases and State Parks and Reserves. Florida, too, has used up its 1500km of coast between Tampa on the west and Jacksonville on the east, except for the Everglades National Park, the Kennedy Space Center and some State Parks.

D Decline: the Spanish 'costas'. Between 1990 and 1993, bookings by British tourists to the Spanish Costas declined by 20 per cent. The positive image of cheap and guaranteed sun–sea–sand–sangría–sex is being replaced by negative images of pollution, crowding, crime, poor accommodation and over-packaging. Resorts are making vigorous attempts to upgrade the natural and built environment in an effort to restore image and hence market share.

D

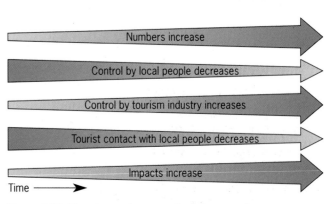

Figure 6.34 The change in types of tourist over time

Numbers increase

Control by local people decreases

Control by tourism industry increases

Tourist contact with local people decreases

Impacts increase

Time ⟶

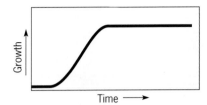

A *planned* resort: built in a previously undeveloped location. There is rapid growth to a planned capacity (e.g. Languedoc–Roussillon, France).

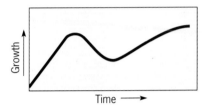

A *multi-phase* resort: a second surge of growth is generated (e.g. by relaxation of planning regulation; by improved access (new airport); additional attractions/facilities (marina)) which broadens the market sector.

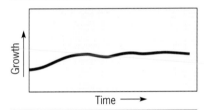

A *specialist niche* resort: controls and maintains its niche market (e.g. spa towns, élite island destinations). Facilities and amenities are progressively modernised but the 'image' and the market segment is sustained.

Figure 6.35 Alternative resort life cycles

England; the resorts developed around the several Disney theme parks. So, resort life cycles may follow different paths (Fig. 6.35).

6.8 Dimensions of impact

As tourism in a destination region develops and changes over time, so the impacts change. Careful study of the evolutionary processes illustrated in Table 6.8 reveals three dimensions to the impact of tourism – economic, socio-cultural, environmental. There may be both positive and negative components to each dimension. This idea of dimensions and components provides a framework for the analysis of any destination region, and can be expressed in terms of a matrix (Table 6.8).

Such analysis highlights several critical understandings. First, the dimensions and components are closely interrelated. For example, in order to achieve economic gains, there may be inevitable environmental losses. Second, the

Table 6.8 A matrix of tourism impact

	Positive (i.e. gains)	Negative (i.e. losses)
Economic	Increased investment More jobs and income Economic diversification Foreign currency, and improved balance of payments	Greater dependence upon foreign capital Seasonality of employment Decline of traditional activities and industries Leakage of income from tourism
Socio-cultural	Contacts with other peoples and cultures Modernisation of social attitudes Revitalisation of traditional crafts, art forms and cultural pride Reduction of out-migration	Loss of family and community lands and rights Weakening of family and community structures Commercialisation of traditional culture Increased crime
Environmental	Upgrading of infrastructure Conservation of ecosystems and heritage buildings Modernisation of settlements and homes	Loss of agricultural land and natural resources Destruction of natural features and vegetation Water, air and noise pollution Removal of traditional settlements

Note: The items in each box of the matrix are examples only.
Thus, other impacts may be identifiable for any specific destination.

Figure 6.36 In Bali, Indonesia, dance is an important element in traditional culture and religion. It has also become a popular attraction for tourists. Does this commercialisation or commodification degrade sacred culture and cause it to lose its real meaning, or does such marketing revitalise pride in traditional beliefs, skills and ceremonies which would otherwise disappear?

THE WORDS and imagery are persuasive: they speak of dream holidays, friendly local people, an unspoilt, palm-fringed paradise. But the reality is drug abuse, child prostitution and widespread environmental destruction.

The Indian coastal state of Goa was singled out yesterday as a lesson in how mass tourism to 'exotic' locations has gone badly wrong. According to the pressure group Tourism Concern, Western tour operators are causing much of the damage but are 'washing their hands' of responsibility.

Goa, which became a Western tourist destination after being discovered by hippies in the 1960s, is now the scene of acid parties, raves and increasing child prostitution. Tourist buses have been pelted with

THE CONFLICTING VIEWS

The place	The image: *What the brochures say*	The criticisms: *What local people say*
Taj and Fort Aguada holiday complexes	'Relaxed . . . laid back . . . beautifully and peacefully positioned.' (Inspirations India)	Local people denied beach access and access to water pipeline
Leela Beach Hotel	'Walk about in the extensive grounds and the predominant noise is birdsong' (Inspirations)	Refuses to rent out coconut trees to tappers, damages trees, illegal wells built, villages displaced from land, beach access denied
Cidade de Goa Hotel	'Lovely, beachside setting . . . comfort, elegance and friendly service' (Cosmos)	Beach access denied by wall, sewage dumped, court orders taken out against it
Dona Sylvia Hotel	'Excellent location . . . alongside a wonderful beach' (Sunworld)	Illegal fence built, dunes damaged to give guests seaview.

rotten fish and cow dung, and police mount drives against drug-taking Westerners.

Women protest at their portrayal in tourist literature – at how 'they and events like the local carnival are being commoditised at the expense of their dignity and culture'. Children skip school to peddle drugs to Western tourists, who affront the morality of villagers by sunbathing in the nude.

Many local groups are also angry at the special treatment tourists receive, according to a Tourism Concern survey. Hotels, many foreign-owned, receive subsidised water and electricity. Yet one five-star hotel consumes as much water as five villages and one 'five-star tourist' consumes 28 times more electricity per day than a Goan.

Figure 6.37 Newspaper report on 'Paradise lost in Goa' (Source: The Independent, 27 January 1993)

26 Read Figure 6.37 carefully.
a Summarise the key social, economic and environmental issues identified.
b Place Goa on the model in Figure 6.32.

27 Use the matrix of Table 6.8 to compare and contrast beach resort tourism with ocean cruise tourism in terms of their impacts upon a destination.

28 Decision-making exercise: Use the information in this chapter to write a brief report to the Development Minister of an LEDC, who intends to develop tourism. You are asked to recommend beach resorts *or* ocean cruise tourism as the basis of this development. (Suggested geographical background for your report: a Caribbean or Pacific island country, with a population of less than 5 million, and currently largely dependent upon subsistence and commercial farming; there is an airport, but not capable of taking large jet aircraft. NB: Add any other features you think will be helpful.) Your report should include the pros and cons of each form of development before setting out and justifying your decision.

same element of an impact dimension may appear as both a gain or a loss in the matrix. Thus, within the socio-cultural dimension, the impacts upon traditional crafts and cultural practices such as carvings and religious ceremonies may be seen as either positive or negative (Fig. 6.36). Third, the matrix for any specific destination region is a form of balance sheet. The gain/ loss ratio will depend upon the values, attitudes and priorities of the people constructing the balance sheet. For instance, the government of an LEDC, an international tour operator and an environmental campaign group will each prioritise and measure impacts differently – they each have different perceptions and goals. The extract in Figure 6.37 illustrates this contrast between the 'image' marketed by the tourism industry and the 'reality' as perceived by Tourism Concern, a British environmental and human rights organisation. The issues raised by the impact matrix model are explored further in Chapter 7.

Summary

- People travel for many reasons.

- The scale and continued growth of tourism make very large demands upon natural and human resources in all parts of the world.

- Tourism is the world's largest industrial sector, and is strongly influenced by processes of globalisation.

- The tourism industry provides a diversity of products and services, aimed at a number of market segments.

- Most countries are attracted to tourism development because they believe it will generate foreign exchange, investment, income and jobs.

- Ownership and control are vital factors affecting benefits from tourism. Many LEDCs have found it difficult to gain this control.

- In many countries, tourism has been developed as an exploitative industry, and so passes through a product-cycle of growth, followed by stagnation and decline.

- A pleasure periphery surged outwards across the globe from tourist-generating regions during the twentieth century.

- Tourism impacts may be measured in terms of economic, social and environmental dimensions.

7 The search for sustainable tourism

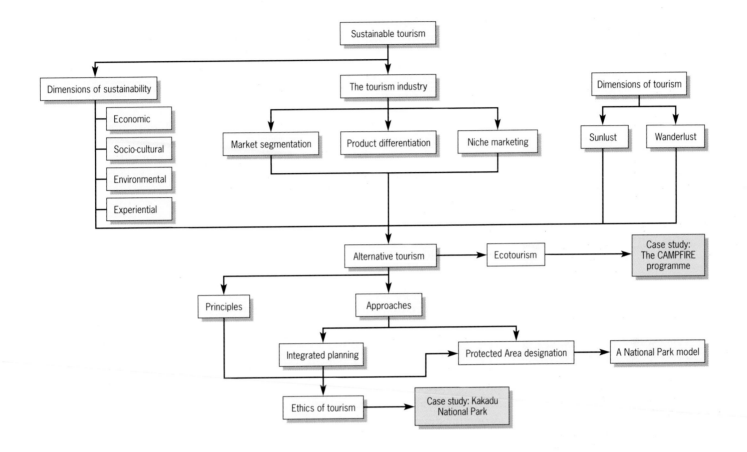

Figure 7.1 Spain: repairing the damage – and the image
(*Source: Time*, 21 September 1998)

For many countries, sustainable growth is an objective. In the 1960s and early 1970s, speculative development in Spain despoiled hundreds of miles of coastline. Now Spain – the world's third-largest tourist destination in 1997 with over 46 million visitors – is trying to repair the damage. The Balearic Islands (Majorca, Minorca, Ibiza and Formentera) have put a limit on beds. Anyone opening a new hotel must close an old one and can then accommodate only an equal number. As Pedro Pasual, director-general of tourism on the Balearics, puts it: 'We're giving licences for the construction of top-category hotels and running down the lower-category ones.'

And none too soon. In the Balearics (population 768 000) the impact of 9 million foreign visitors each year was undermining local identity. 'In some places we Spaniards had begun to feel like foreigners in our own country,' says Pepe Negrón, spokesman for the Balearic Islands tourism office. Initiatives like this will find an echo elsewhere as travel and tourism continue to expand into the ever more remote areas.

7.1 Is there life after tourism?

One important idea developed in Chapter 6 was that a holiday is *product*, which is assembled from resources in a destination region, *supplied*, *marketed* and *sold* by tourism companies and *consumed* by a purchaser at the point of production. As with all products, demand and hence profitability are dependent upon the attractiveness of the product, relative to the competition. Furthermore, because holidays are fashion products influenced by style, status and prestige, any destination faces the spectre of 'boom-and-bust' predicted by the product cycle process (Fig. 6.32): holidaymakers travel to new destinations to consume new products, and tourism companies focus on marketing and selling these new products. It is this process that has hit many traditional British 'bucket-and-spade' resorts as their products have become unfashionable (see Chapter 5).

This nightmare scenario sees tourism as an exploitative industry, that is, exploiting resources in one location before moving on to more attractive and profitable resource locations.

It is not surprising, therefore, that both existing and new tourist destinations are making increasing efforts to avoid the decline phase of the product cycle and to make their tourism industry sustainable (Fig. 7.1). This chapter examines the potentials and problems of the search for sustainability.

1 From Figure 7.1, what dimensions of tourism impact are the Balearics authorities attempting to change, and how are they doing it?

7.2 What do we mean by 'sustainability'?

Sustainability means 'meeting the needs of the present without compromising the ability of future generations to meet their own needs' (the Brundtland Report, World Commission on Environment and Development, 1987).

This definition makes it clear that the economic perspective of tourism outlined above in Section 7.1 is too narrow. Sustainable development must include consideration of people and the environment. From this broader perspective, sustainability consists of three dimensions, comparable with those identified for tourism impacts in Chapter 6 (p.135):

1 *Economic sustainability:* A dynamic, flexible system which encourages continued investment and sustains businesses and jobs over time.
2 *Socio-cultural sustainability:* Development which sustains and enhances the quality of life for families and communities over time.
3 *Environmental sustainability:* Development which conserves the character and quality of physical and ecological resources over time.

Because of the distinctive nature of tourism, we can add a fourth dimension:

4 *Experiential sustainability:* Forms of tourism development which sustain the quality of visitor experience and satisfaction over time (Fig. 7.2).

There is little doubt that, today, all components of the tourism system (tourists, destinations, the industry) accept the desirability of adopting strategies whose goal is sustainability rather than short-term exploitation (Fig. 7.3). This sounds fine, but key problems lie in the sheer scale, complexity and dynamism of the industry (Fig. 7.4). Each of the many forms of tourism has its distinctive resource demands, impacts (Fig. 7.5), and hence potential and problems associated with efforts to achieve sustainability across all dimensions. For instance, the 1992 Winter Olympics brought huge investment and economic development to parts of the French Alps, but caused severe environmental damage. Protected forests and rare wetlands were violated.

Figure 7.2 Poros, Greece. Maintaining visitor satisfaction is vital for economic sustainability, and requires the maintenance of both high-quality environments and the quality of life of local communities

Figure 7.3 Exploitation versus sustainability in tourism development

Figure 7.4 Attempting to match growth with sustainability

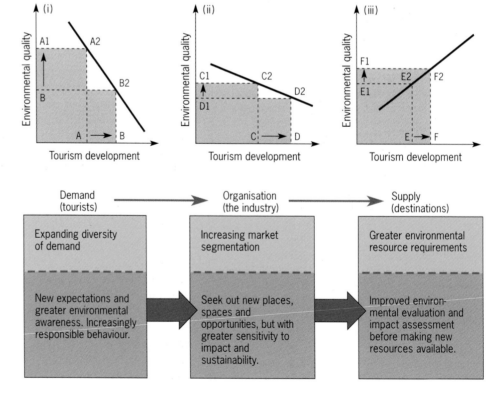

?

2 The graphs of Figure 7.3 illustrate possible relationships between tourism and the environment. In graph 1, at stage **a** of tourism development, environmental quality is measured as **a1**. As tourism develops further to stage **b**, environmental quality declines to **b1**. In this example, even a modest increase in tourism development causes significant negative environmental impacts (**a2–b2**). This form of tourism–environmental relationship is exploitative and non-sustainable (e.g. the deterioration of coral reef ecosystems around a number of Caribbean and Pacific islands as tourism has expanded).
a Describe the tourism–environment relationships illustrated in graphs 2 and 3.
b Which, if either, of these graphs illustrates a process of sustainable development? Explain your choice.
c What is the crucial difference between graphs 1 and 2?

3a Discuss briefly how you would construct similar sets of graphs to illustrate exploitative–sustainable scenarios for the economic and socio-cultural dimensions.
b Draw sets of such graphs.
c Add a brief description of the relationships shown on your graphs. (Think carefully of the options you have for selecting the pairs of variables you will use for your *x* and *y* axes, from the four possible: tourism development; economic change; socio-cultural change; environmental quality. A software package with a graphics facility will be helpful.)
4 Using the example of a Caribbean beach resort, discuss the relationships between experiential sustainability and the other three dimensions of sustainability.

5 With reference to Figure 7.6, describe the economic/ environmental impact changes for phases I–V.

One million cubic metres of earth were moved from mountain slopes for the various ski-runs, ski-jumps and infrastructure. Runoff and drainage regimes were disturbed. In one village, residents were issued with gas masks because of fears of toxic leaks of ammonia from a bobsleigh run. (Fig. 7.5.)

It is equally important to understand that relationships between the dimensions are likely to change over time. The model set out in Figure 7.6 employs economic and environmental variables. It uses the example of the Spanish resort of Torremolinos, but by using different timescales it also has wider application.

Figure 7.5 Eroded ski slopes at Chamonix, France, venue of the first Winter Olympics in 1924 and a popular ski resort

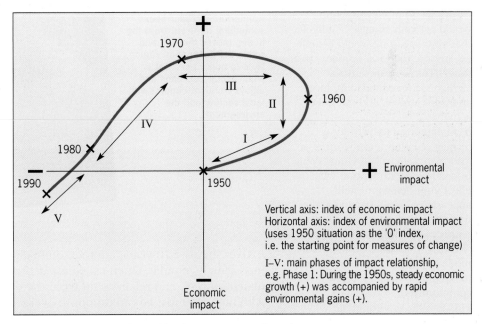

Figure 7.6 Changing relationships between economic and environmental impacts – the example of Torremolinos, Spain

7.3 The many faces of modern tourism

One of the outstanding features of modern tourism is its incredible diversity. In sheer volume, mass tourism remains dominated by what has been called *sunlust* tourism: holidays spent in resort enclaves (**enclave tourism**) with the central attractions of 'sun, sea, sand, sangría, sex' (Fig. 7.7). It is this form of tourism development which has been most criticised as being exploitative. However, if you scan travel agents' shelves, the Travel sections of newspapers, TV programmes and advertisements, and the growing number of Web sites, a wide range of products emerges. Furthermore, not all enclave mass tourism is beach-based (e.g. ski resorts, and cruise ships are a mobile form of resort).

Figure 7.7 Sunlust → enclave → concentrated → packaged tourism. The sunlust tourist seeks facilities and amenities that are better than at home. All aspects of the holiday are tightly organised by the tour operator – transport is from airport to airport to the resort enclave, where all the tourists's time is spent. There is little contact with the local society or environment, except the beach and sea. The tourist exists in an 'environmental bubble'

?

6 Assess sunlust and wanderlust holidays in terms of:

a Spending patterns: what you would spend money on; who would get your money; is it likely that your spending would benefit, i.e. sustain, the local economy over time? (Think of the various elements: accommodation, food and drink, travel, entertainment, activities.)

b Making contact with local people: on what terms (formal or informal); where you would come into contact; with whom; what effect your behaviour and appearance would have (e.g. the demonstration effect whereby young people in particular see 'wealthy' tourists as desirable role models). Would such contacts help to sustain or weaken local communities?

c Use of the environment: what resources you would use and in what way; what your impact would be upon the environment; in what ways your presence might make sustaining **environmental quality** more difficult.

d Place each of the types of holiday on one of the graphs in Figure 7.3.

7 Analyse *either* a TV advertisement *or* a Web site *or* a holiday brochure to illustrate what is meant by (a) market segmentation; (b) product differentiation; (c) niche marketing.

Figure 7.8 Wanderlust → touring → penetrative → dispersed → semi-independent travel. The wanderlust traveller seeks something different from the home, moves through and within the destination region, likes to make personal or small-group decisions and enjoys frequent contact with local society and the environment

Over the past 20 years, another, quite distinct form of tourism has become increasingly popular. Often called *wanderlust* tourism, this involves closer penetration of, and relationship with, the destination environment (Fig. 7.8). Although we must be careful not to overgeneralise, certain contrasts with enclave tourism are evident: we expect different experiences, we go to different places, our holidays are organised differently and our impacts upon the destination are different.

The increasing complexity and sophistication of both *demand* (what we expect from holidays) and *supply* (what is on offer) is illustrated by three important trends in the tourism industry:

1 *Market segmentation:* breaking down the market into an increasing number of specific segments, each with identifiable characteristics (e.g. young people, 18–30s, families with children, senior age groups, economic categories, activity interest groups, etc.).

2 *Product differentiation:* provision of a broadening range of holiday types and options, each tailored for specific market segments.

3 *Niche marketing:* promotion of the 'tailored' products through targeted marketing to specific market segments (see the North American ocean cruise case study in Chapter 6).

Figure 7.9 Concerns for sustainability from two tour operators, World Expeditions and Kuoni

7.4 Sustainability and alternative tourism

Sustainability is an idea central to the array of emerging forms of tourism generally grouped under the umbrella term of **alternative tourism**, which means alternatives to existing mass tourism. Terms such as 'green tourism', 'nature tourism', 'ecotourism', 'responsible tourism', 'agro-tourism', 'rural tourism', 'adventure tourism' are increasingly common. We see the signs in the growing number of specialist tour operators who organise what are marketed as environmentally sensitive trips to distant and exotic locations. These types of tourism attempt to achieve a better balance between conservation values and development values. Increased sensitivity is being shown, too, within the mainstream industry, although as the scale of tourism increases so it becomes more difficult to limit impacts and to sustain resources over time.

Four main forces help to explain this rapid expansion for alternative tourism:

1 Visitor dissatisfaction with certain forms of standardised mass tourism.

2 The growth of global environmental awareness and the conservation movement.

3 The realisation by destination populations and governments of the dangers arising from the negative impacts of tourism.

4 The increased acceptance by tour operators of changing demands, attitudes and the need for greater environmental awareness (Fig. 7.9).

Principles of sustainable tourism
As the examples and case studies in this chapter show, six principles underlie policies for sustainable tourism:

1 Planning and control of the spatial distribution and character of tourism developments – where they will be located and what they will look like (e.g. using local architectural styles and materials for hotel design).

KUONI 1993

FRIENDS OF CONSERVATION

Kenya is home to some of the most spectacular game parks in the world – it is here that many of our client's experience the thrill of seeing, at first hand, wildlife roaming free.
But if the parks and the wildlife they support are to survive, the Kenya Wildlife Service needs help. The Game Parks and Reserves of Kenya are under intensive pressure from a rapidly increasing human population and unless they can be proven to be worth saving, they will be forced to yield to this pressure. We believe that tourism can help stop this disaster from happening.

In conjunction with the registered UK charity **Friends of Conservation**, Kuoni supports the joint projects of Friends of Conservation and the Kenya Wildlife Service, under the personal management of Dr Richard Leakey. A donation of £2 on behalf of every passenger travelling on safari with us to Kenya will be our 1993 contribution to the Kenya Wildlife Service. This enables us to support the following projects:

* Wildlife Protection Unit. This unit's tasks include anti-poaching activities, rescuing injured animals, monitoring of tourist vehicles relative to animal harrassment and care of wildlife.
* Rhino Translocation and Wildlife Veterinarian Programme – support for veterinary expertise and the translocation of endangered rhinos into protected sactuaries.
* Community Conservation and Educational Projects – support for local conservation groups and the production of educational material for use in schools.

Should you wish to make an additional contribution to the Kenya Wildlife Service, more information is available from:

**Friends of Conservation
Sloane Square House
Holbein Place
London SW1W 8NS
Telephone: 071 730 7904
Registered Charity No: 328176
(Patron: HRH The Prince of Wales)**

... Thank you for your help in supporting Kenya's Wildlife.

8 For each of the six principles for sustainable tourism listed on pp.141–2, give one example illustrating why adherence to the principles becomes more difficult as the scale of tourism increases. (You may find it helpful to complete this exercise as a group activity.)

2 Surveys of resource evaluation and impact assessment before development takes place (e.g. study of key nesting and breeding sites of seabird populations before selecting the location of marinas).

3 Integration of tourism into other aspects of regional planning (e.g. locating tourism developments to fit in with plans for regional transport infrastructure).

4 Continued involvement and control by local and regional communities (e.g. finding ways to encourage and assist local people to invest in and run tourism businesses).

5 Identification of the type of tourism appropriate to the resources and the environment (e.g. low-density, low-impact tourism wherever possible in protected areas such as National Parks).

6 Establishment and maintenance of a **carrying capacity** that balances conservation and development values (e.g. determining how much environmental modification is acceptable in the development of a ski resort, and hence the size and character of that resort).

Adherence to these principles becomes more difficult as the scale of tourism increases.

7.5 Approaches in the search for sustainability

Tourism planners believe that, for many destination regions, sustainability may not be achievable if it relies on alternative tourism alone. Thus, despite the well-known problems caused by mass tourism, the best solution may be an integrated combination of both mass tourism and alternative tourism (Fig. 7.10). Genuine alternative projects and businesses are small to medium in size and so may have social and environmental advantages. However, they may not bring in sufficient money or create enough jobs to help a country to satisfy its development needs (e.g. investment in expensive infrastructure). Mass tourism, therefore, can be used as a vehicle for income and job generation, providing, of course, that 'leakage' can be minimised (see Chapter 6, pp.126–7), and that projects are carefully planned and controlled.

Impacts from mass tourism are inevitably severe, but can be concentrated in relatively small areas. For instance, in Barbados, resorts and their associated infrastructure are concentrated along the west coast, partly because the east coast seas can be very rough and dangerous, but also because they minimise

Figure 7.10 A model for integrated tourism development

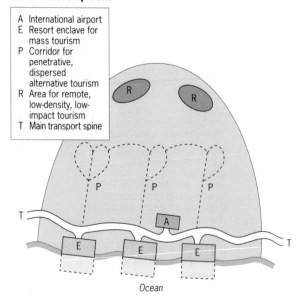

A International airport
E Resort enclave for mass tourism
P Corridor for penetrative, dispersed alternative tourism
R Area for remote, low-density, low-impact tourism
T Main transport spine

Ocean

Some generalised characteristics

Mass tourism	Alternative tourism
• Concentration in planned, controlled enclaves	• Dispersion to a variety of locations
• High level of environmental modification and land-use change	• Low to moderate visitor densities
• Large-scale projects	• Low levels of environmental and land-use change
• Fundamental restructuring of the local economy, strong dependency on tourism	• Small-scale projects
• Severe and rapid social and cultural change	• Strengthening of the local economy by adding tourism while retaining traditional activities
• Capital-intensive – major investment requirements in infrastructure	• Gradual social and cultural change
• Concentrates economic benefits	• Relatively low levels of capital requirements; infrastructure upgrading improves quality of life
• Labour-intensive – creates more jobs	• Disperses economic benefits
	• Creates jobs but does not dominate

a Tour patterns

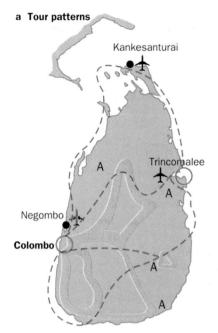

b Tourist facilities : general plan

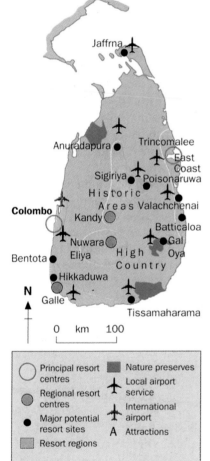

Figure 7.11 Regional planning for tourism in Sri Lanka (*Source:* Baud-Bovy and Lawson, 1977)

Figure 7.12 The urban growth of Torremolinos, Spain (*Source: Tourism Management*, August 1993)

impacts upon the rest of the island. We must remember, too, that sustainable development involves diversifying industry and broadening the economic base. Thus, whatever balance of mass and alternative tourism a country chooses, there must not be overdependence upon this one industrial sector.

Integrated regional planning
Since the mid-1970s, Sri Lanka has based its tourism development upon the plan shown in Figure 7.11. Sri Lanka is a tropical island of over 64 000 sq.km, with a core of forested mountains in the south and lower country towards the north of the island. The 1997 population was 18 million, and the country has a long and rich cultural history. During the 1980s, tourism grew steadily to reach 300 000 arrivals by 1990. Since then, political unrest has interrupted growth (e.g. killing of tourists during 1997).

The tourism plan identifies three key resource areas, each with a distinctive potential: coasts with beaches, forested hill country and areas of historic cultural interest. These attractive resources are made available in two ways: first, through enclave tourism based on resorts accessible to infrastructure, and cultural and natural attractions (e.g. the main international airport at Colombo (the capital) has links to the south coast resorts). Second, the three resource areas and resort enclaves are connected by corridors along which access and facilities are concentrated. This 'cores-and-corridors' approach provides a range of tourism experiences for a number of market segments, while protecting other parts of the island from tourism impacts.

Modern integrated resorts
In the rush to benefit from the explosive growth of mass tourism from the 1960s onwards, many resorts expanded with little planning or development control. Well-known examples include Torremolinos on Spain's Costa del Sól

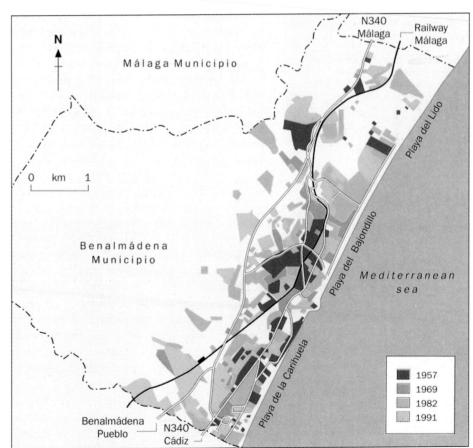

Figure 7.13 An inadequate road system (the N340) in Málaga, Spain. The transport infrastructure has not kept pace with the tourism growth along the Costa del Sol

(Fig. 7.12). Criticisms focus on the piecemeal growth, the uncontrolled scale, the inadequate infrastructure (Fig. 7.13) and poor environmental standards. In contrast to such uncontrolled disasters, six planned resorts, called *unités touristiques*, have been built along the Languedoc–Roussillon coast of southern France, with a capacity of 350 000 visitors (Fig. 7.14). They are part of France's approach to regional planning, in this case aimed at reviving a relatively undeveloped region (Languedoc–Rousillion) and taking pressure off the Provence coast to the east.

Port Leucate–Barcarès is one of six *unités* (Fig. 7.14). The plan shows clearly that, although the environmental impact is, inevitably, extreme, this type of modern resort is very different from the fragmented development of Torremolinos or the traditional 'bucket-and-spade' resort (see Chapter 5). As ever, the aim is to maximise access to the key attractive resources of the beach and the sea. However, the accommodation, the range of facilities and above all the transport network are distinctive. The map shows clearly how the resort is built around the spinal road that runs the length of the sand spit. The environment of this spit is totally transformed, and the impact is highly concentrated. None the less, the extensive area required, the increasing quality and range of facilities and attractions demanded by such planned, integrated resorts, need huge capital investments. MEDCs such as France can raise this capital, but LEDCs must often rely on foreign capital.

Tourism and natural environments

Many forms of alternative tourism require access to and use of environments of outstanding natural quality (e.g. scuba diving around coral reefs; climbing in the Andes; wilderness camping in Alaska; wildlife-watching in Antarctica). As long as such destinations remained at the outer edge of the pleasure periphery, visited by a small number of 'adventurers', few problems arose. Today, however, there are few places on earth where specialist tour operators and expedition outfitters do not offer to take us (e.g. for £5000 or more you can be guided to the summit of Mount Everest). Advances in technology increase our ability to penetrate remote and difficult places (e.g. specialist vehicles; lightweight equipment, clothing and food; communication devices such as mobile phones and Geographical Positioning Systems (GPSs)).

The outcome is that an increasingly large and broad market segment is being attracted into regions once protected by remoteness and inaccessibility (Fig. 7.15). Environments vary in their fragility and ability to withstand visitor impacts, but there is increasing concern over the environmental impacts. There is increasing questioning, too, of *our right to be there*: a debate about the *ethics of*

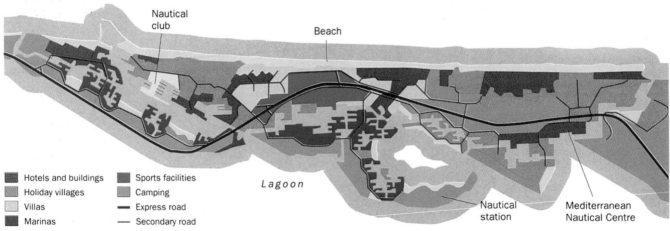

Figure 7.14 Tourism planning in southern France. The six unités touristiques, with the resort of Port Leucate–Barcarès in detail (*Source*: Baude-Bovy and Lawson, 1977)

?

9 Using the model of Figure 7.10, discuss:
a the advantages and limitations of alternative tourism;
b the potential of the model as a basis for the development of sustainable tourism;
c the extent to which the model illustrates the concepts of concentration and dispersion.

10 Using the examples of Torremolinos and Port Leucate-Barcarès, analyse the key differences between unplanned and planned integrated resorts in terms of the four dimensions of sustainability (see p.138)

Figure 7.16 Grand Canyon National Park, USA. This spectacular canyon attracts more than 3 million visitors a year from all over the world

It is the height of summer in the immense arid region of Central Australia. A smart four-wheel drive (4WD) vehicle has stopped. Inside is a white Australian family. With the engine still running the air conditioner keeps the temperature pleasant, almost cool. The man switches on the radio and tunes directly into a cricket Test Match from Barbados. Meanwhile, the woman is using a state-of-the-art electronic navigational device incorporating a global positioning system to guide her family to the area where they have planned to set up camp. In the back seat, the son is playing a game on the powerbook personal computer which his father has bought along to finish off some work while on their ecotour adventure. Their daughter fiddles with the forty-channel citizen-band radio, trying to pick up any messages. Elderly parents refresh themselves with iced water from the latest thermoelectric coolers, before using the digital-networked mobile phone to ring their neighbours, via satellite, back in Sydney.

Figure 7.15 Wilderness, anyone? This is a scenario written in 1996 by an Australian environmentalist. His purpose was to raise the alarm about threats to the wilderness

tourism and whether there should be places on planet earth which should remain natural, 'wild' and the home of non-human species free from human interference (see Section 7.7, p.153). This has generated a variety of policy and management responses.

The Protected Area approach

One of the most widely used methods of environmental conservation is designation as a *Protected Area* (e.g. National Park, National Wildlife Refuge, World Heritage Site, Nature Reserve, World Biosphere Reserve, National Seashore, etc.). Most of these designated areas have the dual purpose of conservation and providing for visitor enjoyment. For example, in the USA, the 1916 National Parks Act states that National Parks are:

> *To conserve the scenery and natural and historic objects and the wildlife therein and to provide for the enjoyment of the same in such manner and by such means as will leave them unimpaired for the enjoyment of future generations.*

There are National Parks in almost every country. They include some of the world's most spectacular landscapes, and it is not surprising that they have become major tourist attractions (Fig. 7.16). The great parks of North America such as Banff/Jasper in Canada and Grand Canyon, Yellowstone and Yosemite in the USA, today each attract 3–6 million visitors a year, over 80 per cent in the May–September period. Although these figures are lower than the much smaller Lake District and Peak District parks in the UK (see Chapter 4), they create serious management problems for the National Parks Service (NPS), the government agency which manages the parks.

In Denali National Park and Preserve, Alaska (Fig. 7.19), the NPS bases its management plan on accessibility control. Remember that in this example, as in many of the North American parks, (a) the area has few inhabitants and (b) the government owns the land and water, making resource management straightforward. The centrepiece of Denali (2.43 million hectares) is Mount McKinley, at 6194 metres the highest peak in North America. 'The park exemplifies Alaska's character as one of the world's last great frontiers for wilderness adventure' (Park Handbook). The central unit of this huge area is the Denali Wilderness (Fig. 7.19) and, although it contains the park headquarters, the visitor centre, a hotel, the only campsites and the only road, it is primarily a wildlife refuge (e.g. bears, caribou).

Vehicles which bring the 110 000 visitors a year must be left at the park entrance unless the group has a special camping permit. Shuttle buses take visitors on a four-hour trip along the gravel road, 100km to Eielson Visitor Center (Fig. 7.17). Tourists can get off and pick up the buses at any point, but

Figure 7.17 The Eielson Visitor Center, looking south towards the Alaska Range

Figure 7.18 The variety of visitor types at the Eielson Visitor Center

Figure 7.19 Location and features of the Denali National Park Wilderness, Alaska, USA

there are no marked trails across the tundra. From Eielson, reached by 65 000 visitors a year, there are magnificent views to Mount McKinley. Thus, the 'look-snap-and-go' tourists experience 'the wilderness' within a day, while serious walkers and climbers can disperse for weeks for *their* perceived 'wilderness experience'(Fig. 7.18). Thus, the carrying capacity of the fragile environment is firmly controlled by restricted access and remoteness. Because of the strict development control within the park, commercial development is growing rapidly close to the park entrance. Such *gateway settlements* are increasingly common and, where planning regulations are weak, can be of low quality.

Alaska illustrates well the difficulties of sustaining quality of visitor experience and environmental resources. The combination of transport technology, the popularity of the wilderness experience and accessibility from the huge, affluent markets of North America and Japan bring ever more

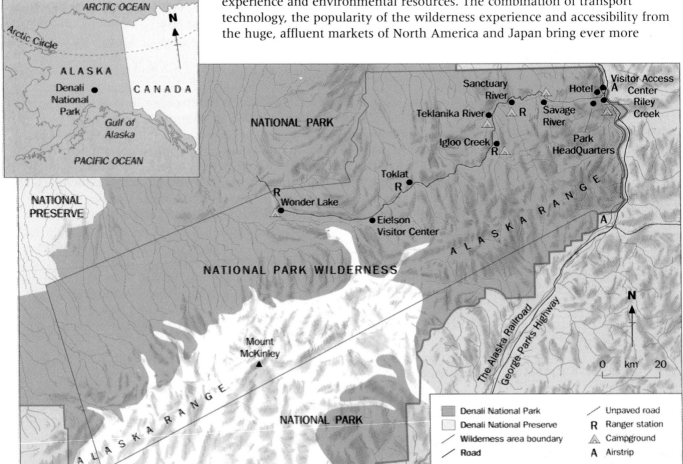

?

11a Define what we mean by 'remoteness'.

b Why is it increasingly difficult for managers of protected areas such as National Parks to retain 'remoteness'?

c Give two reasons why 'remoteness' is a valuable concept in National Park management.

12a Outline the methods used by managers of Denali National Park, Alaska, to provide high-quality experiences for a wide variety of visitor types.

b What problems do they face as numbers increase?

Figure 7.20 The zoning solution: a park superintendent explains

Our problem is this. On the one hand, we have to conserve the quality of the park environment. On the other hand, we have more and more tourists who want to enjoy the park in all sorts of ways. Our solution has been to match the environmental setting with the recreational needs of our visitors. Take two examples. First there is what we call the 'look-snap-and-go' or 'windscreen' tourist. He or she wants to drive through the park in one or two days, enjoying the scenery, stopping at viewpoints to take pictures, visit shops, cafés and restrooms [toilets]. Then there is the 'wilderness lover' who comes to walk and camp deep in the park for several days or more, to get away from people, noise and so on. If they are to go away happy, each needs quite a different environmental setting. What we try to do is to do this while fulfilling our role of conservation. We need to provide a 'spectrum of recreation opportunity' – opportunities for people to enjoy themselves in many different ways. This means dividing the park up into a set of zones. Each has a different balance between conservation, environmental modification and types of acceptable recreational activities. We set a recreational carrying capacity for each zone.

tourists and, equally important, a wider variety of visitor types with differing needs. These trends place increasing stress upon the fragile forests, tundra, wildlife, glaciers and rivers, as well as threatening the quality of visitor experience.

A model for National Park management
Zoning systems vary, but the model in Figure 7.21 sums up the common features. The model shows a park divided into two main

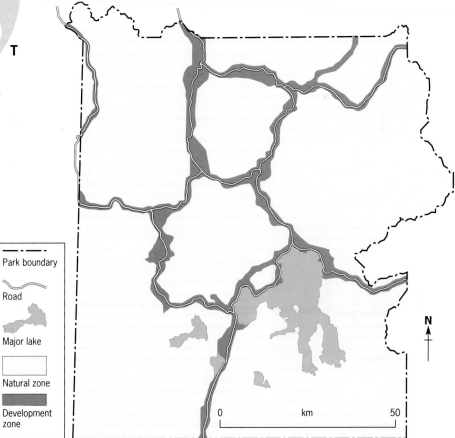

----- Surfaced road
ⓒ Campground
°o°o°o° Trail
Ⓢ Services
T Wilderness trailhead
Ⓥ Visitor centre
HQ Park Headquarters administration

----- Developed experience corridor or frontcountry

Backcountry/wilderness

* Interpreted attraction; car park; footpath, etc.
Ⓖ Gateway settlement
↗↙ Two-way regional relationships

Figure 7.21 US National Parks: a general model for national park management

----- Park boundary
Road
Major lake
Natural zone
Development zone

Figure 7.22 A map of Yellowstone National Park

0   km   50

N

Figure 7.23 Managing the front-country:
a Walkways built to give high-density visitor access at Old Faithful geyser basin, Yellowstone National Park, USA
b 'Windscreen' tourists experience close contact with an 'icon' species – the buffalo in Yellowstone National Park. Park rangers manage the resulting traffic jams!
c Shuttle buses in Yosemite National Park, USA. Environmental modification is undertaken to increase visitor-carrying capacity

zones: a development corridor or *frontcountry* and the wilderness or *backcountry*. In most parks the wilderness zone covers at least 90 per cent of the total area (Fig. 7.22). The other components of the model are built upon this framework.

Frontcountry

This is a zone of visitor concentration, managed to accept mass tourism. The high carrying capacity is achieved by significant modifications to the natural environment (e.g. surfaced roads, built facilities). For this reason, it is known to park managers as 'the sacrifice zone' – naturalness is sacrificed in order to protect the rest of the park. As the model shows, facilities and recreational opportunities for the 'look-snap-and-go' tourist are threaded along this development corridor (Fig. 7.23).

Backcountry

This zone is managed as a wilderness, where naturalness is conserved. Recreational opportunities are restricted to self-reliant (walk-in; ski-in), low-density, low-impact activities (Fig. 7.24). Low carrying capacities are set, controlled by entry permits and trailheads ('T' on the model). Trailheads are entry points to the wilderness; when a visitor purchases a backcountry permit from a visitor centre, each trailhead is allocated a certain number of permits at any one time. In Yosemite National Park the at-one-time capacity for the wilderness zone is set at less than 2000, distributed among 104 trailheads. In this way, visitors are dispersed at acceptably low densities around the park. Bookings for the peak season may have to be made a year in advance.

The backcountry plays a vital role in the policy of conserving the ecosystem of a park and in the survival of threatened species (e.g. bears and wolves). Thus it is important that where the development corridor divides the wilderness, *faunal pathways* should be included, i.e. places where the corridor is narrow enough for wildlife to cross.

Gateway settlements

Located along the main approach roads to a park, gateway settlements have several valuable roles. First, they supply tourists with a range of services (e.g. accommodation, shopping, food and drink, entertainment, vehicle servicing). Second, they take development pressures off a park. Third, they provide income and jobs in often remote areas. To allow such developments within a park would be contrary to park policies. Unfortunately, many are developing as long, ugly commercial strips (e.g. West Yellowstone). Some parks are using the gateway settlement concept to reduce existing development and congestion within the park. For example, the main visitor honeypot in Yosemite National Park is the Yosemite Valley, which is currently closed to further traffic on several weekends each summer because of congestion. The new park plan

Figure 7.24 A wilderness trailhead and runner in Saguaro National Monument, Arizona, USA

13 Define what is meant by (one sentence for each):
a zoning;
b development corridor;
c wilderness;
d gateway settlement.

14 Summarise the positive and negative impacts of (i) visitor concentration and (ii) visitor dispersion.

15 Explain how the management strategy set out in the model (Fig. 7.21) helps managers to 'match the environmental setting with the recreational needs of our visitors' (Fig. 7.20).

16 Group discussion: How would the following tourists enjoy a four-day holiday in and around a National Park managed according to the model in Figure 7.21?
a A family with two teenage children on a touring holiday with their car.
b Three young backpackers on a camping holiday.
(Think of resources and facilities; activities they would enjoy; parts of the park they would penetrate; where they would stay; how the park zoning policy would influence the quality of their holiday.)

17 What options do park managers have when (i) visitor numbers and (ii) range of desired activities continued to increase. (Think about the dimensions of sustainability (p.138) and the way the zoning model works.)

proposes to reduce accommodation capacity (lodges and campsites) and access by private vehicles in the valley. At El Portal, the gateway settlement at the main entrance to the park, additional accommodation, park maintenance buildings and facilities for a park-and-ride scheme will be built.

Regional relationships

A park is not an isolated island, but a vital component in an economic, social and ecological region. As indicated by gateway settlements, a popular park is an important generator of economic activity for the surrounding region (e.g. the tourism industry associated with Yellowstone National Park is the third largest source of income for Wyoming). It must be remembered, too, that a park is a high-quality recreational resource for people who live in the surrounding region. Furthermore, a park boundary is administrative, not ecological. For example, North American bison (buffalo) are protected inside Yellowstone. When they wander outside the park in search of food they may be shot by ranchers, who believe that they carry disease to cattle. Conversely, one aim of the park managers is to retain or restore the ecosystem to as near a natural condition as possible. This is made more difficult as exotic (non-native) flora and fauna enter the park from surrounding farmlands and settlements. As a result, ecological management for Yellowstone Park is seen as part of a sub-regional plan known as the Greater Yellowstone Ecosystem.

Native claims

In many countries, National Parks include the traditional homelands of Native peoples. In some cases such peoples have been forced to move outside a park (e.g. the Masai in Kenya). Elsewhere, until recently, they were given few rights and little role within the parks. Today this is changing. Native peoples are increasingly re-establishing their rights to traditional resource uses in parks and are becoming directly involved in management (e.g. the visitor centre and ranger service in the Canyon de Chelley National Monument, Arizona, are run by the local peoples). For the sake of simplicity, this 'Native Claims' element has not been included in the model, but does influence conservation and tourism policies within many parks (see the Kakadu National Park case study, p.155).

7.6 The ecotourism option

Ecotourism and its close relative nature tourism are among the most popular forms of alternative tourism: purposeful travel to natural areas to understand the cultural and natural history of the environment, taking care not to alter the environment, while providing economic opportunities that encourage local communities to conserve natural resources.

Ecotourism is claimed to be 'environmentally friendly' and to have 'green credentials'. The tourist experience is more than enjoyment; it includes *understanding* (Fig. 7.25) and *education* (Fig. 7.26). Essential attractive resources are natural and semi-natural ecosystems (e.g. rainforests and high-profile species), especially when they are threatened with extinction (e.g. the mountain gorillas of Rwanda, Central Africa). Clearly, sustainability is crucial in this type of tourism – no gorillas, no tourists!

'Wildlife stays where wildlife pays'

A major problem is that many of these attractive ecosystems and species are found in areas where the local population, i.e. the resource owners, do not

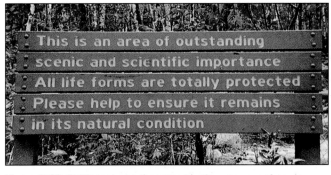

This is an area of outstanding
scenic and scientific importance
All life forms are totally protected
Please help to ensure it remains
in its natural condition

Figure 7.25 Putting across the conservation message in Mossman Gorge National Park, Queensland

Figure 7.26 Ecotourism – a guided walk in the Mt Kinabalu National Park, Sabah, Malaysia

necessarily see the value of conservation, or the potential for tourist income. For example, in Rwanda, population pressures and intertribal conflicts are slowly destroying the mountain forest habitat upon which the mountain gorillas depend.

There is, therefore, a close two-way relationship between conservation and ecotourism. We can see an excellent example at work in the small Central American country of Belize. As population has grown, so communities have been removing rainforest to extend their crop and grazing land. This has reduced the habitat of a number of species, including Howler monkeys. In one area the villagers, with the encouragement and support funding of the WWF (World Wide Fund for Nature), have been persuaded to set up a wildlife reserve for Howler monkeys (locally called 'baboons') known as the Community Baboon Sanctuary (Fig. 7.27). This means that corridors of rainforest bordering streams are left to provide sufficient habitat to support colonies of the monkeys. The local people are benefiting economically from this conservation by running an ecotourism project. They lead guided walks through the forest, focusing on the Howler monkeys, and provide simple accommodation in family homes. By 1997 the project, which had begun with one village in 1985, involved eight villages, attracted 6000 visitors, and the Howler monkey population had doubled to 1800 animals. The villagers gain extra income and the tourism supports some part-time jobs.

The crucial principle is the involvement of the local people as stewards of their precious resources – they must see that conservation is worth their while, and that they can control the tourism development themselves. This idea of local control, responsible stewardship and economic benefit is gaining popularity and acceptance. For example, there is increasing evidence that the safari tourism industry of East and Central Africa, especially as organised in Kenya, has been exploitative rather than sustainable (e.g. environmental degradation, displacement of local peoples, high leakage). Today, community-based schemes such as Zimbabwe's CAMPFIRE Programme have economic, social and environmental sustainability as their primary goal (see case study opposite).

Figure 7.27 The visitor centre at the Community Baboon Sanctuary, Belize. The project manager talks to visitors, while some of the local guides look on, at the end of a guided walk

Is it ecotourism or 'ego-tourism'?

The Belize and Zimbabwe examples illustrate two key problems that alternative tourism faces: carrying capacity and numbers. The type of tourist who seeks an 'authentic' experience (e.g. 'the real Spain') tends to be crowding-sensitive and expects small numbers, not mass tourism (Fig. 7.26). Furthermore, the attractive resources themselves are often fragile and sensitive to impacts (e.g. coral reefs), and have a low carrying capacity. Similar characteristics apply to many traditional cultures. The most obvious way to control visitor numbers and impacts, and so sustain the quality of both the resource and the experience, is through *remoteness* and *inaccessibility*. This approach uses the time–cost–distance factor as the control mechanism – you have to travel a long way and it is expensive in terms of time and money. Yet the supply of ecotourism 'products' may not require large capital investments (Fig. 7.28).

Such features assist the goal of sustainability but open ecotourism to criticisms of élitism: high-cost pleasure for a privileged few. This is, of course, a claim sometimes made about all tourism, that it is founded on relatively rich people enjoying themselves at the expense of poorer people. In many types of alternative tourism it can appear in an extreme form.

There is the further criticism that international companies use the 'eco' label as a marketing ploy rather than as an indication of a genuine policy of 'responsible tourism' and sustainability (Figs 7.31, 7.32).

Figure 7.28 Much ecotourism and adventure tourism is organised by small, specialist companies, often based in regional towns from which the trips start

The CAMPFIRE Programme, Zimbabwe

The issue: Zimbabwe is an LEDC with low per capita income: two-thirds of its 11 million people live in rural areas and are largely dependent upon subsistence agriculture. Population growth is 2.5 per cent a year and land pressures are growing, especially on the 40 per cent of the country which is classed as Communal Lands, i.e. owned by the nation and home to the majority of the rural population (Fig. 7.30). (Most other land is under individual ownership by white commercial farmers.)

The needs: To broaden the base of the rural economy; to provide jobs and income; to conserve the environment; to bring in foreign currency.

Available natural resources: Tropical savannah landscapes and associated wildlife.

Potential: Safari tourism based upon continued access to quality environmental resources.

Problem: As rural population expands, people and wildlife compete for the same resources; as more land is cleared and settled, so there is progressive loss of wildlife habitats. Yet safari tourism depends upon the continued availability of wildlife.

Policy responses:

Model A: *The Kenyan 'top-down' approach*
National Parks and Reserves are set up by the government to protect the natural environment and wildlife, and become the destinations for safari tourism. Village communities are moved from their traditional lands and resettled on Communal Lands outside the parks. This increases existing land pressures. At national level, valuable foreign currency is earned and businesses supported. However, local communities have little say in park management decisions and see few benefits from tourism (e.g. most tourist accommodation is owned and run by non-local companies).

Model B: *The 'bottom-up' approach*
In 1988 the government introduced the CAMPFIRE

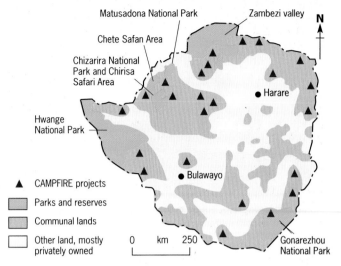

Figure 7.30 Land categories in Zimbabwe

- ▲ CAMPFIRE projects
- Parks and reserves
- Communal lands
- Other land, mostly privately owned

Programme (Communal Areas Management Programme for Indigenous Resources). Development projects are drawn up and run by committees made up of representatives from a group of villages, plus government officers and advisers to assist with expert advice on development options for their Communal Lands. By 1997 there were 24 CAMPFIRE projects working, with photographic and hunting tourism the main source of income and jobs. Local members of a committee are advised by park and wildlife officials about conservation techniques, the wildlife-carrying capacity of local ecosystems and hence how many game animals may be hunted by tourists. Tour operators negotiate with the committee about numbers of tour parties, financial arrangements and the price of hunting permits. The amount of accommodation provided by local communities varies widely. Profits from the tourism are distributed to village leaders who then discuss with their people how the money will be spent (e.g. buying agricultural equipment, introducing cash crops or animals, building schools or clinics (Fig. 7.29)).

?

18 Why has the Zimbabwe government identified tourism as an option for development, and what is its purpose?

19 Define what is meant by 'top-down' and 'bottom-up' models of development, and outline how they relate to the principles of alternative tourism. (In your answer, bear in mind the concepts of exploitation and sustainability.)

20 Write a brief report on how the CAMPFIRE Programme and the Community Baboon Sanctuary Project (Belize) illustrate the principles upon which sustainable tourism should be based.

Figure 7.29 Children outside their community hall, built with profits from the CAMPFIRE scheme which grants money made from photographic and hunting tourism to local communities

Figure 7.31 This 'eco lodge' in Belize is owned by a US company in Texas. It accommodates 100 guests in considerable comfort (air-conditioning, hot water etc.), uses diesel power, most of the food and drink is imported; it creates over 100 jobs, but senior managers are not Belizean (as at 1996). Is it 'ecotourism'?

Figure 7.32 Rondavel accommodation at the upmarket Maruba Lodge eco-resort. These may look authentic – but thatched rondavels are not found in traditional Belizean villages!

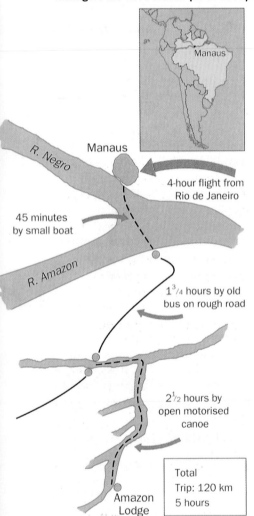

Figure 7.33 Location and route to Amazon Lodge

Figure 7.34 Amazon Lodge: this small, floating lodge is made of local materials, sleeps 25 guests and employs 14 local people

An ecotourism example from Brazil

The tropical rainforests of Amazonia and the communities that live there are attractive resources for ecotourists. The main starting point for such trips is the regional capital of Manaus (Fig. 7.33), allowing tour operators to offer easy excursions from the comfort of city hotels. However, tourists seeking a closer association with 'the jungle' and its inhabitants are catered for at a number of more distant lodges.

One such operation is Amazon Lodge (Fig. 7.34), where the tour operator (based in Manaus) and lodge owners (Portuguese) sustain the experience and the environment by (a) restricting the lodge capacity to 25 guests, (b) keeping the lodge 'simple' (e.g. no air-conditioning or hot water), and (c) making the five-hour journey from Manaus adventurous rather than comfortable – for instance, water surfaces are wide enough to use seaplanes, which would reduce the journey to 30 minutes. The lodge is run on ecological principles (e.g. solar power is used, all waste is taken away in containers, local food is used wherever possible). Trips are made by small boats using low-emission outboard motors and to a number of different locations to reduce impacts. Tourists are taken to visit local families, but no one family is visited regularly, which minimises intrusion while providing a small income (Fig. 7.35).

Amazon Lodge has been operating since 1979, and its programme seems to be sustainable on two counts: in terms of the destination resources and the

Figure 7.35 A *caboclo* (settler) family preparing their staple food, manioc flour. Groups of visitors never number more than ten and are brought infrequently. They stay for up to one hour. Preparing manioc is not a 'staged event', but part of the family's day-to-day life

?

21 Why is it claimed that eco-tourism is 'élitist' and sometimes known as 'ego-tourism'?

22 The type of tourism offered by Amazon Lodge is becoming more popular. Assess the potential economic, social and environmental impacts of doubling the size of the lodge and upgrading the facilities. (Use this exercise to revise your understandings gained in this chapter, especially those concerning the relationships between scale, type of tourist and sustainability.)

quality of experience for the tourist. None the less, in order to survive it must make a profit for its Portuguese owners, and it is élitist.

7.7 The ethics of tourism

Asking key questions

The big question arising from the global explosion of tourism is not '*Can* we get there?' but '*Should* we be there?' Put simply – 'Do we have a *right* to visit where and when we wish?' There is, too, the related issue of our expectations and behaviour when we travel as tourists. Do we and the tourism industry have *responsibilities* and *obligations* as well as rights? These concerns are central to the debate about sustainability and the development of 'responsible tourism'. Examples from the three dimensions of tourism impact (p.135) illustrate the issues.

Economic: Should large international tour operators be able to use their economic power of renting blocks of hotel rooms through the summer to squeeze rental prices so low that they threaten the survival of family businesses? (Fig. 7.36).

Social: We have paid for our holiday and the destination has accepted our money. So – do we have the right to behave as we wish? (Fig. 7.37).

Figure 7.36 This hotel (100 rooms) on the Greek island of Poros was built and is owned by a local family. They would like the block booking contract from an international tour operator, but cannot make an acceptable profit at the rates offered. The family knows that the tour operator can take its trade elsewhere (*below left*)

Figure 7.37 In some societies, scanty clothing, physical contact and noisy behaviour in public offend local customs and religious belief (*right*)

Figure 7.38 Macquarie Island, sub-Antarctica: a great experience for the tourists – but what about the wildlife?

Environmental: Do we have the right to intrude on the lives of wildlife at will? (Fig. 7.38).

Seeking answers

Economic forces will always drive tourism: tourism businesses aim to make profits and tourists want value for money. None the less, there are increasing signs in all components of the tourism system of a shift towards a more ethical, sensitive position (Fig. 7.9). Laws are the most powerful tool (e.g. planning, health and environmental legislation), but *guidelines* and *codes of conduct* are widely used (Figs 7.39, 7.40). They are well intentioned, but are permissive and open to abuse or neglect. They rely on public opinion, acceptance and pressure by tourists, tourism businesses and destination populations if they are to succeed. Owners of resources attractive to tourism must also consider their responsibilities as well as their rights, as the example of Kakadu National Park, Australia, shows (see opposite).

- Book with a qualified tour or ground operator.

- Ask the guide's qualifications.

- Don't book into fragile areas during prime courtship and mating seasons or in the first weeks of rearing young. If you don't know when this is, ask the tour operator.

- Refuse to enter a protected environment with more than 15 people in your group. Recommend splitting the group or discuss alternatives.

- Stay on marked trails, no matter what others say.

- Report anyone taking biological specimens.

- Don't smoke in canopied forest or near wildlife.

- Whisper or communicate with hands when near wildlife – don't talk loudly.

- Don't use flash in an enclosed forest environment, especially if the subject is rare or endangered.

- Don't throw or drop anything beside trails, even biodegradable materials.

- Don't play radios or electronic devices that make foreign sounds in protected areas.

- Don't enter a private or public protected zone without the permission of the guard on duty or in the company of a licensed qualified guide.

- Keep off anything that might resemble a field research project in a park or reserve. This might include a net, box, screen enclosure, cloth cover, etc.

- Don't purchase orchids, artifacts or biological specimens.

- Don't drink water from an open source.

Figure 7.39 A visitor code for Costa Rica

By following these simple guidelines, you can help preserve the unique environment and ancient cultures of the Himalayas

Protect the natural environment

- Limit deforestation – make no open fires and discourage others from doing so on your behalf. Where water is heated by scarce firewood, use as little as possible. When possible choose accommodation that uses kerosene or fuel-efficient wood stoves.
- Remove litter, burn or bury paper and carry out all non-degradable litter. Graffiti are permanent examples of environmental pollution.
- Keep local water clean and avoid using pollutants such as detergents in streams or springs. If no toilet facilities are available, make sure you are at least 30 metres away from water sources, and bury or cover wastes.
- Plants should be left to flourish in their natural environment – taking cuttings, seeds and roots is illegal in many parts of the Himalaya.
- Help your guides and porters to follow conservation measures.

The Himalayas may change you – please do not change them

As a guest, respect local traditions, protect local cultures, maintain local pride

- When taking photographs, respect privacy – ask permission and use restraint.
- Respect Holy places – preserve what you have come to see, never touch or remove religious objects. Shoes should be removed when visiting temples.
- Giving to children encourages begging. A donation to a project, health centre or school is a more constructive way to help.
- You will be accepted and welcomed if you follow local customs. Use only your right hand for eating and greeting. Do not share cutlery or cups, etc.. It is polite to use both hands when giving or receiving gifts.
- Respect for local etiquette earns you respect – loose, lightweight clothes are preferable to revealing shorts, skimpy tops and tight-fitting *action wear*. Hand-holding or kissing in public are disliked by local people.
- Observe standard food and bed charges but do not condone overcharging. Remember when you're shopping that the bargains you buy may only be possible because of low income to others.
- Visitors who value local traditions encourage local pride and maintain local cultures. Please help local people gain a realistic view of life in Western Countries.

Be patient, friendly and sensitive. Remember – you are a guest!

Figure 7.40 The Himalayan tourist code

Whose land is it anyway?
The case of Kakadu National Park

Kakadu National Park, at Australia's 'Top End' (Fig. 7.41) is also a World Heritage Site, one of the very few designated for both cultural and natural values. The region has been the home of Aboriginal peoples for at least 50 000 years, has great religious significance for them, and contains some of the world's finest rock art (Fig. 7.42).

Between 1979 and 1987 the Aboriginal owners signed three leases with the Australian government, allowing the creation of the national park. However, they also leased a block of land to a uranium-mining company. This mining lease is surrounded by the park lease (Fig. 7.41). The Ranger Mine is nearing exhaustion, and the mining company has applied to develop a new working at Jabiluka (Fig. 7.43).

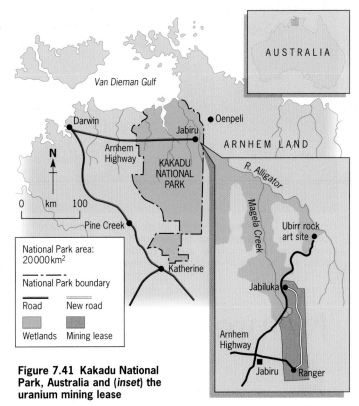

Figure 7.41 Kakadu National Park, Australia and (*inset*) the uranium mining lease

Figure 7.42 Aboriginal rock art, Nourlangie, Kakadu National Park

The park attracts approximately 300 000 visitors a year (Fig. 7.44). The three main attractions are the Aboriginal culture, the wetland ecosystems (Fig. 7.45) and the wilderness environment. The park managers and environmental groups oppose the continuation of mining because of the threat to environmental and experiential sustainability. They fear that toxic wastes from the mine and processing plant will enter the streams and pollute the fragile wetland ecosystem downstream from the mines. They believe, too, that road development and noise will threaten the 'wilderness experience'. The Aboriginal owners supported the original mining, but most of the 500 people now oppose the developments (Fig. 7.46).

The ethical issues focus on the rights of the stakeholder groups. The *owners* of the resources of the park and the mining lease are the Aboriginal people. The *leaseholders* are the Australian government and the mining company. The special-interest groups include environmentalists and the tourism industry. The economic, cultural, environmental and experiential dimensions of sustainability are entangled here. Do the rights of ownership overrule the responsibilities of stewardship?

Figure 7.43 The Kakadu wetlands and billabong, from Ubirr rock art site. The proposed Jabiluka uranium mine and road would be in the distance beyond the billabong

Kakadu National Park

Figure 7.44 A park ranger interprets the Ubirr rock art site to tourists. The paintings are on the protected walls of the overhang. All rock art sites are sacred, and the Aboriginal peoples allow access only to a few of the hundreds of sites

Figure 7.45 Wetland birds along the Alligator River, Kakadu National Park. This drainage basin and fragile ecosystem are downstream from the uranium-mining base

Nature rates second to uranium mine

ABORIGINAL and green groups say the Australian government faces international embarrassment after a United Nations World Heritage committee called for the scrapping of a controversial uranium mine.

A damning report said the proposed mine would pose a severe danger to the cultural and natural values of the nearby world-famous Kakadu National Park. But the federal government has dismissed the report as biased and unbalanced.

The Jabiluka uranium mine and mill has been subject to months of blockades and legal challenges by environmentalists and local Aborigines, who objected to the underground workings, and the UN committee's report was their last hope.

The week-long investigation found the world heritage values of Kakadu in the Northern Territory were threatened by the mine, and that the environmental regulations laid down by the government were not rigorous enough.

But Robert Hill, the federal environment minister, said: 'We reject this finding. We are greatly disappointed by the superficial assessment.'

He said the report had no legal capacity to stop the project, and said Australia would oppose moves to place Kakadu on the world heritage 'in danger' list.

The report said the mining lease threatens Aboriginal culture and sacred sites and repeats the concerns of some top Australian scientists about the 'unacceptably high degree' of uncertainty surrounding the mine's design and radio-active-waste dam. It also seriously questions the compatibility of uranium mining upstream from the park which attracts tourists from around the world to its extensive wetlands.

Phillip Shirvington, of the mining company Energy Resources of Australia, which is developing the lease, said his organisation had been given a clean bill of health by independent Australian scientists, and it appeared that the UN committee had a pre-set agenda.

The traditional owners of the Jabiluka mine site said they were relieved that the UN team had listened to their concerns. And they claimed that the news would give the 27-strong clan the power to keep up the fight. Christine Christopherson, spokeswoman for the Mirrar people, said:'We're thrilled, but it's still such a shame that the Australian people or the government can't come to the same conclusion.'

Figure 7.46 A World Heritage site is under threat, but the Australian government rejects a UN committee's report. The photograph shows the site of the uranium plant (*Source: Guardian*, 26 November 1998)

Some final questions for discussion

Is it acceptable that tourists intrude on homes and family life? (Fig. 7.35). If so, how should we behave?

Should the promotion of sex tourism be permitted just because there is a market for it (e.g. Thailand)?

Should tourists and the tourism industry boycott countries where there is evidence of serious human rights violations (e.g. Myanmar (Burma))? And what do we regard as 'serious' – where do we draw the line?

At what point does visitor presence produce stress on wildlife, and how do we know (e.g. penguin colonies in Antarctica)?

Should ability and willingness to pay be the sole measure used by a tourism operator in accepting business, and what are the 'rights' of the paying customer? For example, each year, growing numbers of tourists pay large sums to commercial expedition leaders to take them to the summit of Mount Everest, the world's highest mountain. In 1995, nine people, including two of the leaders, died. Whose responsibility is it to decide who is fit to do what, where, when and with whom?

Figure 7.47 Should we really be here? Is it an enriching experience or an intrusion? Campers in an ancient-growth forest in the Chugach National Forest, Alaska

Summary

- Increasing efforts are being made to encourage tourism development that is sustainable rather than exploitative.

- Sustainable tourism includes four dimensions – economic, socio-cultural, environmental and experiential.

- Alternative tourism is an 'umbrella' term often used to include the various forms of tourism whose aims are sustainability.

- A set of principles has been identified to provide a basis for the development and monitoring of sustainable tourism.

- Integrated planning and Protected Area designation are popular methods used for balancing conservation and tourism development goals.

- A model for National Park management uses a frontcountry–backcountry structure.

- Ecotourism and nature tourism are popular forms of alternative tourism, where sustainability depends upon the conservation of natural resources.

- Sustainability is likely to be achieved only when destination communities are involved in the decision-making process, benefit from the outcomes, and accept stewardship responsibilities.

Glossary

Access The right to visit and use a resource or facility. This right is dependent upon the terms under which the resource/ facility owner makes them available.

Accessibility 'Relative opportunity of interaction and contact' (Johnston, 1990). The ease with which people can reach and use a site or attraction in both locational and economic terms.

Alternative tourism A general term used to cover forms of tourism set up as alternatives to existing mass tourism with the primary aim of achieving an acceptable balance between conservation and development values. Examples include 'green tourism', 'soft tourism', 'ecotourism', 'responsible tourism', 'agrotourism' and 'rural tourism'.

At-one-time capacity The maximum number of people that a site or facility can accommodate at one time.

Attitudes Sets of beliefs that predispose a person to perceive and act towards people, environments or situations in a particular way.

Carrying capacity The maximum level of use that a site, facility or resource can support without suffering significant environmental deterioration (ecological capacity) or before the quality of visitor experience begins to decline (perceptual capacity). *See* Physical carrying capacity.

Catchment area The area from which users are attracted to a particular resource or facility.

Central Business District (CBD) The main commercial, professional and entertainment core of a town or city, containing an assemblage of high-order facilities.

Commercial sector The component of private sector supply whose primary motivation is to sustain profit levels.

Conservation The management of environmental resources and the built environment in such a way as to ensure their sustainability for future generations.

Country Park An area created under the provisions of the Countryside Act 1968 to provide urban dwellers with increased opportunities for informal outdoor recreation in country surroundings. Key features are free access and easy accessibility, with the supply located close to demand (i.e. usually within 15km of a town or city).

Critical mass The proposition that in order to survive and thrive, a traditional resort must attain a certain 'mass' which can be measured by the quantity, range, character and quality of its attractions.

Demand People's desire for a product, facility or experience and their ability and willingness to pay for it.

Demand-based A term used to describe a facility or attraction that has been located close to the origin of consumer demand.

Dual-use The provision of a leisure facility for both educational and leisure purposes. A dual-use facility is shared by students and the community, and is often funded jointly from local authority education and leisure services budgets.

Enclave tourism A form of tourism where the tourism experience is concentrated at one location, usually a resort or hotel complex.

Environmental quality This term has two possible meanings: (a) the quantifiable conditions of a resource or resource set, e.g. water or air quality; (b) the level of value that is placed on an environment, e.g. beauty, variety, rarity etc.

Facility An indoor or outdoor amenity or attraction that is provided for leisure use and enjoyment.

Footloose industry An industry that is not constrained in its choice of location by factors such as resource location, transport availability or market source, and thus can operate profitably in a wide range of locations.

Gross National Product (GNP) The total value of the goods and services produced by a country, including the value of its investment abroad.

Heritage tourism A form of tourism whose primary product and attraction is the historical legacy of a destination, e.g. industrial heritage.

Honeypot An especially attractive site or facility which, because of its popularity, is likely to experience high-intensity use and significant environmental impact and modification.

Integrated resort A planned assembly on one site of all the resources, facilities and attractions – accommodation, restaurants, entertainments, transport infrastructure etc. – necessary for the total touristic and recreational experience.

Investment The process of putting money into an enterprise with the aim of making a profit (private commercial sector), or of improving the quality of life for a group or the whole community (voluntary and public sectors).

Leakage The proportion of tourism income that is lost from a destination country and from which it therefore does not benefit, e.g. repayment of foreign loans, payment for imported goods, non-national workers sending money home etc.

Leisure Relatively freely-chosen activity and experiences which take place in time free from work and other obligations.

Less economically developed country (LEDC) A country with a relatively low standard of living and GNP, and that is attempting to move towards a developed status by enlarging and broadening its industrial base.

Management The rational allocation and control of resources and facilities according to a pre-determined set of criteria or objectives, e.g. to make a profit; to conserve an ecosystem.

Manufacturing industry An industry that involves the production of usable goods from raw materials and partially completed components using industrial processes.

Market segment A specific category of consumers, identifiable by their possession of a distinctive set of attributes, interests and spending patterns, e.g. 'Dinkies' – 'double income, no kids'.

More economically developed country (MEDC) A country that has achieved a high standard of living and GNP by developing the primary, secondary, tertiary and quarternary sectors of its economy.

Multiple use The management of a given set of resources and facilities for a variety of purposes.

Multiplier effect Spending in one area that produces a greater level of spending in many other areas. The multiplier effect can be a negative chain reaction (decreases in spending) or a positive reaction (increases in spending).

National Park An extensive area of countryside that has been given a special status because of the perceived quality and rarity of its environment, and so is managed in such a way as to conserve this quality. (NB this is an informal definition only. Formal definitions are given in the text on page 72.)

Newly industrialising country (NIC) A country that has undergone rapid and successful industrialisation within the last 30 years.

Physical carrying capacity The maximum number of users that a facility or site has been designed to hold at one time.

Pleasure periphery A concept that depicts the boundaries of tourism as a tidal wave surging outwards across the world over time, progressively incorporating new, more distant tourist destinations.

Private sector The component of the economy that is made up of privately-owned enterprises. *See* Commercial sector and Voluntary sector.

Product cycle The life cycle of tourism at a destination over time, from 'discovery' to 'decline'. The product cycle model depicts tourism as an exploitative industry comparable with mining – using an attractive resource while it lasts or is in demand, before moving on to exploit another location.

Public sector The component of the economy that consists of government-owned enterprises.

Pull factors The perceived attractive features of a recreational site or holiday destination that draw people to it.

Push factors The perceived negative features of the home environment that motivate people to 'get away' from that place.

Quality of life The social and economic well-being of a community or an individual and their perceived levels of happiness, satisfaction etc.

Recreation Leisure time activity that does not take place within a formal setting of rules and that may or may not involve travel away from the home environment. (Contrast with sport, which is enjoyed within á framework of rules and possibly formal competition.)

Resort An urban settlement whose primary purpose is the provision of leisure experiences. Resorts have distinctive locations, forms and functions.

Resource-based A term used to describe a leisure attraction or facility that is located at the site of the attractive resource (supply-based), e.g. a rockface for climbing; a natural ski slope.

Rural tourism A form of tourism that promotes the attractiveness of the natural and cultural resources of the countryside. It gives high priority to sustaining rural economies and to developing the conservation values of the visitor, and so is an example of the trend towards 'responsible tourism'.

Secondary industry An industry that produces goods using raw (i.e. primary) materials. *See* Manufacturing industry.

Service industry An industry that provides services rather than manufacturing or assembling goods.

Supply The amount of a commodity that is made available.

Supply-based *See* Resource-based.

Sustainability Maintenance of the quality and productivity of an attractive resource base over time. This resource base includes the natural and built environment, the character of society and culture, and the economic viability of the communities.

Sustained yield The use of resources in such a way as to sustain their quality and quantity over time and so sustain the amount of visitor satisfaction, i.e. quality (yield) of visitor experience.

Tertiary industry An industry that involves providing services for other people or industries. *See* Service industry.

Theme park A large leisure facility that is built around a distinctive and focused theme, that charges some form of all-inclusive fee, and offers a broad enough range of facilities and attractions to occupy a family for the whole day.

Throughput capacity The maximum number of users a site or facility can accommodate in a given period of time. It is the relationship between the physical design capacity and the length of individual/group/team participation time, e.g. if a car park at a beauty spot has a physical capacity (at-one-time capacity) of 10 vehicles, is open for 12 hours a day, and the average length of stay per car is 20 minutes, then the throughput capacity is 360 cars per day.

Tourism Activity/experience for business or pleasure that involves travel and temporary stay away from the home environment for at least one night.

Transnational company A large corporation that has subsidiaries in a number of different countries.

Values Enduring beliefs that a particular mode of conduct or way of living is personally or socially preferable to alternative conduct or ways of living.

VFR 'Visiting friends and relatives', a significant component of travel and tourism.

Voluntary sector A sub-group of the private sector whose primary motivation is the provision of social and recreational benefits for individuals and communities. It incorporates a wide range of self-run organisations, e.g. drama societies; sailing clubs; the Caravan Club.

Zone A defined area whose resources are allocated and managed to provide specific kinds of recreational activity and experience, appropriate to the environmental character of the area, e.g. water-ski zone; wilderness zone.

Zoning A management strategy for the spatial differentiation of recreational activities/experiences according to the character of the environmental resources.

Index